PO Box 601

C McReynolds
~~cocountywildgoatlake lr~~
Rhinelander, WI.
54501

Strategic Leadership
for Schools

John J. Mauriel

in collaboration with
B. Dean Bowles
and
Barbara Benedict Bunker

Strategic Leadership for Schools

Creating and Sustaining
Productive Change

Jossey-Bass Publishers
San Francisco • Oxford • 1989

STRATEGIC LEADERSHIP FOR SCHOOLS
Creating and Sustaining Productive Change
by John J. Mauriel

Copyright © 1989 by: Jossey-Bass Inc., Publishers
350 Sansome Street
San Francisco, California 94104
&
Jossey-Bass Limited
Headington Hill Hall
London OX3 0BW

Library of Congress Cataloging-in-Publication Data

Mauriel, John J., date.
    Strategic leadership for schools : creating and sustaining
productive change / John J. Mauriel ; in collaboration with B. Dean
Bowles and Barbara Benedict Bunker.
      p. cm. — (Jossey-Bass education series)
    Includes bibliographical references.
    ISBN 1-55542-184-9
    1. School management and organization—United States.
2. Educational planning—United States. 3. Educational innovations—
United States. I. Bowles, B. Dean. II. Bunker, Barbara Benedict.
III. Title. IV. Series.
LB2806.M375 1989
371.2'00973—dc20   89-45592
                                           CIP

JACKET DESIGN BY WILLI BAUM

FIRST EDITION

Code 8958

*The Jossey-Bass
Education Series*

Contents

Preface   xi

Author and Contributors   xvii

Part One: Developing an Effective Strategy   1

1. Strategic Leadership: A Framework for Orchestrating Successful Change Efforts   3

2. Major Challenges Facing Schools Today   15

3. Recognizing Opportunities and Threats   45

4. Assessing the School District's Capabilities and Limitations   75

5. Discovering What Constituencies Want from Schools   95

6. Formulating a Strategic Plan   131

Part Two: Implementing the Strategy   161

7. Gaining Support for Change: The Politics of Strategic Leadership
   by B. Dean Bowles   163

8. Developing a Marketing Plan   211

9. Instructional Leadership: Providing Quality
    Educational Services   229

        **Part Three: Evaluating
        and Revising the Strategy**   **259**

10. Leading School Systems Through Transitions
    by Barbara Benedict Bunker   261

11. Accountability: Determining How Much
    Performance Is Improving   287

12. Leading Schools into the Future: Managing the
    Ongoing Process of Strategic Change   314

    Resource: Management Report to Stakeholders   331

    References   339

    Index   345

Preface

Strategic Leadership for Schools is for those executives with the challenging, rewarding, and often frustrating job of providing leadership and direction for local school systems. Success in the job of leading a public school system today requires the school executive to carefully guide multiple stakeholders—including parents, educators, and students—toward the development, acceptance, and achievement of worthwhile organizational goals. Additionally, in today's environment, the public also demands a voice in shaping the specific social and educational goals and purposes of a public school system. Because of public expectations, the central office has the responsibility of shaping goals to make them consistent with the values and needs of the school system's various constituencies. It may have been possible at one time to perform these tasks by fiat. Now broader skills are needed. *Strategic Leadership for Schools* delineates these skills and provides help in developing them.

Why I Wrote This Book

I had two purposes in mind when I wrote this book. First, even if the current literature available to assist school administrators was adequate to meet their needs, very little is aimed at the central office executive. Most books written for education administration are either aimed at a higher governmental level—at state and federal educational policymakers—or are written for the principal or building-level administrator. I argue that the problems of running a school system present a different kind of management and leadership challenge than those faced by building principals and higher-level policymakers. These problems require a different kind of treatment, and that is one reason I wrote *Strategic Leadership for Schools.*

Second, this book takes what has been learned about managing successful business organizations and applies this knowledge to the leadership of school systems. I attempt to understand both the uses and the limitations of the wisdom available from business literature and practice. Public school officials have tended either to overlook the lessons from business organizations or to swallow popular concepts whole, turning them into fads that come and go. *Strategic Leadership for Schools* shows what is useful for school policymakers and executives to borrow from the extensive business literature.

Intended Audience

This book is written for people who have some responsibility for overall governance and management of a local school system. This includes those who have a major role in establishing policies, in determining goals and objectives, and in guiding, leading, and managing the multischool educational organization. This includes members of the following groups:

- Members of boards of education
- Superintendents and other central office executives of local schools
- School principals in their role as members of the district executive team
- Other administrators preparing for central office positions
- Executives of other local and regional education agencies

The following individuals, although not the primary audience, may also find *Strategic Leadership for Schools* useful:

- State policymakers
- Citizens, especially parents, interested in assessing the operation and performance of their local school systems
- Members of search committees for local superintendents

Overview of the Contents

Strategic Leadership for Schools is divided into three parts. Part One, which includes Chapters One through Six, describes how to identify a strategic plan for a school system and how to think about strategic leadership.

Chapter One provides a framework for understanding and applying the concept of strategic leadership to school districts. In Chapter Two, I discuss eleven major issues and problems facing schools today. Included are issues such as the impact of demographic shifts on funding, growing poverty among underclass children, and staff motivation.

Chapter Three introduces readers to a framework for identifying and organizing key environmental trends shaping public education. Chapter Four then shifts to internal analysis, providing a process for assessing the strengths, weaknesses, resources, and capabilities of a school district.

Chapter Five discusses the nature of the market for school services and examines how specific market research tools and techniques can aid school executives.

In Chapter Six, I walk readers through a process for developing and implementing a strategic plan. This chapter also introduces readers to the insights necessary to go beyond strategic planning to strategic leadership.

Part Two, consisting of Chapters Seven through Nine, takes the reader through some of the intricacies involved in implementing a plan.

Chapter Seven discusses stakeholder politics, consensus building, and applying political skills to develop policies acceptable to various constituencies.

In Chapter Eight, I discuss the marketing functions of service design and delivery, advertising and sales promotion, pricing and costing, and consumer/client analysis.

Chapter Nine discusses how to involve teachers and others in improving performance. I examine participative techniques and the assumptions necessary for successful consensual decision making.

Part Three examines how to change strategic direction and how to assess results of a strategic plan's implementation.

Chapter Ten is crucial for those involved in change efforts in school systems. It describes leadership methods necessary in periods of transition and discusses the forces that promote or inhibit change.

In Chapter Eleven, I discuss the need for various kinds of accountability systems and provide a comprehensive list of accountability measures. Readers are shown how to develop and use performance indicators to produce an annual report to stakeholders. (The resource, which follows Chapter Twelve, provides an example of such a report.)

Chapter Twelve provides suggestions for the next steps a school district might take after it has launched its strategic leadership program, begun its implementation programs, and introduced assessment, improvement, and change processes.

My major thesis is that a school executive in these times must be equipped to inspire and direct a school district by applying a broad range of leadership skills. Merely managing an ongoing process or doing strategic planning is not enough. In the face of uncertainty and society's continually changing demands and expectations, the chief executive and the central office must articulate a strategic vision for the school system and inspire groups and individuals to act in new ways, even though the formal authority of the executive position is not adequate for the task required. It is my hope that *Strategic Leadership for Schools* will help school executives accomplish these difficult and important tasks.

Acknowledgments

Stanley Shepard, senior program officer, and Humphrey Doermann, president, of the Bush Foundation of St. Paul, Minnesota, were responsible for getting me involved with the leadership process in public schools. They sought me out in 1975 and asked me to plan and design an executive development program aimed at enhancing the leadership and management skills of midcareer public school central office executives. They then suggested that I manage the operation of the six-week residential course that resulted from our early planning effort. Their views about what might be possible for school leaders and their willingness to finance a kind of educational experience that previously was available only to business executives were truly visionary. I hope *Strategic Leadership for Schools,* which comes out of my thirteen years as the director of the Bush Public School Executive Fellows Program, will serve as partial repayment to the foundation for the trust and generosity with which they have supported this unique activity.

John Maas was the codirector of the Bush Program in the early years and provided me with much practical knowledge of the realities of life in the central office of a school system. He also provided ideas on what was important to and missing in the education of school superintendents. Sharon Gannoway, associate director of the Bush Program, kept it running smoothly so I could devote major blocks of time to writing. My department provided support and reduced teaching assignments that helped me in the finishing stages.

Many others contributed to the writing of *Strategic Leadership for Schools.* Obviously, the work of B. Dean Bowles, who wrote Chapter Seven, and Barbara Benedict Bunker, who is responsible for Chapter Ten, is most important to acknowledge. Their outstanding contributions represent two of the highlights of this book.

Faculty members who teach in the Bush Program helped out by reading selected chapters. Dan C. Lortie, whose scholarly achievements and teaching ability I greatly admire, and C. William Rudelius, whose knowledge and wisdom both in the field of marketing and in the ways of communicating to executives, were of great help to me. Michael Patton, a most prolific and well-known scholar in the field of qualitative evaluation methods, also reviewed parts of the manuscript and provided extremely helpful criticism.

The participants of Bush groups X, XI, XII, and XIII read earlier versions of the text, and their comments and reactions made it better each year. The accomplished and extremely capable people with whom I served for three years as a member of the Golden Valley, Minnesota, school board during very difficult times for the school system were also great teachers of mine. Our superintendent, Robert Johnston, who was a true statesman during that period when we were reviewing the decision to consolidate, was very patient in answering my questions and was very helpful in the preparation and teaching of the Golden Valley cases, which were written so well by JoAnne Klebba, now a professor of marketing. These cases provided the raw material for many of the applications discussed in *Strategic Leadership for Schools*.

When the final crunch was on to complete the word processing, proofing, and formatting adjustments, Jay Adams, the word processing specialist in my department, stayed late many evenings and would not leave on the final evenings until we were finished.

Finally, my wife, Mary Anne, was instrumental in teaching me much about school/community relations and in my being elected to the school board in Golden Valley, Minnesota. She has always been an invaluable assistant, a person with whom to discuss, test, and refine ideas. She has also tolerated many long absences of mine when I was away to manage the Bush Program sessions and on retreats to write parts of *Strategic Leadership for Schools*.

The shortcomings of this book are my own responsibility.

Minneapolis, Minnesota   John J. Mauriel
August 1989

Author and Contributors

John J. Mauriel is associate professor of strategic management in the Carlson School of Management at the University of Minnesota, where he founded and directed that school's first major residential advanced management courses. He is also director of the Bush Foundation's Public School Executive Fellows Program, an intensive six-week residential program of study in leadership and strategic management that he designed for central office administrators of local school systems in Minnesota. In addition Mauriel directs a similar program designed for public and private school principals and heads, also funded by the Bush Foundation. He received his A.B. degree (1953) in economics from the University of Michigan and his M.B.A. (1961) and D.B.A. (1964) degrees from the Harvard Business School.

Mauriel has published in business journals (including the *Harvard Business Review*) and has written several business case studies. Recently Mauriel has begun active research and writing on school administration issues. His first book, *The Logic of Strategy* (with D. Gilbert, E. Hartman, and R. E. Freeman), was published in 1988. He is currently a principal investigator on the Minnesota Innovation Research Project. He has coauthored a chapter based on a longitudinal study of site-managed schools, which is included in that project's extensive volume on the management of innovation.

B. Dean Bowles, author of Chapter Seven, is professor of educational administration at the University of Wisconsin,

Madison, where he teaches courses in the politics of education, school/community relations, and qualitative research design and methods. He has been a teacher in the California public schools, a staff adviser in the California legislature, mayor of a Wisconsin city, and deputy state superintendent of public instruction in Wisconsin.

Barbara Benedict Bunker, author of Chapter Ten, is associate professor and director of graduate studies and admissions in the Department of Psychology, State University of New York, Buffalo. Her research subjects include commuting couples, executive leadership of women and men, the teaching of psychology at the high school level, and experiential learning. She is a partner in the Portsmouth Consulting Group. A director of the National Training Laboratories (NTL) Institute for seven years, she was for three years chairperson of the board of the NTL Institute.

Strategic Leadership
for Schools

Developing an Effective Strategy

Part One of *Strategic Leadership for Schools* consists of Chapters One through Six, which describe a methodology for formulating a school system's mission and strategy. Since the requirements for implementing a strategy are important influences on the kind of strategy that can or will be formulated, it is somewhat artificial to separate the formulation process from the implementation process, which is the subject of Part Two of this book. Yet it is necessary first to start thinking about the issues and trends one must identify and work through in developing a preliminary cut at selecting strategic options before one gets immersed in the operating problems involved in pursuing these options. With the knowledge that the problems of implementation and ownership must be dealt with early in the planning for strategy development and the knowledge that strategies can be modified as they are pursued, we proceed in this section of the book to explore the process of strategy formulation.

Chapter One provides an overview of the strategic leadership framework that is the guiding structure for the entire book, and Chapter Two identifies major strategic issues facing local school executives today. Chapters Three and Four discuss environmental trends and forces that are shaping the kinds of strategies school systems must follow to be successful, and the two chapters describe a process for further defining and apply-

1

ing these trends to the local district. Chapter Three focuses on external trends, and Chapter Four is concerned with the analysis of internal strengths and weaknesses.

Chapter Five describes marketing research and needs assessment so that the final chapter in Part One, Chapter Six, can deal with how one puts the trends, issues, and local needs together to develop an inspirational mission and a viable strategy.

strategic leadership ?

skills - leadership - vision

♂ 1

Strategic Leadership: A Framework for Orchestrating Successful Change Efforts

Success in the job of leading a public school system today requires an ability to articulate its mission and purpose to its constituencies and to engage them in establishing an overall strategy. It also demands an ability to manage and direct a process that ensures that the organization is working toward the achievement of a set of key goals that move it in a direction consistent with its mission, purpose, and strategy. Engaging in these activities successfully is what I call strategic management, or strategic leadership.

Some Definitions

Strategic Leadership. What is a strategic leader? How does one provide strategic leadership? What are the steps that executives take in providing strategic leadership? First and foremost, strategic leaders are people who have a clear vision—based on a widely shared set of values and aspirations—of where their organizations should be heading and who can clearly articulate that vision in a manner that motivates others. They are an inspiration to others both external and internal to their organizations. Second, strategic leaders are sensitive and effective listeners tuned to hear and understand well the needs and demands of their constituents, to understand the significance

of their constituents' evaluations of the organization's performance, and to interpret and clarify the trends that indicate future
needs and directions for their organizations. Finally, strategic
leaders are analysts and assessors of their situations in terms
of politics, markets, and finances. They understand the value
and impact of the services provided by their organizations in
political, market, social, human, and financial terms. But more
importantly, they know how to use that information to adjust
the mission and vision, to mobilize resources, and to generate
action. They do this by modifying as necessary the strategic plan
and then moving the organization to achieve the results necessary
to make the strategic plan happen, thus bringing the vision closer
to realization.

It is perhaps this last point that distinguishes what I call
"strategic" from other kinds of leadership in the field of education. An ability to employ the strategic thinking processes involved in analyzing trends and outcomes and then using the
results of these analyses to modify or amplify or redirect organizational efforts is a key attribute of a *strategic* leader. Put another
way, it is the ability to move from strategic planning to strategic leadership to make things happen—not just anything called
for in a "plan," but the kinds of things that help people and
organizations make the dramatic changes necessary to move
closer to achieving their common vision and fulfilling their lof-
tiest mission.

Mission and Vision. As Bunker points out in Chapter Ten,
one of the difficulties in the planning and leadership world of
today is the ambiguity involved in the definitions used for key
concepts. Words like *mission, strategic vision, goals,* and *strategy*
can have multiple, sometimes vague, and often different meanings for different people. For the purposes of this book, here
are some operational definitions that I will use throughout,
recognizing that in practice and use in your school district the
same terms may take on somewhat different meanings.

I tend to use *mission* and *vision* interchangeably to mean
a statement that expresses the dominant values and feelings
about what the school system should be about or what in a broad

and general way it should be trying to accomplish and what it should stand for. For example, one school superintendent states that it is the mission of his school district "to help its children to achieve their full potential and to live healthier, happier, and more productive lives by facilitating the development of their academic, artistic, and athletic knowledge and skills." This is both a mission statement describing the purpose of the school system and a vision of what the system can be for all its students. Chapter Six discusses the development of vision statements in a variety of school settings.

Strategy Formulation. Strategy is the main theme of this book and is defined to include broad objectives and goals, a guiding philosophy, key operating policies, and also the organizational design and global plans of action devised to achieve the mission, purposes, and general objectives. In other words, the definition of strategy includes both objectives, or goals, and the means for achieving them, unlike the more common usage that typically includes only the means of attaining objectives. A definition of strategy formulation flows from this. I use one provided by Hrebiniak and Joyce (1984, p. 29), which states that "Strategy formulation is a decision process focusing on the development of long-term objectives and the alignment of organizational capabilities and environmental contingencies so as to obtain them."

Strategy Implementation. I define strategy implementation as the process of developing and activating policies, programs, marketing plans, operations, and financial plans and then — *tactical plans* assessing results in order to influence future strategy formulation.

Leadership and Management. At this point it may be fruitful to address the currently popular topic of leadership versus management. In current discussions, the customary definition of *leadership* includes a wide variety of change-making activities. Often leadership activities are directed ultimately toward changes in instruction or curriculum or major improvements in educational delivery systems. According to the more commonly used definition, leadership might include engaging in such actions as the following: significantly altering the direction of a system, articulating a new vision, guiding the process of redefining goals and policies, shaping new attitudes and action programs, inaugurating new approaches to discipline or transportation or financial management, and introducing other major changes.

On the other hand, *management,* in the public sector lexicon, refers to the orderly maintenance and supervision of the support functions of the school and of the structural administrative processes that are vital to the continuing operations of an effective school. Managers, according to this definition, carry out the policies of the school district, supervising or organizing the systems that are in place to plan, direct, monitor, and control the processes by which strategies established by others are "implemented" or goals established by others are achieved. This involves such things as class scheduling, school discipline, transportation planning, personnel and financial administration and record keeping, salary negotiation, facilities planning, and general supervision of the activities of the school system and its programs. Sometimes the word *management* has a negative connotation in the public sector, whereas *leadership* has a positive, active, and dynamic ring to it among educators.

In the private sector, upper-level executives have a high regard for the term *management.* They recognize that good management is vital to the success of an enterprise. One does not think of good leadership existing in an organization that is poorly managed. Leadership and management tend to be intertwined and reinforce and often attract each other. The public sector—specifically, school systems—might do well to reassess its attitude toward management as a discipline and thus recognize its relationship to effective leadership. It is difficult to identify great leaders of poorly managed systems. A superintendent must have order and discipline not only in his or her classrooms and schools but also in the management of administrative affairs, budgets, hiring practices, transportation systems, policy administration, and the like. In some organizations, effective and proactive leadership behaviors might include the redesign and improvement of some or all of these management systems. In other organiza-

tions, the maintenance of an existing good administrative operation might be a vital prerequisite for the introduction of new
leadership initiatives.

The debate about the difference between leadership and
management might better shift to a discussion of how the two
concepts interrelate and support each other. We should also
recognize that the definitions of the two are not as clear and
as sharply differentiated either in theory or in practice as many
would have us believe. A discussion of the meaning of the terms
leadership and *management* has some similarities to the discussion
of *policy* versus *administration*. You know the common wisdom:
''Boards set policy, school officers administer, and each should
not try to do the other's job.'' The next time someone says that,
ask the person to get a key group together and see if he or she
can obtain agreement among its members on which specific actions in a massive curriculum change are policy actions and
which are administrative actions. Furthermore, even if all
reached full agreement on the operational definitions of the two
terms, it would be virtually impossible to run a school where
the board did nothing but set policy and the administration did
nothing but administer policy. While it is important to distinguish these two functions as much as possible and to be sure
that the board does not try to run the day-to-day operations of
the school and make important management decisions, it is
proper for a board to review major administrative programs and
processes, and it is equally vital that a superintendent be involved
in influencing the shaping of policy. Without a joint effort and
administrative support, policy-making is not very effective. The
same is true of management and leadership. Without good
management of the process, leadership initiatives can lose their
power.

In summary, I have not tried to provide conclusive definitions for leadership and management; nor have I tried to distinguish precisely between the two concepts. Rather than debate
whether a superintendent is a leader or a manager, it seems more
fruitful to discuss the quality of the leadership and management.
What are the superintendent and board of education leading
the school district toward? What visions or directions or pro-

posals for improved operation seem to set the agenda for the leadership and management strategy? Is there an emphasis on educational results, equal opportunity and access, and creativity, or is the focus on process, order, and structure with absence of content? Is the chief concern for outcomes, or is it for inputs?

Strategic Planning. Engaging the school board and other key constituents in a strategic planning process is a crucial first step in providing strategic leadership for a school district. The product of such a process—a strategic plan—can provide the framework, direction, and guidelines for strategic leadership. Bryson (1988, p. 48) provides an eight-step process for strategic planning:

1. Initiating and agreeing on a strategic planning process
2. Identifying organizational mandates
3. Clarifying organizational mission and values
4. Assessing the external environment: opportunities and threats
5. Assessing the internal environment: strengths and weaknesses
6. Identifying strategic issues facing an organization
7. Formulating strategies to manage the issues
8. Establishing an effective organizational vision for the future

Outline and Plan of the Book

Strategic Leadership for Schools begins with an approach to strategic planning similar to Bryson's but tailors it specifically for school systems and similar education delivery organizations and then proceeds to provide guidance in implementing, evaluating, and changing strategies in independent school districts. The topics covered in this book take the reader through strategic planning and then on to *strategic leadership*. The objective is to help one get started in doing the thinking and taking the actions necessary to accomplish the strategic management tasks listed in the preface and repeated in Table 1. In practice, these tasks are not necessarily performed in the neat and orderly sequence that such a listing implies. The framework for this book, however, uses these concepts as a model for strategic leadership. The framework for the book is shown graphically in Table 1.

Table 1. The Strategic Leadership Process.

DEVELOPING AN EFFECTIVE STRATEGY

    Identifying the key issues affecting school systems
    Analyzing environmental trends influencing schooling
    Assessing a system's resources and capabilities
    Researching market needs
    Orchestrating the development and implementation of a guiding
       vision and mission and a strategic plan

IMPLEMENTING THE STRATEGY

    Engaging politics, policies, and publics
    Developing a marketing plan
    Providing leadership for improvement in operations and instruction

EVALUATING AND REVISING THE STRATEGY

    Introducing and managing change
    Assessing overall school system performance
    Modifying the vision—the next steps

The first of the three major parts of this book—Developing an Effective Strategy—describes a process for identifying a strategic plan for a school system. This initial chapter elaborates on the framework presented in Table 1 and explains why such an approach can be needed and useful. Chapter Two identifies the major issues facing school executives in the next decades in order to set the stage and highlight the need for a new concept of strategic leadership. Identification of these issues also helps one to limit or focus the search for environmental trends discussed in Chapter Three, which presents an approach for

examining the relevant environmental trends that will shape the
needs and demands that will be placed on the education industry
in general and schooling in particular and, more specifically,
the trends and issues that will affect that local school district
in the decades ahead. This latter activity helps a school system
identify the opportunities and threats that may lie ahead. Chapter Three also deals with an examination of the competitive environment in which a local school district exists.

Chapter Four describes a method for assessing a given
school system's ability to effectively provide the services that
are needed now and will be needed in the future. It provides
a guide for examining a school system's vast resources and potential capabilities as well as its limitations. Next, Chapter Five
introduces concepts and techniques of market analysis that can
assist school systems in the process of needs assessment. This
chapter describes how to identify the alternatives for mission
and strategy most desired by a school system's constituencies
and the public's relative preferences for financing the pursuit
of those alternatives. Chapter Six, the final chapter of Part One,
describes the development of a visionary mission and strategic
plan that respond to the community's needs (identified in Chapter Five) and to the key issues and concerns of education (identified in Chapter Two), while matching the school system's
strengths and weaknesses (identified in Chapter Four) to the
opportunities and competitive environment (identified in Chapter Three).

Part Two of the book—Implementing the Strategy—
includes Chapters Seven through Nine, which deal, respectively,
with politics, marketing, and operations and finance. Chapter
Seven discusses politics, policies, and publics and includes processes employed in identifying and working with the appropriate
stakeholder groups. Chapter Eight elaborates on the marketing
concept first introduced in Chapter Five, taking the reader
through the process of developing a marketing plan. Finally,
Chapter Nine deals with operations or instructional delivery
functions. Included in operations management is the job of instructional leadership and the management of the delivery of
educational services. Since operations management is a people-

intensive activity in education, Chapter Nine deals with issues of motivation and participation of staff in the instructional improvement process.

The third and last part of the book—Evaluating and Revising the Strategy—deals with leadership methods involved in introducing strategic changes and in assessing the impact of the old and new strategies. Pursuing the strategy can sometimes involve only minor additions or revisions to what is already being done, along with some improvements in how well it is being accomplished. In such cases, the advice and approaches presented in Part Two are generally adequate for the task of implementing the strategy. Often, however, a strategic analysis, such as prescribed in Part One, leads to the conclusion that some overall organizational change is needed. Leadership approaches for introducing major changes are discussed in Chapter Ten. Whether major change is needed or not, methods for evaluating the performance of a school system and its strategy are vital in helping an effective executive assess his or her work. Chapter Eleven discusses the use of information systems and assessment processes for evaluating, monitoring, and improving strategic performance. Chapter Twelve summarizes the key elements of the job of strategic leadership; discusses how and when the vision, mission, and strategy must be modified; and outlines the next action steps for the reader.

Why a Framework Is Needed

The leadership team (board, superintendent, other central office administrators) of a school system must deal with a variety of forces and trends that affect the need for, quality of, ability and willingness to finance, and the public's ability to exploit, assimilate, and use public education services. In addition to the complexity that such forces introduce, an array of constituents with changing demands and needs can impose increasing, often conflicting demands on the school district. To help sort out the array of forces and demands, school system executives need a structure and a process to facilitate their ability to guide the use of the human, physical, and financial resources that exist or can exist in a school district. School executives are also stewards of these resources, which they must use to pursue the purposes of the system. But for whose purposes? How are they arrived at? And is there a rational process that uses unarguable logic to determine purposes and means for achieving them? Unfortunately, or maybe fortunately, there is no logic, no formula, no path to the one *right* answer for determining a school system's mission, purpose, and strategy. Nevertheless, the framework introduced in this book is designed to help executives manage the tensions and conflicts and to guide them through a process that helps them deal with or balance the interests of all their constituents while providing for the long-term survival of the organization's mission. The constituent forces are shown in Figure 1.

A framework is needed to guide the discourse and the development of an action plan for the overall governance and management of a school district that has some hope of surviving the constant tests to which it is put. The (corporate) strategy framework described herein not only provides a structured process for developing a strategy but also a model for testing and retesting the strategy's viability. Thus one can follow the steps used to formulate a strategy to continually asses its potency and to determine whether it might require changing. The steps outlined in Table 1 must be constantly worked through because pursuing the strategy can lead to its modification, reassessment, and reformulation just as formulation can determine or lead to new ways of pursuing a strategy. Examining environmental trends might remind one of a resource or strength of the school system that could be used to counter or exploit that trend. Or the identification of a unique capability or asset of a school system might lead it to pursue an opportunity that the current environment presents.

As one moves through the steps in Table 1, pursuing several of them concurrently, one can benefit from a road map. The strategy framework provides such a general road map. While not guaranteeing that one will end up on the right street at exactly the desired address, it increases the likelihood that one will end up in the right city or at least in the right general part of the country.

Figure 1. Constituent Groups of a School District.

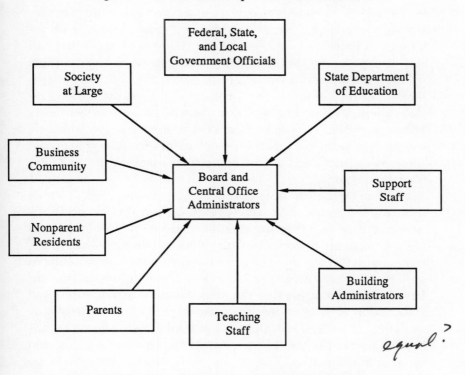

Goal: to balance the interests of all while achieving system goals

The process used includes a consideration of the personal values of the leadership group of the school system and of each of its constituent groups. One cannot follow a rigid decision process that comes to a single logical, rational "right" answer precisely because one can and must make important value choices. Some values are part of our free democratic heritage, such as equal opportunity and access, the right to an even chance to learn and succeed, and the protection of certain property and individual rights, all of which one would consider as reflecting the "right" values. However, there are no *specific* "right" values when it comes to choices of learning styles, delivery modes, courses to be offered, sizes of classes to be paid for and made available to the current cohort of students.

Many consultants on "strategic planning" are emerging on the school scene today. Beware of a consultant who provides too sure a "recipe" for preparing the "plan." This book attempts to inoculate you against the dangers of quick fixes in strategic planning, while still providing powerful and simple (though not simplistic) guidance in developing not only a strategic plan but a system for formulation, implementation, reassessment, redirection, and execution of a long-term strategy. Following such a system or process is the task of a strategic leader. The utility of this framework comes from its conceptual rigor, its simple elegance, its comprehensiveness, and the flexibility it provides.

To say that there is no *one* demonstrably "right" value that can determine the correctness of certain specific decisions with precision is not to say that there are no means for assessing the congruity of decisions with values or that there is anything wrong with having some clearly stated values or an articulated philosophy that guides the choices of a public school system. In fact, I would argue that the identification, articulation, and elaboration of these values are a crucial part of the strategy formulation process. The values of a school system should be imbedded in its mission. The process of formulating a vision and mission statement is part of the early phase of the strategy development process.

Without a guiding philosophy buttressed by a firm set of values and beliefs, an organization's strategy can become the victim of every current whim or fad or succumb to the pressures of every minor constituent person or group. Figure 1 illustrates the variety of constituent group interests that must be balanced by the school system's leadership group. Thus, the strategic decision framework presented in Chapter Six explicitly considers personal values. The fact that there are often no objectively "right" values is not an excuse for relativism or wishy-washy catering to all pressure groups. It is a call for stating and debating and then living firmly with some guiding value choices.

The remaining chapters of Part One discuss the subsequent steps of the strategy formulation process, starting with the identification of key issues facing the school system.

2

Major Challenges
Facing Schools Today

This chapter briefly describes eleven significant issues or challenges facing school superintendents. The list includes some of the major concerns elicited in interviews with more than 200 school superintendent attendees at a six-week executive course funded by the Bush Foundation of St. Paul, Minnesota, from reading current administrative journals, and from the author's general observations in working with school systems over the past fourteen years. The issues are heavily interrelated, and in some cases one leads to or is a major cause of the next. The list may not be exhaustive, but it does include some of the most overwhelming concerns voiced in recent years by local school superintendents from across the United States.

Developing such a list of issues is an important first step in the strategy formulation process. The eleven issues noted here may provide a starting point for discussion by a district involved in the early stages of strategic planning. Subsequent chapters will discuss the management and leadership processes useful for dealing with these issues. At this stage, however, I recommend your staying with the broad issues and trying to identify—by means of a brainstorming approach with local community and educational leaders and perhaps some outside resource person(s)—the key national, state, and local issues that are part of your context. At first it is helpful to focus on the more basic and enduring problems and fundamental realities that exist. Each local district should go through this exercise. The following sequence is recommended, though it should be modified to take advantage of local conditions and available resources.

1. Assemble a strategic planning committee. This committee should include at least one board member, some staff members, the superintendent and one or more other administrators, and key citizens.
2. Have each person on your planning committee read and think about this chapter.
3. Call one or more meetings of your strategic planning committee to discuss the eleven issues listed in this chapter and to work through steps 4 through 6 below. Ask the group members to state what each of these issues means to them and to your local school system.
4. Ask for additions to the list, especially for those that focus on your own state and local community or local school district. Brainstorm for twenty to thirty minutes, listing issues on a chalkboard without discussion or critique at this point.
5. Spend as much time as you find useful synthesizing the key issues and discussing their meaning and relevance for your system.
6. End the first session by telling the group that the next meeting will focus on a discussion of general and specific trends facing the school system, and ask members to read Chapter Three of this book before the next meeting.

The next series of discussions of the strategic planning committee should involve an analysis of the external trends facing your school system and an examination of your district's strengths, opportunities, resources, and limitations. You may want to use Chapters Three and Four of this book as a starting point for these discussions.

Before proceeding with an elaboration and discussion of the eleven issues, I should point out that although these are fundamental and long-term issues not subject to frequent change, it would be helpful for anyone using this list to consider updating it from time to time. I recommend every five years or whenever a fundamental shift in the economy, social values, or political or legislative circumstances or attitudes takes place.

The eleven issues are listed in Table 2 and are discussed below.

Table 2. Major Challenges Facing Schools Today.

1. Ownership of the schools
2. Reexamining goals, purposes, and mission
3. Involving community and staff groups—participative decision making
4. The impact of demographic shifts on funding
5. Growing poverty among underclass children
6. Staff motivation—rewards for merit
7. Product quality—providing leadership for instructional improvement
8. Obtaining capital (human and physical) to enter the information age
9. Defining and pursuing new market segments
10. Assessing and reporting results—accountability
11. Articulating the strategic vision

Issue 1: Ownership of the Schools

˙ Perhaps the most crucial and pervasive issue facing school executives is one involving ownership or control of the local school district. Over the last two decades there has been a gradual shift in ''ownership'' of the authority to establish a school system's mission, purpose, and direction. This transference of ''ownership'' has not been obvious because in a formal sense no change has occurred. Each state still has the authority and responsibility to provide educational opportunities to all its citizens. It, in turn, delegates this authority and responsibility to a local elected (or in some cases appointed) school board or school committee, of which there is one in each of the approximately 15,000 public school districts in the United States. The final delegation of formal authority has been and continues to be from the school board to the chief executive officer or school superintendent.

What is changing is the ''informal'' authority structure, the structure that determines who in reality exercises the power and authority that actually influence and/or set the direction and plan for an independent school system. (Perhaps private schools have also been undergoing this kind of change, but this book is chiefly about the leadership and management issues facing public school executives.) Until the 1950s there was a deference to the authority of the "educational professional." School boards exercised jurisdiction over budgetary matters and had final approval in a formal sense over appointments, salary, and educational policy. However, the decisions concerning who the superintendent hired to administer and teach in the schools, what programs the schools would offer, especially in the academic curriculum, and what the educational philosophy and procedures would be were generally considered the prerogative of the "professionals."

Later, especially in the 1960s and 1970s, along with a general societal questioning of all forms of authority (family, church, government, and so on) came a questioning of the professional educator. Ironically, the freer use of and possibly even the greater effectiveness of our public schools (and colleges) led to a higher level of awareness and a greater ability to think critically on the part of a better-educated populace, which in turn contributed to this challenge of traditional authority structures.

Ownership and control of the local school system are being impacted from all directions. In 1954 *(Brown v. Topeka)*, the federal government asserted controls over school systems' enrollment policies in an effort to ensure equality of educational opportunity to all. In addition, federal and state funding of special education and vocational education programs and the passage of Public Law 94-142, pertaining to rights of the handicapped and the school's responsibility toward them, provided more prescriptions and mandates relating to how the local school must allocate resources and what it must do to provide services. Some of the school's goals (beyond providing a basic education) were being mandated by outside forces and groups.

It is difficult to say which contributed most to the demand that some of the goal-setting authority be transferred to parents, staff, state, nation, and the community at large: (1) dissatisfaction with the professional education establishment stimulated by such books as *Why Johnny Can't Read* (Flesch, 1955) and *Crisis in the Classroom* (Silberman, 1970), or (2) the general societal challenges to institutional authority and professional "expertise," with an attendant willingness to speak up at public gatherings. In any event, in the 1970s, many PTAs and other parental and community organizations began changing from social and fund-raising groups to activist groups demanding some say in how their children were dealt with in schools—not just in terms of discipline but also in terms of education. In addition, many states passed sunshine laws requiring that board meetings and records be open to the public. Finally, in the wake of this eroding local power, teachers' associations (unions) emerged, with great strength in negotiating salaries and working conditions. In most states, control of more than 70 to 80 percent of a typical school's budget (professional salaries) is now in the hands of a collective bargaining process, a process that sometimes proceeds with little or no influence from the central office. Often, either the school board takes charge of this process or a hired outside negotiator becomes involved. In some districts not only has the authority to set salaries or to decide who is to be laid off if a reduction in the number of teachers is needed been transferred to a collectively bargained formula (based purely on two simple criteria—education level and seniority); in many instances certain key management rights and responsibilities, such as setting class size and schedules, have also been bargained away by school administrators. For teachers, the collective bargaining process provided some of the control and influence over their own work situations that a more understanding, skillful, and perhaps less resource-constrained management might have been able to provide.

Although one can point to formal erosion of local school district power and autonomy because of an increase in the influence of federal and state governments and the rise of teacher associations or unions, a substantial change in the school superintendent's freedom to change policy or direction has also occurred because of demands made by local constituencies at the grass roots level. Chemical dependency programs, athletics leagues, computer literacy courses, career preparation, "relevance," classes for the gifted, and so on have been requested

or initiated as the result of demands from consumers as well
as staff members and various interest groups at the state and
local levels.

Which stakeholders should influence the mission, purposes, and goals of schools? Our democratic society at large?
The state? The local municipality? The citizens residing in the
local school district? The parents of children ages five to eighteen? Education leaders or administrators? Teachers? Students?
Faculties of teacher preparation institutions? Just who are the
clients of the local school system? These questions are being addressed by myriad school system stakeholders in power-, author-
ity-, and influence-wielding processes in a variety of local settings. Later chapters (especially Chapter Seven) discuss these
stakeholders and influence processes and suggest some action
steps superintendents may consider in guiding and working with
them.

Issue 2: Reexamining Goals, Purposes, and Mission

What is and what should be the role of the public school?
This question is of course closely linked to the question of who
owns the schools. A typical public school pursues a variety of
knowledge, social, cultural, physical, and emotional development objectives. The role of the public school in the history of
American society is a unique and vital part of the grand social
and political experiment inaugurated in 1776.

The providing of free public education to all citizens served
many purposes in the nineteenth century. Not the least of these
purposes was acculturating the children of immigrant parents,
imparting to them the values of the middle-class establishment,
training them to be ''good citizens,'' and equipping them to
be functional in the world of work in the new industrial society.
Thus the combination of social and educational objectives has
long been a part of the American school scene.

Recently, many education administrators have complained
that the schools are now being asked to solve problems in the
greater society above and beyond their capacity to do so or at
least beyond the funding authority's willingness to provide

resources to deal with these "extra" responsibilities. Problems such as racial inequities, drug addiction, family breakups must now be at least addressed, if not solved, by schools. Schools are asked to become welfare counselors, drug prevention centers, baby-sitting agencies, nutritional meal providers, mainstreaming forces for the severely handicapped, and the like, in addition to fulfilling their more traditional role of providing basic education for good citizenship.

To repeat the question: What is and what should be the role of the public school? It seems that all constituencies or stakeholders of the American public school system agree that at least one function of schooling is to teach the basics—reading, writing, and computing—and to graduate children who are functionally literate to live in and productively contribute to the complex and sophisticated economy of today and tomorrow. There may be some disagreement as to how much computer literacy is essential and just how well children must be able to write and read, that is, how advanced their knowledge and skills ought to be in these areas. There may also be some disagreement as to how some of these skills ought to be taught. However, there is little disagreement over the fact that a primary goal and purpose of a school is to provide basic education. Related to this basic goal is the desire to have schools prepare a child for the world of work or for further schooling (college or vocational). Again, there is little controversy over this objective of public schooling. In addition to teaching the basics and preparing students for the world of work, there seems also to be a great deal of agreement, though not unanimity, on the need for schools to be places where children experience discipline and learn obedience or appreciation of the need for order in social organizations. In other words, schools are expected to contribute to the process of "socialization" and teach children to be good "citizens." There is, of course, some controversy over what good citizenship is and how much "conformity" is good, but in general, citizenship and respect for authority are usually high on the list of goals most stakeholders would have the schools pursue.

Teaching people how to work cooperatively is a third objective of schooling on which most people would agree. Children should learn to get along with one another. The need to develop a facility or ability for teamwork is considered by most (though not all) to be one of the purposes of schooling. Many parents who might publicly espouse this aim for schools would in practice prefer to have their children learn to "win" and "compete" and individually achieve. At some level, cooperation and competition become conflicting goals. If schools in our society teach children individual achievement and competition more effectively than they teach cooperation, they may be more a reflection of our broader social ethic. If they teach cooperation more than competition, some people may say the schools are imparting countercultural values.

A great deal of agreement seems to exist on the need for public schools to contribute to the development of the "whole child" by providing opportunities for extracurricular activities, especially athletics. The community also seems to feel that the schools ought to help prevent or at least deal with the key social problems of the day. Therefore, community support for drug education programs, hot breakfast and lunch programs, preschool programs, and some of the other items listed in Table 3 has been forthcoming in many districts. What is still unknown is how important these objectives are when they demand resources that are essential to the maintenance of a minimum academic program. As the financial resources of many school systems continue to decline, we will see who steps forward to fund programs aimed at special-interest groups, sometimes serving only small numbers of the school population.

On the academic side, the question of how much our schools ought to really challenge and push children beyond basic knowledge and skills is much more controversial in practice than in theory. In theory many people, especially parents, are in favor of teaching beyond the basics. Yet the more advanced educational goals of teaching critical thinking and skills of analysis and synthesis probably get more lip service than actual support. Demands from both parents and central administrations for higher test scores and more efficient and effective teaching of reading and math are not typically aimed at trying to improve a child's ability to think creatively and to analyze and synthesize information and knowledge.

Table 3. Some Services Provided by Public Schools.

Basic education
Career preparation
Advancement of analytical, critical, and synthesizing skills
Personality development
Physical and athletic skill development
Artistic and esthetic expression
Human interpersonal skills
Motivation (desire to learn and grow)
Cooperative attitudes (obedience to authority, and so on)
Understanding of self, improved self-concept
Chemical dependency prevention and treatment
Hot breakfasts and lunches for the poor
Hot breakfasts and lunches for all
Parent effectiveness training
A full range of opportunities for the handicapped
Baby-sitting services
Bicultural education for those from family backgrounds from other cultures
Community education
Preschool programs
Individualized special education programs allowing students to be
  "mainstreamed" where possible
Band, orchestra, choir, drama, and a whole range of "cocurricular"
  programs

Finally, though somewhat controversial, is the question of what proportion of a school system's resources ought to be spent on special education programs. State and federal funding to individualize instruction for handicapped children and a thrust toward getting them as much as possible into the "mainstream" with their peers are evidence of the belief that a goal of the school is to try to make every child a productive member of society. No matter how strongly previous environmental and congenital factors may have rendered a child less able to "compete," the school is required to provide an educational program tailored to that child's needs, sometimes without careful consideration of and provision for the funds involved and the method and sources of payment. Even more controversial is the allocation of major segments of a school's resources to rehabilitation work, such as chemical dependency programs, AIDS education, and other related kinds of programs, not to mention more traditional athletic and cocurricular activities.

What are the appropriate goals for schools? It is hard for anyone to say that any one of the goals identified above is inappropriate. Yet in a time of limited resources it is necessary to examine priorities and ask questions that elicit answers about the best or optimum resource allocation mix. What is the *primary mission* of the school? What are its primary purposes? To what extent must these primary objectives be served before other objectives are pursued? Can we afford not to address any of the major issues listed in Table 3?

The answer to the question of who owns the schools is closely related to or at least influences the answers to the questions of goals, purposes, and mission. It is time, in the 1990s, for each local school district, if it has not already done so, to examine its basic purposes and priorities and how its actual funding and resource allocation processes are consistent with or contrary to these stated purposes.

Issue 3: Involving Community and Staff Groups

As a way of addressing the challenge to his or her power and influence, the chief executive officer must learn to work constructively with community groups, manage the inevitable conflicts, and in general obtain constructive involvement in a positive goal-directed process. The central office and other school administrators and staff members *can* work to facilitate processes that allow management to maintain some degree of control and influence over the direction and results achieved. But it is much easier to manage with formal power and authority. Greater skill is required in employing participative processes. They require patience, a great tolerance for frustration, an ability to respond and change direction, and enormous amounts of intellectual and emotional energy. Some of these processes and some of the methods for utilizing them are discussed later in this book.

In many organizations, both business and public, attempts at broader involvement in decision making have turned into exercises in sham participation at one end of the spectrum or into abdication of responsibility at the other end. A participative executive responsive to multiple and competing publics must neither impose her or his own monolithic solution nor abdicate to the group's wishes in the name of "responding to market needs." The human need to obtain closure or task completion can and often does pervert or abort the process of participative decision making. The result is "efficiency" American-style at the expense of long-run effectiveness. In industry we have seen how the patience of the "Japanese" approach (committees, discussions, involvement, consensus building), which to some U.S. executives seems extremely inefficient, leads to successful achievement of purpose. The Japanese process, which is less efficient at making decisions, is frequently far more efficient at successfully implementing the decisions.

More than ever we need skillful educational leaders who are comfortable with the job of managing the ongoing process of working with committees, community groups, and a variety of individuals in constantly examining goals and purposes, mission and delivery, programs and procedures. Some people now in leadership roles in industry and in our public schools have not received the kind of training that might equip them for this kind of leadership task.

Issue 4: The Impact of
Demographic Shifts on Funding

The shrinking size of the public school system's traditional target market (five- to eighteen-year-olds) is a demographic fact that no one can dispute. This phenomenon has affected schools in the 1980s. For two reasons at least, however, it is arguable whether the size of the total school market has really shrunk: (1) the customer age range has widened (for example, there is a demand for preschool education and adult education programs offered by public schools), and (2) the range of services desired by the target market has widened some. Current debates are trying to sort out the difference between what the consumer desires and what the true economic market demand is (that is, what the client is willing to pay for). It seems reasonable to conclude, however, that even after the dust settles on the latest round of revenue cuts for public schools, the remaining list of "must"

services will be broader than the list one might have drawn up
in the 1950s. In most states a large percentage of a school
system's revenue is directly related to the number of school-age
children residing in its geographic district. This combination
of taxation formula and demographic reality has meant fewer
real dollars for many school systems. Even though per pupil
revenue allocations have gone up, the total funds available to
most school districts after allowing for inflation have decreased
because of enrollment decreases. The deep recession of 1981–82,
the federal government's withdrawal of funds for state and local
use in the early 1980s, large deficits in state budgets (created
by or exacerbated by the recession), and the cries for tax relief
(Propositions 13 in California and 2½ in Massachusetts) all led
to an even tighter squeeze on funds, which affected many local
school districts in the 1980s.

    While the chief executive officer of the school system was
intensely busy responding to these forces, outside bodies were
attempting to document the serious charges against the quality
of the performance of the nation's schools in such reports as
A Nation at Risk (National Commission on Excellence in Education, 1983). Ironically, the conditions that tend to promote the
kinds of innovative responses needed to cope with and overcome
the problems created by declining markets, declining resources,
and inflation are least present when they are most needed.

Issue 5: Growing Poverty
Among Underclass Children

    The large group of underclass children consisting of a
disproportionately high percentage of minorities and of offspring
of single teenage mothers and potentially headed into a life of
poverty, crime, and drugs presents one of the greatest social,
political, and economic challenges facing the nation in the 1990s.
Even traditional opponents of welfare programs agree that
society has an economic interest in working with these helpless
children engulfed in the cycle of poverty. In order to make it
possible for such children to become contributing members of
society, some programs even recognize a need to begin while

the child is in the womb, with prenatal care programs, followed by infant care assistance, parenting classes, and preschool Head Start programs. Corporate leaders also recognize the competitive issues and personnel staffing problems businesses will face if qualified, literate employees are not available to them in the early part of the next century. In many cases these leaders are willing to support welfare and self-help programs for poor children with both money and personal time and effort.

State and local governments are beginning to realize that it is much cheaper to educate children properly in their early years than it is to incarcerate those same children for drug-related and other kinds of crimes. The cost of keeping a prisoner in one state penitentiary with only normal security was quoted recently and conservatively as $20,000 per year. Add to that the waste and loss involved in any crimes and drugs and the costs of arrest, trial, and protection purchased by other members of society. In comparison, $4,000 a year for an outstanding preschool or day-care program that would include some education and opportunity for growth seems cheap.

In the 1980s, the increase in the percentage of children at the poverty level, apparently fueled by such factors as the rising number of teenage pregnancies, the loss of many higher-paying semiskilled jobs, the growth in drug traffic, and reductions in federal, state, and local welfare programs, was significant. This increase was documented by a U.S. senator from New York State (Moynihan, 1986). Visionary business leaders were concerned about the long-run economic and social impact of such a situation, and governments were beginning to see the wisdom of funding preschool programs for poor children, along with day care, parenting courses, and nutritional assistance for teenage mothers. Some suburbs were even considering proposals for sharing programs and students with contiguous inner-city schools. The problem appears to have the potential for spilling over into schools outside the core ghetto areas of the major cities.

As the last decade of the century approached, the gap between children at the poverty level and those from higher-income families seemed to be widening. The latter children start with access to computers and television and probably reasonably good nutrition and mental stimulation at home; to the former, the competition at school presents an almost hopeless feeling. Most school officials will be affected by this issue directly or indirectly, though it may not now be of direct concern to the majority of districts and their educational programs.

Issue 6: Staff Motivation—Rewards and Incentives

Why Most Current Merit-Pay Proposals Will Fail. The issue of rewards and incentives for meritorious service or excellence in teaching unfortunately becomes oversimplified and misconstrued when labels such as "merit pay" are applied. Merit pay is then very narrowly defined as a financial reward for an individual teacher based on that teacher's special worthiness. This kind of popular definition brings on opposition from teachers' associations. It should also be opposed by management, though for different reasons than those advanced by teachers. Merit pay systems based on individual incentive "bonuses" for individual teachers would probably do more harm than good to both performance and satisfaction.

Perhaps because of our "individualist" tradition, we tend to think of individual incentives as powerful stimulants to greater performance. In spite of a great deal of evidence to the contrary, industry leaders and other executives tend to believe that individual incentives are superior to group incentives as a means of increasing productivity. In a few select situations, such as in individual selling, that may be true. It is usually not true for a work team, for professional groups, or for any other group that must work interdependently to produce results.

In the wake of the recommendations of many of the "reform" reports of the 1980s that call for the institution of merit pay for teachers, most of the proposals being advanced are not the kind one could expect to improve educational performance. The key element of many of the proposals involves the selection of a small percentage of the "most productive teachers," who would be singled out to receive some small dollar bonus for the period during which they excelled. The research on motivation and productivity indicates that such an approach would probably be counterproductive.

There is also an implicit assumption in most merit pay proposals that professionals will work harder for a very small increase in pay and that after receiving that increase, they will continue to work harder and better than they might otherwise have done. Empirical evidence indicates that this is a fallacious assumption. Factors others than pay can be powerful motivators for teachers.

Age Distribution. One chief motivation issue in terms of public school faculties arises from the fact that they are getting older. The average age of the instructional staff members of almost all public schools increased steadily in the 1970s and 1980s. In decreasing the size of their teaching staffs, most school systems were forced by state laws and/or collective bargaining agreements to accomplish reduction in force (RIF) according to seniority, with the most junior members being laid off first.

Undoubtedly, in many cases experience and maturity lead to improvement in teaching skill and effectiveness. On the other hand, after people have been teaching for more than ten or fifteen years, it is also possible that they may settle into a regular routine and substantially reduce their rate of learning or improvement. Some teachers may even cease to keep up-to-date in their subject areas or, worse yet, get tired or burned out as working conditions deteriorate and resources available to them become scarcer. More important than the average age of staff is the lack of age mixture among teachers in many school buildings. Young teachers may bring into a system new enthusiasm, new ideas, and the latest theories to be tested in practice, and they can boost the morale of an entire staff.

Of course, in recent years the decline in student population has been arrested; in fact, some schools are growing in size. Furthermore, as the older teachers who were hired in the fast-growth years of the 1950s and early 1960s begin to retire, a much better age balance in school teaching staffs may be achieved. In fact, there are predictions that we will have teacher shortages in the 1990s, though the accuracy of these predictions will depend on what school executives do about pay and working conditions for teachers and on what policymakers do about teacher certification requirements. Market forces will correct the problem eventually, and in fact the pendulum will swing the other way because market forces in a long lead time system tend to overcorrect. Enrollments in colleges of education declined drastically in the late 1970s and early 1980s. For the ten-year period from 1973 to 1983, the number of students enrolled in degree programs declined 53 percent, from 135,000 to about 70,000. Not only have enrollments dropped in colleges of education, but the intellectual quality of the student body in some states and some colleges is alleged to have dropped significantly as other opportunities have expanded, especially for women.

The End of the "Gender Subsidy." The liberation of women has opened new options to females, and some of the best of them are pursuing careers in medicine, law, and business. No longer can schools count on the middle-class second-income wife or the upper-class educated woman to provide her services at below-market rates for the "privilege" of becoming a teacher. As career options became more widely available to female college graduates in the 1970s and 1980s, pay for beginning teachers in many states became less competitive. Fortunately, this problem now shows signs of changing as beginning salaries for newly graduating education majors are rising in some areas and on an annualized basis can compete favorably with beginning salaries in business and industry.

The problems of maturing staff and loss of the "gender subsidy" are not ones with which a local school district can easily cope. As noted earlier, in most states schools have already given up the right to lay off teachers on some basis other than seniority. As for the second problem, social and economic trends beyond the control of a local school system will play themselves out. The pendulum swing of market forces described above can only be dealt with on a state and federal policy level. This issue— providing pay that is competitive with other opportunities now available to young college-educated individuals—involves teacher preparation institutions and state departments of education. Critical, however, is reexamination by leaders across the population and by taxpayers who ultimately foot the bill or suffer the consequences if schools are substandard.

Staff Development and Differentiation. School systems must find ways to maintain the quality and performance levels of their teaching staffs. This means designing staff development plans to introduce current ideas and methods and to reignite the enthusiasm and zest for learning and teaching that lie within most people who enter the teaching profession. It may also mean establishing separate categories or levels of teaching staff members, such as master teacher, lead teacher, intern, and so forth. Staff development and differentiation programs can be much more productive than merit pay programs and may have a greater potential for improving the morale and performance of mature staffs. (One must recognize that improvements in morale are not necessarily directly correlated to improvements in performance and so must consider both satisfaction and productivity in designing any kind of staff development program.) More effective instructional leadership by the building management (the principal and her or his administrative staff) to bring out the best in the current teaching group is also a potentially rewarding area for improving staff motivation. This issue is identified and described next.

Issue 7: Product Quality—Providing Leadership for Instructional Improvement

The product that a school provides can be described in several ways. First, it might be defined as *teaching* or *instruction* or *instructional methods.* Second, it might be defined as *student learning.* Finally, it is often defined in terms of *measurable results* or *student outcomes* as measured by standardized test scores, dropout rates, participation rates, and so on. Student outcomes are most often used by the public to evaluate the effectiveness of a school's production process. Conventional wisdom is that the principal is the key to more effective educational results. Scholars involved in the so-called "effective schools" research (see, for example, Brookover and Lezotte, 1977) have defined effectiveness in terms of student outcomes—specifically, standardized reading and math scores. Because of this and similar research, it is now widely accepted that certain behaviors and attitudes of the building principal lead to better student outcomes. However, it is not clear how these specific behaviors and attitudes are identified—or developed—in people.

One characteristic of successful principals identified by this research is a strong interest in and commitment to improving the instructional program. Other characteristics associated with effective leadership at the school building level are the existence of curriculum and educational goals, order and discipline, regular student evaluation and monitoring, and the active involvement of teachers and community in setting goals and working on schoolwide problems.

While the effective schools research has produced many useful insights about the role of the principal and about the characteristics of a successful academic learning environment, it has two major deficiencies. First, the measure of success used by the researchers is strongly related to the socioeconomic status of a school's student population. As discussed in Chapter Eleven on accountability, test scores, while an essential part of performance measurement, are almost meaningless as an indicator of a school's result-producing effectiveness unless they are adjusted for the natural ability level of that school's student population. A school's effectiveness (at least in that very narrow part of learning measured by standardized tests) should, then, be gauged on the basis of how much it can affect scores above or below the expected scores for its particular student population.

A second serious deficiency in the literature on effective schools, however, is that it gives little recognition to the influence of the central office in enhancing school performance. It is the thesis of this book that, contrary to current belief among some educational researchers, the superintendent or the central office can influence the quality of the instructional leadership in a school system, whether by the seemingly simple act of selecting the "right" principal or by the more complex set of actions that help shape the environment in which the principal operates. The superintendent can provide leadership models, support for instructional evaluation/improvement programs, and policy and board guidance and support for educational achievement. Chapter Nine describes how the central office can influence instructional improvement.

Part of the reason why central offices are not given much credit for positively affecting educational performance is that school superintendents and boards are often preoccupied with financial and budget problems, special government grant and compliance programs, facilities planning, cocurricular issues and policies, collective bargaining, and other "administrative" matters that do not seem to have a direct bearing on the chief products schools were established to turn out—instruction, learning, and student outcomes. The amount of time a school board and central office spend in responding to these problems as opposed to the time they spend on educational policy questions is sometimes rationalized on the basis that the former "are important in order for us to have an educational program."

The public is now saying that school systems have to pay more attention to their education production process and perhaps take a closer look at the quality of that process (teaching and learning) and its product outcomes (measurable results). There may be a lesson to be learned from the problems U.S. industries encountered when their competitive advantages began to erode in the face of foreign competition. U.S. companies tend to give less weight to production and quality issues than they do to financial and administrative concerns. Japanese companies, driven by production and quality concerns, with finance and marketing either merely equal to or subsidiary to the need to produce something better and cheaper, gained a reputation for quality that helped them capture many world markets that were traditionally dominated by the United States. Now U.S. industries and all forms of service businesses as well are looking at quality and emphasizing its prime importance. One of the most popular industry training courses these days is a nationally publicized seminar on the subject of quality.

If the chief product as defined by the clients of the system is measurable learning outcomes and if product quality is of real concern, then board agendas and central office goals ought to include some attention to issues of learning quality and the efficiency and effectiveness of various instructional processes and programs. In the next section, a closely related issue, that of obtaining the resources to invest in instructional improvement, is discussed.

Issue 8: Obtaining Capital (Human and Physical) to Enter the Information Age

New information processing and transmission technologies provide an unusually powerful opportunity for revolutionizing the production and delivery processes of public education. In effect, the revolution in education as a whole has already begun. Yet schools and colleges may be the last to really understand and become part of it. Television, with only a small amount of guidance and/or use by the public school, already takes up more of the average school-age child's time than does attendance at school. The fact that preschoolers and school-age children receive so many kinds of stimuli—information, misinformation, awakened desires for material possessions, for sex, violence, and fame—has had a profound effect on both the curriculum and outcomes of schooling.

When one adds the potential of very inexpensive microcomputers and direct satellite communications technology to the already potent force of television and links these all together, one can envision powerful and potentially explosive forces on the horizon for public schools (if large amounts of capital are made available for training and equipment). These forces have already begun to affect the world of work and the world of industrial training and business communication.

What happens when a school's library becomes, in addition to a collection of books, a set of computer programs, videotapes, and computer-controlled videotape simulation exercises? More tragically, what happens if the school does not make this change and only the people who can afford their own home computers and communication devices have access to the software and potential learning impact of these new tools? How can and how will the general public and our school systems support and respond to new technology? This may be the most important question of the 1990s for public schools. Indeed, the whole question of how society uses the new information technologies may be the key story for the history books in the last part of the twentieth century.

But innovation needs resources and personal champions who have power, time, and funds to nurture new ideas and approaches. At the start of the 1980s, conditions were extremely tight. Budgets were strained for reasons previously discussed, and the job outlook for new teachers and for those with less than ten to fifteen years of tenure was gloomy. Teachers often felt insecure. This insecurity led to defensiveness, that is, to people's becoming adamant about defending old positions. Some teachers understandably clung to past successes and ways of working as colleagues around them were being laid off. Top school system executives who might otherwise have been willing to take some of the risks associated with supporting new or innovative ideas were caught in the struggles of short-run survival and were in the midst of fighting crisis after crisis. Many felt that they could not take the long view when their school boards were demanding short-run performance in dealing with immediate problems.

It takes real courage on the part of a school board and the chief school executive to do what has to be done to create some "risk capital" by reducing or eliminating expenditures on a worthy program—a program that may already be suffering under the wounds of previous budget cuts. Yet effective school executives must ask their school boards to set priorities that may lead to cutting programs or services that are considered very important to some of their constituencies and even considered essential by some "customers," who may threaten to leave the school system. Reducing budget requests by an amount greater than required simply to balance the budget is an essential step toward making resources available to support new and innovative programs and procedures crucial to the long-run health and success of the public educational system. Community involvement, discussed in issue 3, is a vital part of cutting the budget and setting program priorities and is extremely useful to school systems facing decline and financial problems. What superintendents and others in positions of authority must be careful to avoid is only asking for help when they are in trouble or in a budget-cutting mode rather than also asking for community help and involvement when there is new money or opportunity to make positive choices.

At this stage the outlook is mixed for public schools. Their finances are under more pressure than they have ever been. The

declining enrollments and excessive reductions in force most
school districts have experienced in the recent past and the increasing age of the teaching staff tend to make the climate for
change less than encouraging. Even where enrollments are rising again, memories of past financial pressures and the existence
of current constraints on tax increases make it difficult for the
public to provide funds for needed capital improvements, the
benefits of which may not be visible for several years. In the
face of powerful pressures to improve schooling as reflected in
reports such as *A Nation at Risk* and with the knowledge that
technology can provide some help, what can the school executive
do to effectively deal with the introduction of technological
change and the related structural, curriculum, and staff changes
that must inevitably accompany major technological change?
The whole issue of introducing change—an ever present and
more general issue for schools than merely the immediate technological advances—and the leadership required in times of
change are dealt with in Chapter Ten.

Issue 9: Defining and
Pursuing New Market Segments

The first eight issues lead to an important conclusion concerning the definition of a public school and its market. Serious
problems and major opportunities are facing school superintendents of the 1990s, and they will have to take strong action
and display real innovation to maintain their market position.
Education is a growth industry. Although the demand for public
schooling in its traditional form aimed at its traditional market
with its traditional products may be declining, or at best growing only slowly, a great number of opportunities for growth are
available to a school district organization. As society becomes
more complex and knowledge advances geometrically, the population vies for learning and growth just to keep up. Most of this
learning is provided by businesses, colleges, books, television,
and now the computer.

There must be a place for the school organization, with
its teaching expertise, its physical plants, and its management

structure, to participate in several segments of this growing market. This is the new marketing challenge that the chief school officer and school board face. The key challenge is not simply how to sell the current program's value to the community or how to defend a program against budget cuts from taxpayer groups through more aggressive sales and promotional efforts; it is learning how to identify and exploit new market opportunities through study and research and community involvement. This leads to a consideration of the *marketing function,* which is discussed more fully both in Chapter Five and in Chapter Eight. Marketing is identifying and assessing client needs and then developing, pricing, promoting, selling, and providing services that respond to those needs. Note that selling and promotion are just two of the many aspects of the marketing function. Unfortunately, most people think of marketing and selling as synonymous. This error has led to seriously dysfunctional consequences for many nonprofit organizations.

The *first* function of marketing is called market research in business terms or needs assessment in school terms. Some services that school districts are providing and other services that they might be in a position to provide if they were able to identify customer needs and to design products that responded to them include the following:

- Adult education classes
- Preschool education and day care
- Computer literacy training
- Language training
- City recreation programs
- Senior lunch and dinner service
- Counseling services to the public
- Subcontracting of business and industry training
- After-school recreation; social, educational, and day-care services for the student body and the wider community
- Athletic training and coaching for adults (for example, ski lessons, tennis lessons)
- Health and fitness programs
- Meeting facilities and services for corporate use

- Personal computer training and usage labs
- Testing services for corporate use
- Corporate training services (consultation, program design, teaching, and so on)
- Drug rehabilitation services

These services are only a beginning. The important concern is for school executives to keep in touch with changing social and living trends and the educational and human service needs of their communities and then to think hard about the kinds of capabilities their systems have or could readily and easily develop. The kind of two-step process that many businesses go through when they develop a corporate strategy and that schools could well follow involves (1) analysis of environmental opportunities (and risks) and (2) assessment of the organization's capacities (and limitations) to exploit those opportunities. Methods for accomplishing these two steps are described in Chapters Three and Four, respectively.

Schools must look more at opportunities than at constraints. They are too used to saying, "We've never done that" or "That is not part of our traditional function" or "The city or county or some other organization should do that." The fact is there are many needs out there that are not being adequately met, needs that people are willing to pay money to have satisfied (or in some cases government agencies or foundations are willing to fund or contract for) and that an aggressive and innovative school organization can efficiently and effectively meet.

In examining and providing for community needs beyond the traditional schooling services, school systems may have to work with other governmental and private agencies. The question for schools to ask of other agencies then becomes "How can we extend their services, subcontract for them, replace their function with something better or cheaper, help them operate more efficiently, or obtain some of *their* funding and support for *our* programs?"

Reviewing Social and Economic Trends. The process of examining market opportunities (and risks) involves reviewing general social and economic trends and then focusing on how

those trends apply to the local school system. Here are some
of the general trends:

- A sharp increase in single-parent families
- A growing percentage of working mothers of both preschool
  and school-age children
- A growing percentage of retired and senior citizens
- An increasing rate of job obsolescence
- An increasing feeling of aloneness in the population
- A declining respect for authority of church, home, and
  school
- Increasing state and local control of federal programs
- Growing state and federal control of educational policy
- Rising international business competition
- Increasing technical and professional specialization
- The growing number of smaller families
- The movement of the demographic graph's ''bubbles''
- An increasing use of computers
- The reemerging impact of television (with cable capability)
- An increasing emphasis on diet, health, and fitness
- The ongoing need for improvement in reading and writing
  skills
- An increasing sensitivity to adult functional illiteracy
- A continuing shortage of math and science teachers
- A growing surplus of professionals (doctors, dentists, lawyers)
- A continuing surplus of teachers in some fields

The list could continue. This is just a springboard from
which school staffs can begin a discussion of what is going on
around them and how they might develop and use their special
strengths and competencies to meet emerging and important
human needs.

In examining environmental opportunities, an organization should also analyze prospective competition. A school
system must ask who else can and might provide a particular
service. Can the school provide it better, more cheaply, or with
some special advantage for a segment of the market? Schools
must ask these questions even as they relate to their primary
product, basic education for children.

Examining the School System's Capabilities. In assessing a school system's capacities to determine what markets it could potentially serve, we might examine the following:

> *Teaching staff* and its subject matter knowledge, teaching skills, special training, interest in children and knowledge of learning and growth processes
> *Administrative team* and its ability to design, organize, and deliver programs
> *Community reputation and image*
> *Physical plant*—buildings, grounds, cafeteria, auditorium, labs, workshops, classrooms, athletic plant, media resources, libraries
> *Specialist staff,* including nurses, special education personnel, janitors, cafeteria personnel, psychologists and other counselors, athletic coaches, librarians, music and art teachers, and so on
> *Relationships with state and federal departments* of education and with local colleges and universities

The list could go on, and the degree to which the above resources are real strengths will, of course, vary from school system to school system. The point here is that every school should conduct a resource analysis, as described more fully in Chapter Four, and an environmental analysis of opportunities, as described in Chapter Three.

Issue 10: Assessing and
Reporting Results—Accountability

Issue 10 is essentially about accountability, but since that term has taken on a very specific and perhaps narrow definition in educational language, the broader managerial terms of assessment and reporting are used to describe accountability, the topic discussed briefly in this section and then more fully in Chapter Eleven. In this information age the public is not going to continue to let schools get by with the kind of informal and random reporting of results that most school systems now provide. (Test scores are featured this year, a special report on the band or the debate team that went to the state tournament is featured another year, the drop in absentee rates is reported in yet another year, and so on.) As citizens are given more choice in the selection of schools and programs, they will require even more information about a school's performance. Moreover, they will want that information presented in a regular and systematic fashion, in layperson's terms (not in state department of education report jargon), and in a way that will allow them to compare schools on a variety of dimensions.

School boards, staff members, students, parents, and the public at large need information about the resource costs and the benefits obtained from their investment of time, money, and talents. In focusing on the question of accountability for obtaining good value for the dollar spent, it seems logical to raise questions about any school district's chief expenditure: teaching personnel. Over 80 percent of the typical school budget is for personnel, and the largest single item in this category is for certified instructional staff members, including both classroom teachers and specialists. It follows, then, that one of the most important accountability questions to raise with a superintendent is "How well is your teaching staff performing?" One can assess the effectiveness of a teaching staff by attempting to evaluate what members do and how well they do it and also by examining the results of their work in terms of learner outcomes.

The outside constituents of schools tend to look at outcome or result measures. How should one assess student outcomes? This question ultimately leads to a discussion of test scores and other measures of student growth, achievement, affect, and attitude. Before getting into the controversy over the narrowness of standardized reading and math test scores and the dangers of their overuse (clearly they are often used as the exclusive external reporting device and in that way provide the public with much too narrow a view of what schools are achieving), one must ask what it is the public really wants tests to measure or, more broadly, in what learner outcomes they are truly interested. This leads to an analysis of the market demand and needs for education and schooling and to an analysis of the purposes of school systems. This in turn leads back to some very basic questions about the reasons for the existence of schools. One can only answer the question ''What are schools for?'' or ''Why do schools exist?'' after answering some other questions addressed to the marketplace.

Some possible items for which the public might hold school systems accountable and about which they will ask for reports include the following:

1. Standardized test scores
2. Criterion-referenced tests
3. Achievement against goals
4. Affective measures—the need for systematic collection of data on motivation, citizenship, cooperative and social skills, and the like
5. Client satisfaction measures (for example, the number of parental complaints from their classes or the number of student complaints from their classrooms)
6. Dropout and attendance rates
7. Outside awards and recognition
8. Participation rates

The communities of a school system might request that the foregoing indicators be presented in a simple and easy-to-interpret format in any or all of the following media commonly used by superintendents in communicating with their constituents: (1) annual reports to the public, (2) newsletters and other written communications, (3) meetings, and (4) speeches and other oral communications.

Furthermore, the school district will be asked how well it is doing in relation to other similar districts and to regional, state, and national averages and compared to how well it did last year. Chapter Eleven is devoted to the topic of accountability.

Issue 11: Articulating the Strategic Vision

One of the key differences between strategic leaders/ managers and administrators is the former's ability to <u>excite</u>

the imagination, to inspire and uplift the spirit, and through the use of symbols, language, and behavior, to mobilize energy directed toward achieving nobler and longer-run ideals or objectives. Chapter Six provides some guidance to superintendents for developing strategic vision and mission statements for their school systems. This is a process whereby one appeals to deeper human longings and drives to incite action to achieve organizational goals.

In the field of primary and secondary education, the opportunity to link the organization's goals to higher human and social purposes is almost limitless. Men and women who are drawn into careers as educators often are motivated by ideals of service to humanity. Typically, parents' most unselfish desires to "give" are brought to the surface by their need to "help" their children. An entire community can be moved by the thought of helping its "precious" children become the builders of a "better tomorrow" for us all.

Despite the inherent opportunity to inspire and lead, some school executives shy away from the use of the symbols and behavior that might coalesce groups into pursuing constructive change and improvement in a school system. Why? Some may feel that they lack the skill; after all, ability to lead and inspire in the fashion just described only exists in a very few rare "charismatic" individuals, so it is believed. Yet the evidence suggests that this apparent charisma is at least in part situational and that given the right situation, a much wider range of people in our society possess potential skill to lead and inspire.

Another reason people may not lead is that they feel it is safer to *manage efficiently* the status quo. The risks are lower, or so it is believed. The path of managing a given course of action—planning, organizing, and tabulating and ensuring that predetermined procedures and processes are followed—appears to be easier. To many, the risks here seem lower than those of embarking upon bold new actions.

For many potential "leaders," one obstacle is the fear that inspiring words may turn into empty rhetoric. This has happened often in education, as well as in other human organizations. Words, beautiful words, jargon, rhetoric far exceeded the actions. Indeed it is true that the rhetoric of leadership must come from a deep conviction. The leader must also be energized to follow up and make things happen. Later chapters in this book discuss leadership methods for energizing the school system's stakeholders into taking constructive action to help achieve the organization's goals.

Dealing with the issue of articulating the strategic vision and the other issues cited in this chapter requires visionary strategic leadership. A strategic leader is a person who is willing to take local action on some of the eleven issues raised here. Such a leader is willing to do so even though he or she will suffer some short-run pain or discomfort and will have to devote precious energy to overcoming the resistance to change from the advocates of the status quo while at the same time addressing the issues.

3

Recognizing Opportunities
and Threats

The next four chapters are concerned with a process for developing a long-term strategy and direction for a local education organization. This chapter deals with identifying external trends, Chapter Four with assessing the organization's capabilities, Chapter Five with identifying market needs, and Chapter Six with putting together the elements from Chapters Two through Five to develop and articulate a mission and vision and to formulate a strategy. Again, strategy means more than is normally considered in the military definition; here strategy is defined as the pattern of purposes, long-term objectives, goals, and plans and also the implementation processes of organizing, marketing, influencing, managing operations, and evaluating performance. This definition and the notion of systematically assessing both opportunities and threats and capabilities and limitations draw heavily on the work of Andrews (1987) and his colleagues at the Harvard Business School, who developed the framework and concept of corporate strategy so widely used in business and government today.

Defining the Schooling Business or Industry

An important first step in the formulation of strategy is an assessment of the external environment. This assessment involves an examination of the key economic, market, political, social, and technological trends that significantly affect the business or industry in which an organization operates. Thus, in order to determine which trends are relevant for a school system to examine and monitor, it is important to identify the scope of the business or industry in which schooling operates.

The more broadly the industry or business is defined, the wider the range of environmental forces and markets one has to consider in analyzing relevant external factors that could have an impact on a school system. Too broad a definition could diffuse the efforts at strategic analysis. It could require one to examine and understand the complex interrelationships of too large a number of environmental forces and compel one to consider too wide a range of potential school products (services) and markets. Too narrow a definition could restrict the scope of strategic analysis and cause one to miss significant trends and important forces that may now be only indirectly affecting the business of schooling but directly affecting the activities and businesses that have a future potential for competing with schooling. In business, the most serious competitive threats often come from outside an industry that defines itself too narrowly (for example, steel invaded by aluminum, railroads derailed by the trucking and airline industries, and typewriters replaced by computers).

With these cautions in mind, let us proceed to develop a definition of the industry in which the business of schooling operates or competes. Are the service markets for public schooling set in the context of an industry viewed as broadly as the following definition implies?

> The education ''industry'' is concerned with the acquisition, development, and transmission of knowledge, skill, and attitudes to any individual or group.

Or is the industry in which school systems operate better described in terms of the definition of a school system with the narrowest possible service portfolio, as follows?

> Education is imparting basic skills and information to children in the five- to eighteen-year-old age-group.

This discussion employs a definition of the public schooling business that falls somewhere between those two extremes but much closer to the first, broader definition. The delivery of education is imbedded in a complex array of social, political, and technical factors. Schooling itself is a very complex process. Oversimplifying its mission and character could be dangerous to our society in the long run and dangerous to the survival of a local school system employing such a narrow view. Therefore, the definition used to guide this strategic analysis is one that broadly describes the general mission of public schooling:

> The mission of a public school system is to provide opportunities for the development of basic cognitive, psychological, athletic, esthetic, and social knowledge and skills, and the relevant attitudes and motivation, as required by its identified groups of clients, so that these clients may learn to function effectively as productive and learning and caring citizens of a democratic society in a dynamic and changing world environment. In pursuing its mission, a public school will work with families and community groups and agencies when feasible and necessary to achieve community and societal goals for education, to monitor and implement federal and state mandates and goals for education, and to help raise the necessary funds to achieve its purposes.

Why a Broad Definition? Of course, the problem with the above definition is that it is very broad. In developing the definition, my starting point was the narrowest description of the product/service domain of schools, namely, that the business of a school system is to provide basic education for children, to equip them to read, write, and compute so that they may become functional members of society. I then broadened the definition to include the fact that it is the business of schools to provide an opportunity for each child to develop his or her potential abilities and skills.

The discussion will now begin to sound like that found under issue 2, "Reexamining Goals, Purposes, and Mission," in Chapter Two. The two discussions are related because the goals of a specific school system are definitely limited by and one would hope related to the definition of the industry. In fact, the industry definition should be broader than the definition of any one local school's position in it. But this breadth is important because there are other organizations, agencies, and events that compete for the student's attention and the resources that the public will devote to schooling. Failure to understand the nature of these forces and thus to understand the "competitive" arena within which schooling is provided could seriously impede the effectiveness of a school system's current strategy.

The objective is to define the industry in such a way that an examination of trends will allow the strategy formulators to cast a net wide enough to include all the relevant trends that could affect the school system's ability to serve its communities effectively yet narrow enough to be manageable. The chief strategists for a school system cannot be experts in all the areas to be examined, but they must at least know what areas to examine and how deeply to probe in their search for an understanding of the underlying trends that are shaping the future of education delivery.

In terms of the "industry" definition of public schooling, and as stated in Chapter Two, most people would probably agree with the fact that the primary business of the school industry is to provide local delivery of educational services to children in a local geographic area, even though some schools may occasionally deliver services to other clients, some of whom may reside in other locations. The definition is thus expanded to include the option for examining services that are not only related to the primary basic service associated with public schooling but that also have potential major impacts on whether and how constituents will obtain schooling in the future. More controversial, however, is a further broadening of the definition to include services not traditionally associated with public schooling and markets other than children. Thus in addition to providing basic education, the public schooling "industry" in a broader and more liberal definition might be required to examine trends related to the delivery of the following services:

- Career education
- Social, artistic, and athletic skill development
- Socialization of children to become socially and economically functioning citizens
- Teaching children (and if necessary their parents and guardians) to cooperate and communicate with one another and to respect authority
- Attempting to bring all children into the mainstream of society
- Enhancement of self-concept
- Family counseling and health services for children
- Other family social services
- Special programs for the severely disabled, the gifted, substance abusers, unmarried teenage parents, and other special groups
- Custodial care of children
- Other intellectual and personal development and self-improvement opportunities for children and the community at large

In addition to broadening the product-service line definition, one could also broaden the market definition. Thus, a school system might provide the additional services listed above to additional markets—for example, to people younger than five and older than eighteen years of age or to people residing in communities outside the school's geographic area. That means the industry definition of public schooling includes the provision of the services enumerated to any consumer regardless of age or geography. To understand why it could be very useful to employ such a broad definition, consider the following examples.

• A local cable television network installed in the community served by a medium-sized school system in a small town can now receive educational broadcasts from all over the world. Included in the programming are courses in Russian, Chinese, Japanese, and calculus. Some adults in this community are formally studying these languages for credit from a distant university. Do these trends have significance to the school if it does not include adults in its market definition? If it does include adults?

    • A local group is considering opening a franchised day-care center for preschool children. The state government is considering some subsidies to facilitate the start-up of such centers. This particular school community has many dual-career and single-parent families. Is this prospective franchise a competitor, a resource, or an influence on the school's future programs? Is it something else?

    • A recent survey in a middle-class suburb of a large city showed that 60 percent of the children between the ages of seven and eighteen have access to personal computers at home, half of these students using them for word processing and a fourth using them for more advanced computing tasks. A large corporation is considering making software available to personal computer owners with modems (devices that allow the home computer to communicate by telephone with a large-scale computer), which would provide a vast array of elementary and secondary school courses at a very low cost.

    In the cable TV example, if an adult is satisfied with the Japanese course she takes on cable and it is obvious that the same kind of course might be easily made available to her twelve-year-old child, what are the implications? In the case of the day-care example, if the preschool day-care program is successful, how will that affect a parent's willingness two years from now to send his child to your kindergarten? And if he does send his child, how will it affect your ability to educate that child and achieve appropriate learner outcomes? In the personal computer example, is the corporation a competitor? Does potential competition affect only your middle- and upper-income constituents? What if 25 percent of your school's students come from households receiving welfare? Does this change the school's role in employing personal computers?

    The point is that it is important to think about these kinds of questions, and therefore the definition of the schooling industry used in strategic planning must be broad enough to force the district to consider such developments. A moderately broad definition of the business of a school will point to a wide array of appropriate trends to be analyzed and continuously monitored. Of course, no school district will elect to provide services in every market segment of the industry. Each school system must develop its own range of services after considering the needs of its community and the availability of required resources. In doing this it should remain cognizant of the trends affecting the need for and provision of its present and future services in its market segments and of closely related services in related market segments.

While the school system should monitor in a general way a wide variety of trends, it can limit a more detailed examination to trends that affect the business or programs it is actually involved in or wants to be involved in. In other words, the school system does not have to cover the entire industry in detailed fashion. Thus, before attempting to identify which trends are most relevant for it, a specific school system should think carefully about its mission. What business is it in or does it want to be in? What are schools in this community for? How is the primary mission and product/market scope of this school in this community likely to change in the years ahead? Once having thought about these questions, the central office executives and school board are better prepared to define the scope of their analysis or environmental scan. Of course, the Chapter Two discussion about major challenges affecting schooling provides additional guidance concerning the scope and nature of the inquiry involved in environmental trend analysis.

Analysis of External Trends Affecting Schools

For convenience, I divide the external environmental trends that could significantly affect a school system into the following categories: economic, market, political, social-demographic, and technological. I have taken the approach described by Andrews (1987) and designed for business organizations and revised a few of the terms and added a few others to fit the context of the public sector and public schools especially. *Note that it is important to examine each item mentioned not only for its current status and recent trends but also in terms of anticipated changes in these trends.*

Economic Trends. Economic trends include those forces that affect the economic and financial situation that supports the school system. The examination of economic trends may include the following:

• Relevant income and employment levels and growth rates
• Changes in the tax base
• Past and anticipated economic activity in the area
• Plans for and the nature of growth in the school district and nearby areas
• Projected financial status of the state and locality
• Amount of and trends in spending on education and related social services by the local population

Market Trends. Market trends include factors that relate to the size of the prospective customer groups and their buying habits and needs. For schools this may include the following:

• Projections of preschool and school-age populations
• Move-in and move-out rates of families with children
• General population changes in the area and reasons for these changes
• Demands for education services for all age-groups
• Indicators or predictors of future demand for education services such as education levels and occupations of community members
• Socioeconomic characteristics of the district and the immediate area
• Traditions relating to and interest in athletics and other cocurricular activities and programs
• Agendas and strength of any relevant special-interest groups in the community such as the parents' association, business groups, and taxpayer groups
• Demand for related social services and trends in this demand

Political Trends. Relevant political trends are those that may be affecting or could affect the marketplace and the environment for schooling. These include, especially, trends affecting local, state, and national thinking about what should be the ownership and control and accountability mechanisms for schools, what services schools should provide, and who should pay for each service. It is difficult to define a focus in the political area. Since the broad definition of the school "industry" used here might lead one to consider monitoring an almost unlimited number of political trends and forces shaping the lives and behavior of society, it is important for people using this process to focus only on those issues that might have (now or in the future) significant bearing on the nature and operations of schools in their area.

Determining which trends are relevant and important to examine and monitor is one of the major judgment tasks of the central office executive. Here are some examples of the trends and forces in the political area that he or she might examine:

- Federal and state values toward education as they affect issues of equal opportunity, minimum requirements, services to the handicapped, and the like
- Federal and state support for education
- Local attitudes toward schools and their funding
- Changes in the community power structure
- Legislative trends affecting the governance and management of school systems and other public and private social services
- Laws affecting professional staffs and their right to strike and bargain collectively
- Strength and agenda of the state and local teaching professionals' associations

Discussion of techniques for conducting political analysis more focused on a local school system and directed toward the process of executing a strategy is presented in Chapter Seven.

Social and Demographic Trends. Although the next group of trends is labeled social, it is often difficult to separate social and political trends. Social trends pertain to values and attitudes toward education and its management and use. They involve life-styles and attitudes relating to vocationalism, intellectual pursuits, teenage pregnancies, the wisdom of having large or small families, and welfare children, to name but a few.

Consider also demographic trends that include birthrates and changes in birthrates, shifts in population and population location, age distributions and how they are changing in an area. While it should be reasonably clear what constitutes demographic trends, it is apparently not so obvious how to monitor and predict such trends and the resulting population changes to which they lead. Many schools built in the 1960s are now half-empty, perhaps because mathematical projection models (many computerized) assumed past trends would continue and failed to include changes in birthrates since 1959. It is possible that another shift in birthrate trends (this time upward) began in the late 1970s. Failure to foresee this change may have led to some erroneous planning decisions for the decade of the 1980s. A more intelligent use of these models and a better understanding of the assumptions underlying them might prevent grave errors from recurring. Computer projection models using cohort survival formulas can only present the implications of a steady state system, where past trends continue unchanged. We know that is almost never the case. While computerized population projections can provide a useful starting point for developing a forecast of the future that in a very stable community may be quite accurate, there are crucial times and situations when such projections can be very misleading. An effective strategist must be able to foresee a change in trends on the horizon, such as might be caused by changing social values, new industry moving in, or a community changing its socioeconomic characteristics for any one of several reasons. On the other hand, political and psychological forces may push school executives and boards into making facilities planning errors: for example, political forces can dictate that a school be built or kept open because of community pride.

When one focuses on the age distribution of the local community's population, it is especially important to determine the rate of any change. For example, if the rate of decline in thirteen-year-olds or seventh-graders moving on to eighth grade was 5 percent two years ago and 18 percent last year, this raises a flag that indicates the necessity for a closer look at the situation. There may be a perfectly reasonable explanation for the change, but usually the explanations for changes in the rate of change tell us something we should know about the future of a school's market size and character.

Most superintendents know that they must also be sensitive to the prospects of businesses and public organizations moving into or out of the area, new housing developments, changes in the desirability or accessibility of neighborhoods, and of course to the rates of turnover in constituents. More important than the numbers are the reasons for change. Questions such as why people with children leave a school district while other people move into the district should, if possible, be posed to everyone who moves in or out. In addition, school districts should keep a running tally of these answers and trends in the answers for comparison and analysis in total and by neighborhood. It is most important to note whether significant changes occur in the data from year to year or if events change the meaning and importance of some of the data elements. Representative samples of relevant populations should be polled periodically. Exhibit 1 provides some simple questions that might be used for either a mail survey or telephone interview to obtain answers to questions about reasons for moving into or out of a district.

Finally, the school district should make an assessment of how socioeconomic characteristics are changing in the community and by neighborhood. What are the income and education levels and career patterns of the members of the community, and how are these changing? While such data are easy to get by U.S. Census Bureau track for past years, it is sometimes very difficult to get an accurate picture of current trends until a few years after they begin. This means conducting carefully administered surveys by using questions from Exhibit 1. Following are some of the current social and demographic forces that might be monitored for a given school system and its surrounding areas.

Exhibit 1. Questions for Those Moving Into or Out of the School District.

How much did you know about the_____school system before you moved here?
___ Nothing
___ A little
___ Quite a bit

_____
_____

What was your opinion of this school system before you moved here?
___ No opinion
___ Poor
___ Fair
___ Good
___ Excellent

Why did you move into this district?
___ Job
___ Family or friends
___ School system
___ Socioeconomic characteristics
      (kind and quality of neighborhood)
___ Other _____
      _____

If you moved from out of town, why did you choose this specific area rather than an adjacent community or neighborhood?
_____
_____

Marital Status: ___ S   ___ M   ___ Separated or divorced

No. of children you have: ___

If you have school-age children, where will you send them?
___ Public school
___ Private school
___ Other

Ages of children: _____

Why did you move from _____?
                        (Community)
___ Job change
___ Friends or family
___ Different kind of home or neighborhood
      Explain: _____
___ Retirement
___ Different school system

Do you own or rent your new home?
___ Own
___ Rent

Did you own or rent your previous home before moving here or when living here?
___ Own
___ Rent

- Changing life-styles (condominium living, size of families)
- Family structure and values (single-parent families)
- Changes in rates of move-ins and move-outs
- Social attitude toward the importance of any kind of educational experience (arts, humanities, technical sophistication, and so forth)
- Social attitudes and values in ascribing meaning to concepts such as personal development, full potential, substance abuse
- Attitudes toward discipline, regularity, and attendance
- Changes in birthrate trends
- Changes in the number of females of childbearing age and in the age at which they have their first baby
- General values and attitudes as they affect society's views on the appropriate role of public schools

Technological Trends. A great deal of sophistication may be required to understand the engineering specifications and the multitude of uses and applications of new technological phenomena, but little sophistication is required to recognize their power and potential in general social and educational terms. They are just plain awesome. The truth is that most of education's function of knowledge transmission and skill development can be adequately assumed by the use of interactive television and computers. If knowledge transmission and basic skill development are essentially what schools are believed to be for, then schools as we have known them are virtually obsolete.

Nevertheless, to the extent that schools are involved in value shaping, in motivating students to want to learn, and in choosing what they should learn and at what pace and in what sequence, then there will be a need for the school organized substantially as we know it today. The role of teachers will change, however, in this computer/electronic communication age. It may become much more a role of "director of the process" and much less "presenter," as the need increases for teachers to take on the role of "teaching/learning managers." This change will not be without great cost. It will require vast expenditures in staff development to invest in the human capital required to deliver education in the decades ahead, not to mention additional major expenditures for hardware and software.

Are federal, state, and local governments and communities ready to make these enormous investments?

Receiving information in the form of the printed word is much more efficient than listening to it in a lecture. Reading is faster, and one can have the benefit of the best experts by means of their articles and books rather than being limited to the locally available teacher/lecturer. But even though books provide the major portion of transmitted knowledge, the real function of teaching is to see that the right books are selected, assigned, and explained and that students of all ages are motivated through human contact and a reward system (for example, the organization, supervision, and evaluation of learning experiences). That function remains even after the advent of a widely disseminated library of printed information, and it will probably remain—albeit in drastically altered form—in the new information age.

Yet the adoption of technology by education has a long and dreary nonhistory. Some felt that the printing press should have radically altered the function of teaching, but it did not. So why should television and the computer make any more changes in the way teaching is done? The answer for television is that it does provide many of the stimuli that the lecturer provides: sound, color, audiovisual displays, and the like. More importantly, it is widely available to the population as a whole, even to parents who have not been to school. The fact is that this generation has spent an average of eight hours a day in front of a television set, more than the amount of time spent in school. Even though up until now the advent of the television age seems to have had only a small effect on the pedagogical approaches used in schools, new interactive cable and satellite transmission technologies and interactive image-producing laser disc systems may in the future make television a much more powerful actor in the schooling production.

In the case of technology, one must look at all the audiovisual and information-communication areas affecting the transmission of knowledge and data. The computer, especially when it is combined with laser disc interactive systems, could potentially have an even more radical impact on the teaching process. The computer now has the ability to provide two-way inter-action with students: diagnosing knowledge deficiencies, branch-ing and sequencing modules to the special needs of an individual student, altering lessons to focus on areas of weakness, reward-ing students for performance, answering questions, and so forth. In short, the computer could replace most of the functions of the classroom teacher except those involving communication of affect and dealing with the needs for emotional and personal support and stimulation and the communication of human feel-ings as part of the total life experience.

But teachers will still be needed, not only because their function as learning managers becomes more valuable in the computer age but also because those exceptions to what the com-puter can do are so crucial. Indeed, human interaction and com-munication are such an important ingredient for activating the motivation and energy of most students that some would say that if providing a meaning to and drive for lifelong learning were all a teacher did, she or he would still be the most valuable part of the learning process. If motivating and energizing stu-dents are done well, they can lead to their obtaining an excep-tionally good education; if they are not done well, then all the computers in the world will not be able to make a student learn.

I have no specific checklist to offer in the technology area, just an admonition to keep current in this fast-changing area.

Competitive Analysis

Competitive analysis is a special kind of process for en-vironmental trend assessment. For the public schooling "in-dustry," this process involves an examination of the organiza-tions that provide any products or services that could satisfy needs that might otherwise be met by public schools. It also in-volves examining the relative strength and efficacy of the pro-viders of the services that compete with or could substitute for those provided by the public schools. This includes not only ex-amining trends in private and other kinds of schools that could legally provide the state's mandated educational programs for children; it also includes looking at a wide variety of other kinds of alternative providers, such as child-care organizations, health and fitness centers, community education organizations, commercial schools, and social agencies, and examining technological changes affecting providers and prospective alternative providers (TV, home computers, and so on). Obviously, this implies an ability and willingness to identify who these alternative providers are or might be (home schools, computer software companies, business training programs).

Some school administrators do not like to feel that the concept of competition or of the marketplace is appropriate to consider when analyzing the public schooling "industry." Whether it is called "competitive analysis" or a study of how educational and school-related services can be provided in a variety of ways by a variety of organizations, it should be a similar process with a similar result. I will occasionally use the word *competition* in this book even though I know that it is almost a "dirty" word among some public school administrators. Indeed, the attitude of many public educators can be summed up in the following comments from an interview with an anonymous suburban school superintendent: "After all, we are in the public sector and should be cooperating, not competing, with other units of government to provide a needed service to our communities. Furthermore, we shouldn't have to 'sell' our services. We should only provide what people want or need. (Sometimes the need is generated by legislation.) Education is a necessity and people should come to us for it, with the exception of those few who go to private schools and whom we probably can't attract anyway, and we should devote our energies to providing the best service we can rather than to fighting or competing with others."

Only ten years ago, I would have said that the above remarks represented the general attitude of a majority of public educators, who for so many decades had pretty much a monopoly on general primary and secondary education for our society. The seeds of change of this attitude were planted and growing, however, even before the Reagan administration and the deregulation push. As a result, today terms such as *marketing* and *competition* are more acceptable and even discussible in many public school administration circles.

Industry in Which Schooling Operates or Competes. Education, broadly speaking, is a growth industry. The demand for knowledge and professional skills of all kinds has never been greater and seems to grow (faster than the population) every year because of the proliferation of knowledge and our increasing sensitivity to various phenomena occurring in the world around us. Yet in the midst of this growth industry, schooling (just one segment of the education market) is declining or at least seems merely to go along with the population shifts in the five- to eighteen-year-old group. Meanwhile education and education-related needs in an affluent technologically sophisticated economy proliferate. School officials must now think about a market for the schooling ''industry'' that is potentially large and growing and of which their share is fast shrinking rather than thinking about schooling as a market segment of five- to eighteen-year-olds who come to a school building from about 8:00 A.M. to 3:00 P.M. Of the latter market segment, public schools have about a 90 percent share in the United States, and this percentage has been fairly stable over the years. Of the former and larger market, quantification is more difficult, but it is surely true that the public schools' share of the total education market is declining significantly. This seems to be obvious even from a cursory examination of some of the key underlying trends that will affect the size, composition, and activities of the education ''business'' in the twenty-first century.

Thinking about the competitive environment enlarges the scope and perspective for determining which external environmental trends are appropriate to examine. Thus after one completes the competitive analysis step, it might be useful to review the analyses of economic, political, social-demographic, and technological trends to see if one should consider other trends in the environment for closer monitoring.

Who or what are the most significant competitive threats to public schools? Other schools serving the same populations, that is, private schools, home schools, parochial schools? I say no, these are not the biggest competition. It is often true in an industry that the biggest competitive threat to a product or service does not come from the direct rivals in supplying that product or service but from the suppliers of substitute products or related services. For example, as already noted, railroads did not force each other out of business through intensive competition among themselves; other forms of travel, such as the airplane and the private car, federal and state road-building programs, international resorts and travel agencies, air freight, trucking, and giant water transport vessels, were responsible for most of the railroads' troubles. The same could be said of the standard typewriter industry of the 1930s and 1940s. It consisted of blue chip companies with efficient manufacturing and distribution systems and reliable, high-quality products. It was displaced by an industry whose electric and then electronic typewriters were sold as part of total office systems. Direct competitors did not put each other out of business. Other companies from other industries caused the demise of such giants of the typewriter industry as Underwood, Royal, and Remington Rand.

The parallel in education is almost frightening. For example, who has developed and often made a great deal of money from educational software, day-care centers, learning center chains, preschool programs, family counseling services, privately packaged and sold self-help courses and programs, language-training courses for corporate executives? Public schools or organizations from another "industry"?

What are the chief competitive threats to public schooling in today's marketplace for public and private dollars? Consider the following:

- Television, especially cable
- Personal home computers
- Private day-care centers and preschools
- Business and industry education and training programs for employees
- Special self-help courses offered by private organizations in drug prevention, fitness and dieting, exercise and health, self-image development, and how to stop smoking
- Adult education classes in financial planning and myriad other topics
- Present and future vendors of compact laser interactive computer-connected TV ROM discs containing entire libraries, courses, and active simulation exercises

The foregoing list is not necessarily meant to suggest that a school should get into any of these areas. It is meant to help school administrators understand and think about the competition for their services and the context within which their services are chosen and obtained by their clients. Each school system must decide for itself whether it should consider entering some of these markets. It may be forced by legislation or popular demand to enter certain areas (for example, drug abuse counseling and prevention), often without the funding to do so. There are, however, other areas in which citizens are paying a great deal of money to buy private services of the type that the school district has more credibility and public confidence to offer more reliably or safely (for example, day care, preschool programs, adult education classes).

Questions for a Competitive Analysis. A competitive analysis for a school system might ask the following questions:

- Who is the client for this service?
- Why does the client buy or use this service?
- What substitute service can fill this same client need?
- What other agencies or organizations are or can be equipped to fill this need?
- Who can fill the need best and at the lowest economic and social cost?
- What future product or service might be created to help meet this need?
- Who are the suppliers of the raw materials for this service and how can they serve the customer or work with the school to better serve the customer? (Note that the chief raw material of a school system is teaching talent and skill.)
- Could the power relationships between the school system and its suppliers change in the future so that suppliers could become competitors?

In terms of the last question, to take just one example, textbook publishers do not compete with schools, but could suppliers of computer-driven compact disc television courses become competitors or drivers of schooling? My hypothesis is that at this time they could not because they are presently even smaller than book publishing companies. Their size and power could change in the future, however, especially if large commercial television networks or other media companies redefined their businesses as being providers of education rather than just suppliers to the schooling segment of the education market.

Conducting an Environmental Analysis

Let us now turn to a discussion of some practical steps to take to complete an environmental analysis for a local school system. This job is facilitated by having broad participation from people within and outside the school district. Whether or not the district has a planning committee, such as that recommended in Chapter Two, consisting of board, community, and staff members, it will need to obtain input from a variety of specialists. This may be obtained by reading the written works of experts or by meeting with experts, but contributions should come from at least the following fields: political science; sociology, especially demography and cultural values studies; economics, local, state, national, and world; information technology; learning theory; and of course education and education policy. Armed with executive summaries of the relevant materials from these fields or just with a summary of Chapters Two and Three of this book (which is an attempt to select key trends and issues from all these fields as of 1989), one can assign the most knowledgeable people in the district staff and community to brainstorm and discuss the meaning and implication of environmental trends for the local school system. The reason for including a broad range of community and staff people in such an examination is that collective wisdom is more effective in identifying the broadest range of trends and implications than the response of just a small number of people. In larger systems, it might be possible to have as many as a hundred or more people involved in committees, subcommittees, task forces, and so on, gathering and examining these kinds of data. Even in a smaller system, having thirty to fifty people may not be unrealistic. This can be an exciting process in which people feel they are being educated about the trends and issues of the day and during which the superintendent performs an important part of his or her community education function. Another reason for inviting a broad spectrum of community people to assist in the trend identification phase is that they are then more likely to take ownership of later steps in the process, which may require them to make or support significant changes in their schools in reaction to the trends.

One caution! The final analysis and interpretation of the trends, in a world where data are available in abundance to prove and disprove almost anything, require a great deal of help from social scientists and other astute and objective analysts. If you have a very limited consulting budget, it should be focused on the analysis and interpretation of data rather than on their collection. In fact, I would caution against relying on too many outsiders to gather the data. A good library and a few enthusiastic and well-educated community and staff members can do a great deal, starting with reading parts of this book.

Application to the Golden Valley School System

To illustrate the application of the external trend analysis, I will use a specific school district, identifying the relevant external environmental factors and their importance to that school system's strategic planning effort as it faces an uncertain future. The school system is Golden Valley, Minnesota, District 275. A brief summary of the situation in Golden Valley in 1978, the time a series of cases (Klebba and Mauriel, 1978) was written about that system, follows. After summarizing some of the relevant facts from the case, I will apply the framework presented in this chapter to the Golden Valley situation.

The time is 1978. Golden Valley, Minnesota, is a middle- and upper-middle-class first-tier suburb of a reasonably prosperous midwestern city, Minneapolis, Minnesota. It is the smallest school system in its metropolitan area, with 1,400 students K–12. Enrollment has been declining rapidly. Because of the method the state previously used for defining district boundaries, Golden Valley schools include only one-third of the population of Golden Valley, the portion that lies directly west of downtown Minneapolis, is contiguous to the city limits, and is relatively wealthy.

The district's staff is considered to be very good, many of the members having been hired during the boom years of the early and mid-1950s, when this suburb developed. In 1978 most of the staff members have about twenty to twenty-five years' tenure in the system. The community is proud of its school system, and residents are actively involved in its activities. The district was established by neighborhood residents in 1952. The idea put forth was that this small neighborhood could maintain a school system that could be "small and personal" and well financed, combining some of the advantages of a private school with the financing of a public school. The students tended to be very bright, high-achieving children of well-educated parents.

The case information tells us that Golden Valley parents and children are very active in athletics and extracurricular activities. Students have high participation rates, and parents value the fact that their small school system allows for such high rates. A review of the case also indicates that there does not seem to be any specific demand from a strongly mobilized special-interest group. A key bit of evidence supporting this conclusion is that board members campaigned and were elected on general education quality issues and on the basis of their own backgrounds and relevant experience. None were single-issue candidates.

Very few lots are available for the building of new homes in the community, and population growth has stopped. Moreover, younger couples have difficulty buying homes in this area because of inflation in house prices (higher than inflation in general in this area because of concerns about the energy shortage in the 1970s, which has enhanced the value of homes so close to downtown Minneapolis) and high mortgage interest rates. Those who can afford to move into the area are often dual-career professional families who tend to have few or no children.

The district's three school buildings, elementary, middle, and high schools, are geographically very close to each other and located near the busiest highway intersection in the Twin Cities area, a commuter lane from the western suburbs to downtown Minneapolis. The school district's program is considered rich and of high quality, competing favorably in breadth with the neighboring suburban school systems which are three to twelve times its size. Golden Valley was one of the pioneers of the middle school movement in Minnesota and is quite proud of its middle school building, with its modern layout, commons areas, open courtyard, and Olympic swimming pool, as well as of its academic program.

In 1973, the school board formed a citizens' committee to look into the future of the school district and to begin some long-range planning. It developed and mailed a survey to all district residents to gather and assess very specific demographic data and projections about the probabilities of families moving into and out of the district, to ascertain their feelings about the school system, and finally, almost incidentally, to obtain their preference for various ways of dealing with impending financial difficulties, specifically, their choices and relative preferences among alternatives such as larger classes, higher taxes, consolidation with another district, reduced program scope, and the like to solve what was expected to become an enrollment driven crisis.

In general, respondents noted their satisfaction with the schools and their willingness to pay higher taxes (the respondent group was skewed in that it had a higher percentage of people with children in school than the actual 28 percent of households in the attendance area) and their willingness to support a variety of options, even consolidation, as a solution to their problems. On the other hand, the survey indicated that the respondents would strongly oppose any significant reduction in the schools' programs. The survey results also seemed to confirm the worst predictions of a future enrollment decline.

As a result of a levy limitation act passed in 1971 in Minnesota, state aid is based on a formula that in effect limits the tax support of the schools to a set amount per pupil unit, with only some specific allowable adjustments. This presents a potentially severe constraint on the finances of property-rich districts such as Golden Valley. Offsetting this somewhat is a grandfather levy allowing districts to continue funding at the present levels and then a proviso that an additional sum can be obtained from local taxes if a majority of the school district's residents who voted in a referendum election are in favor of an excess levy to support school operations. Golden Valley was one of the first districts in the state to pass an excess levy (6 mills), but the school's administration feels that it cannot ask for the future levy amounts that would be required to keep a broad and viable program operating in the schools as enrollment declines further.

Just prior to the time of the case, the Minnesota legislature presented a bill to consolidate all schools in each county into one county district. Concurrently, there seemed to be a feeling among the leaders in Minnesota's State Department of Education that bigger was better and that the financial problems of schools could be solved by their becoming larger and "more efficient." Golden Valley is above the state median in size but is still the smallest district in its metropolitan area. Indeed, fifteen districts in the county in which Golden Valley is situated presumably would become one system if such radical legislation were passed. The countywide consolidation bill never came to a vote, but it did create a loud stir throughout the state.

Trend Analysis

As superintendent of Golden Valley, what would you do in this situation? Ask for more information from your community? Provide more information to the committee? Present a proposal to the long-range planning committee? Study the situation further? Ask for more information from the committee? If you think you would ask for more information, what specific information would you want, and how would obtaining this information affect your future actions? What are your options?

I suggest that the reader reflect on these questions, using the framework and concepts described in this chapter, before proceeding further. The framework and concepts are applied below to an analysis of the Golden Valley situation.

Economic Trends. The economic data are clear. Wealthy taxpayers in a no-growth community will mean the continuation of decline in the school-age population. However, there are some other important questions not answered by the available data, questions whose answers might help the decision process. For example, how much money could the Golden Valley school system raise in an excess levy referendum? What services could it sell to the community for a profit? What other fees could it charge to parents? Could the school system consider sharing programs with nearby districts? (There are several other districts within a twenty-minute bus ride, and the district already buys the time of a special education director from another district.)

Even though the economic picture is clear (an affluent population but no growth in the area), the economic analysis seems to have raised more questions than it has answered. Yet raising these kinds of questions can be very useful. In seeking answers to them (using some of the methods discussed in Chapter Five on market research), school districts may be able to unveil many helpful clarifications and solutions.

Market Trends. The population projections, move-in and move-out rates, and general demographic trends are fairly clear and fairly gloomy in terms of the decreasing number of people in the five- to eighteen-year-old age-group likely to exist in the near and intermediate future in the Golden Valley attendance area. However, the demand level for general education services must be rising faster than the population at large in a community such as that of the Golden Valley attendance area. For what kinds of educational services? At this time there are no specific data.

Markets for other school-related services could exist in the Golden Valley attendance area and might be served at a profit or at least for a fee that would cover full costs. Day-care services for professional couples, special fee-based after-school programs for gifted students, and self-improvement courses for children or the community at large might be considered. But a limitation of the marketplace in that community is that it sits so close to a major metropolitan area and is surrounded by districts that are much larger and have many service offerings that a small system like Golden Valley cannot easily provide.

There might be some potential for Golden Valley to attract additional public or private school students from other areas. These students would have to come from outside the present attendance area because the number who live in the Golden

Valley attendance area but attend other schools is too small to make a significant difference in the system's future even if they all return to Golden Valley schools.

A possibility might also exist for attracting tax-deductible contributions from the members of this relatively affluent community. (Note, however, that at the end of the 1970s the market was less ready than it is today to provide private support to public schools.)

Political Trends. The brief description of the Golden Valley situation provides us with two important bits of political data. First, there is some current pressure toward consolidation and large-scale efficiency although we do not get an indication of how strong that is. (It later turned out to be quite weak, and faith in the efficiency of bigness lessened over succeeding years.) Second, the state seems to support a commitment toward fiscal equalization in its levy limitation law. Both of these factors seem to offer little help for a small district with an upper-income tax base. Without obtaining a great deal of data about the political situation during the time the case study was written (1978), at the community, county, state, and federal levels, it is difficult to have the "feel" required to make effective political decisions for Golden Valley. A question we should continually ask about this (or any) school's political environment is "What legislation or pressure might be brought to bear in the future that would directly affect the school district's situation?" The point to note here is that while political issues and trends are important factors to consider in most cases, in the Golden Valley situation, political factors are clearly overshadowed by demographics and program and financial projections.

Social and Demographic Trends. Some national macrosocial data are clear at that time: smaller families, a greater need for education as a professional stepping-stone, greater opportunities for women, especially those with advanced education. Other data are less clear. Will the neighborhood school, with its potential advantages of familiarity and personal attention and its perceived ability to build self-confidence in students, outweigh in the minds of the present and future Golden Valley parents the need for the more sophisticated and broader programming that a larger school system can offer? What will be the special needs of any new parents who move into the district or of present residents who decide to have children in their late childbearing years? Demographic data for Golden Valley specifically also seem quite clear: little chance for growth, a declining number of school-age children, fewer young couples moving into the district, and statistical enrollment projections pointing to a reduction in the size of the school district's traditional market population to a figure that appears to be very uneconomical to serve effectively.

One caveat for all of us, including the administrators of Golden Valley, in interpreting enrollment projections is that mathematically developed forecasts are typically not sensitive to sudden environmental changes or new circumstances. One must carefully examine changes in the rate of change and the possible intrusion of unanticipated new events. The accuracy of cohort survival rate projections, or almost any other form of computerized or manual projection techniques for forecasting the future, depends on the continued existence of past relationships.

Any changes in the rate of change or any dramatic events (movement of a new business into town, change in zoning laws, sudden change in retirement patterns or desirability of this community as a residence) could upset past patterns and change the validity of the future projection significantly. Therefore, important human judgments must be added to the interpretation of the statistical projections. This does not mean that one should ignore the computer projection. In the absence of any major new event, it is usually the best prediction we have. But human judgment must be applied in making a careful interpretation of the computer printouts. Finally, it should be noted that each of the suburban districts contiguous to Golden Valley was experiencing a similar population decline at the time. The data for Golden Valley's enrollment decline were confirmed in a variety of ways and proved to be quite accurate as the years went by.

Technological Trends. For many years prior to 1978, the time the Golden Valley case study was written, there had been available to educators many powerful forms of electronic technology. Yet within schools, they seemed then and seem even today, more than twelve years later, to be much less visible than they are in the world outside school. While technology was available to perform efficiently and effectively many innovative instructional acts—and was especially available to a small well-endowed school like Golden Valley—few schools in the 1970s were very far along in adapting television, the computer, or other electronic media for instructional use. The fact that a great deal of potential for the use of technology was available should be considered in any strategic analysis.

Interpretation and Use of the Data

Having collected data on and reviewed the external environment facing the Golden Valley school system, what has one learned? While this external strategic analysis is only a beginning step in a multistep process, one might draw the following conclusions:

- Golden Valley will have to make some drastic changes, either in its program, class size, or corporate structure (for example, consolidate, merge, or form cooperative relationships with other districts).
- The community wants good education and a broad program and is financially supportive, but it lacks the intense local pride and loyalty to its school system that would lead it to demand that the system maintain its independence from other school systems. (The last point is an inference drawn from two facts: first, the respondents to a survey sent out by the long-range planning committee stated that they were willing to consolidate to preserve a rich program; second, this is part of a large metropolitan area where there is typically not the intense community loyalty that usually exists in more isolated small towns.)
- Technology could provide potential help to a school like Golden Valley.

- Markets for other school-related services could exist in the Golden Valley attendance area and might be served at a profit or at least for a fee that would cover full costs.
- There is some potential for Golden Valley to attract additional public or private school students from other areas, but there are many difficulties to overcome in seeking this result. Such students would have to come from outside the present attendance area because of the small number who live in the Golden Valley attendance area but attend other schools.
- The school district may be able to solicit private tax-deductible contributions from the members of its relatively affluent community. While starting a nonprofit educational foundation to collect donations to support the present school system seems like a real possibility in a community like Golden Valley, the difficulties in pursuing such an approach are great.
- The district still has many feasible strategic options to pursue, but the number of such options could diminish within the next few years.

The examination of relevant data on the environment within which a school system must conduct its business is an ongoing process. For each school system, the board and the executives must decide which trends are crucial, which should be monitored frequently and closely, and how the data should be interpreted. This environmental analysis will not necessarily give answers about what to do, but it should help bring to the surface many of the issues that ought to be communicated and discussed widely as the school district develops its strategies and plans. It is important for the community and especially for the current customer groups to understand and discuss the context within which school decisions are being made, programs are being developed, and results are being achieved. Thus, an ongoing discussion and debate on the issues presented in Chapter Two, other issues identified by a school district, and a review of trends highlighted in this chapter should be continuously engaged in by a broad sample of individuals and groups. School boards should see to it that there is public awareness and ongoing debate on these matters.

Next Steps

An analysis of the external environment tells a school system something about the opportunities and threats in that environment. The next step in a strategic analysis is to consider the school system's capabilities and limitations. The internal assessment should tell something about the possibilities that exist within the system to exploit these opportunities to serve the needs of its constituents. The internal analysis attempts to examine in a systematic manner the school system's strengths and weaknesses, resources and limitations, assets and liabilities, both real and potential. The process for engaging in this internal analysis and its application to the Golden Valley school system are discussed in Chapter Four.

4

Assessing the School District's Capabilities and Limitations

This chapter deals with the analysis of the resources, strengths, weaknesses, and competencies of a school system. It tries to answer two basic questions: What is this organization uniquely qualified to do? What can it do especially well? In terms of corporate strategic planning, these questions might be phrased as follows: What is the school system's distinctive competence? What is it able to do or can it become qualified to do especially well and efficiently? What resources does it have (or lack) for pursuing its primary and secondary objectives and any other objectives it might wish to pursue?

Capabilities and Resources of the School System

An examination of the resources (or a resource audit) of a school system would start with a review of the following:

Teachers: the level and quality of the training, experience, competence, and performance of teachers in the system and the working relationships within the teacher group

Administrators: the quality and working relationships of the administrative team

Programs: the type, quality, history, and reputation of the school district's programs

Board and board-administrator relations: the nature of the school district's board of education and the quality of

working relationships between the board and the ad-
ministrative team
Students: the background characteristics and outside en-
vironment of the student population
Physical facilities: the buildings, equipment, playgrounds,
athletic facilities, land, and the like owned or leased
by the school system
Reputation and image of the school system
Special programs and their quality
Student achievement rates: past test scores, dropout rate, at-
tendance, honors attained, and so forth
Student participation rates in programs
Special features of the local community: support for education,
socioeconomic levels, parental characteristics and the
potential level of parental involvement in the schools
Financial condition (especially general fund)
Tax base and future financial and enrollment prospects
Other assets: human resources in particular, leadership,
relationships among the management team, and so on

The following sections of this chapter describe each of the
key assets of a school district and provide some suggestions for
how each might be assessed.

Teaching and Administrative Staff. The most important
assets of a school system are intangible. They reside in the minds
and spirit and abilities of the teaching and administrative staff.
Although the assets that are easiest to see are the buildings and
the financial statements and perhaps the formal credentials of
the certified staff, these tell very little about what makes a school
system perform in a manner that leads to results and useful outcomes for its constituencies. What really determines the potential performance of a school, besides the quality of the student
body input, are the skills and abilities, behavior patterns, and
motivation of the staff, both latent and manifest, potential and
realized.

How can one examine the skills of the teaching professionals more closely? Does one look at the level and quality of

their education, the subject matter they have studied, the degrees earned, the proficiencies demonstrated in previous schooling and training of each staff member? Does one look at the experience of the staff members, what they have taught, what other jobs they have had, what their relevant outside interests and activities are, what their performance record has been? The answer is yes to all of these questions. But that still gives us only part of the answer.

How have they learned to cooperate and work together? How adaptable are they? How quickly can and will they learn new approaches to teaching and new subject matter content? What is their motivation level? Do they willingly volunteer for outside work, for committees? Are they deeply involved with and caring toward the students? Do they regularly attend meetings and conferences to keep up-to-date in their fields as well as with current problems and issues?

Most of the same kinds of questions can be asked about the administrative team. It is also important to raise questions about how well the administrators communicate with teachers and other school constituents, especially parents and students. Do the administrators hold regular problem-solving and goal-setting meetings with staff? What kinds of goals do they set and what kinds of processes for monitoring and reporting on goal achievements do they have in place? Does the administration encourage competency-related workshops and experiences as opposed to only rewarding credit-hour accumulation purely for its own purpose or for degree-seeking purposes? Are the administrators available to parents and students when needed? What kind of rapport do they have with each of their constituent groups?

Some of these questions are not easy to answer. However, an executive must be sensitive to what the questions are and to clues that might give at least partial answers to them. One can examine in any given school system the extent of curriculum change in recent years, as well as changes in formats, schedules, technology use, patterns of community volunteer usage, and other possible indicators to uncover some of the answers to questions on the adaptability of the staff.

Many school people say they can walk into the building and "feel" the spirit, seriousness, dedication, and motivation levels of a school's staff. These key "spiritual" factors, of course, may vary from building to building in an individual school system. But they are the factors these intuitive analysts say produce the learning outcomes and results in a school.

A more scientific (though not necessarily more helpful) examination of the factors that lead to performance results or student outcomes can be obtained from research studies, such as the work on effective schools (Edmonds, 1982). Perhaps the most important contribution of the literature on effective schools is that it provides a very useful checklist for examining the strengths and limitations of the teaching and administrative resources of a school. Since these resources are a school system's most important assets and an examination of them is probably the most important aspect of an internal resource audit, I find it useful to refer to the researchers' identification of the teacher- and administrator-related correlates of effectiveness in schools.

The Minnesota State Department of Education (1984) has distilled from this literature the following attributes of effective schools, which it uses to guide a state department program to increase the "effectiveness" of participating Minnesota schools:

Social Organization Attributes
Clear academic and social behavior goals
Order and discipline
High expectations (of students)
Teacher efficacy
Pervasive caring
Public rewards and incentives
Administrative leadership
Community support

Instruction and Curriculum Attributes
High academic learning time (ALT)
Frequent and monitored homework
Frequent monitoring of student progress
Tightly coupled curriculum
Variety of teaching strategies
Opportunities for student responsibility

All but two of these attributes (the last two under social organization) are largely if not fully influenced by teacher behavior and performance coupled in some instances with leadership at the building level. Since the attributes studied and reported on in the so-called "effective schools" literature are useful aids in examining a school system's resources and capabilities, their use is recommended as a starting point for this examination. Unfortunately, it is much easier to recognize the existence of the above attributes than it is to create them in a situation where they do not exist. Even in assessing their existence, researchers have had to use subjective or perceptual measures in many cases. For instance, how does one assess whether a school has a clearly articulated set of academic and behavioral goals, pervasive caring, or teacher efficacy without asking someone's perception of the existence of this characteristic in his or her school? I should hasten to add that I do in general have confidence in the judgments researchers have made in gathering and interpreting data on these traits; I only wish to point out some limitations that exist in the application of their results.

If it is difficult to assess the degree to which each attribute of the effective school exists in a particular school, then it must be very difficult for an administrator to develop these attributes in a school and then evaluate efforts at making that school "more effective." To know that you must have clear goals tells you little about how to make them clear. To know that "pervasive caring" is one key to effective learning gives you little guidance in pursuing a motivation and staff development program for a typical staff let alone for a staff that is hostile, apathetic, or distrustful of some of its administrator colleagues.

In my view, the biggest limitation of the research on effective schools, however, is that the researchers define effectiveness (their dependent variable) in terms of scores on standardized reading and math tests of basic skills. This means that the research may be most useful for a primary school or for a school that has problems in helping its students perform well on such tests. Unfortunately, the most serious criticisms of U.S. schools relate to their failure to teach people to think critically, communicate in writing, and speak clearly and effectively, not in teaching children how to add and comprehend basics.

A Word About Collective Bargaining. A major force, relatively new on the scene, that has important consequences in dealing with motivation and relationships among the teaching staff and between teachers and administrators is the use of teacher unions or associations to bargain collectively for salaries and working conditions. In some school districts even middle management is organized into bargaining units for purposes of negotiating with the school board on salary and working conditions.

In performing the internal resource audit, one must also examine the nature of the bargaining units and employee associations that exist among teachers and administrators, the past history of conflicts and settlements, the strength of these associations, and the degree of loyalty they command. Who negotiates for each employee group, and how much authority and credibility do they have? When evaluating the human resources of the school organization, it is important to examine both the pros and cons and the strengths and weaknesses of these collectivities. It is also important to look at the history of the relationship between each of the various employee organizations and the school board.

Administrators often cite the existence of strong teacher associations as a reason for not being able to introduce major changes in direction or in personnel practices. Indeed, if it is true that a given position taken by a union on a given issue is considered to be both rigid and detrimental to the education of children, then management has a serious responsibility to address the issue. A weakness often cited for school districts is the fact that teacher unions require the district to pay teachers on the basis of their number of years in the system and their education level, with no consideration for the kinds of professional qualifications they have, for their motivation and performance levels, or for the differing characteristics of their jobs. The first response of many administrators is "We can't do anything about that because the union won't let us change it." The first response should be to attack the problem head on and to discuss how the interests of teachers, children, and administrators can be served by some form of revision in the present arrangement, if that is the need. The problem of introducing change is discussed in

Chapter Ten. The concerns to note in this analysis of a school system's capabilities are the degree of flexibility and adaptability the organization has or can develop in dealing with the changing environmental circumstances and how arrangements such as union contracts and other agreements and norms affect this flexibility.

It is not always easy to tell whether an existing characteristic is a strength or a weakness, much less determine its relative importance in influencing the performance of a school. For example, the existence of a strong and effective teacher association may be a strength for administration if the leadership of that association can be counted on to work consistently to achieve administration goals. Often the goals of a teacher association can be very functional for administrative and student learning and effective school performance. At other times a strong union may be a handicap. Thus, with each resource one examines as part of this strategic audit, one must carefully assess that resource's strength and functionality.

Programs. How does one examine the quality and reputation of a school system's programs? On the surface or from a distance most schools' programs look quite similar. They all have art, music, English, physical education, boys' and girls' interscholastic athletics, and so on. What, then, are some of the factors that make one school's programs different from another's? In attempting to assess the quality of a school's effort, output measures are a natural place to start. Test scores; popularity of courses and teachers as indicated by registrations and student and parent surveys; special awards for performance in interscholastic debates, tournaments, contests, and colloquia; percentage of graduates gaining admittance to highly competitive colleges; job placements; and attendance and completion rates are some of the factors to be examined. But important input and process variables must be examined as well. Factors such as enthusiasm and motivation of teachers and students, range of course offerings, and variety of special activities and performances staged by the student body may tell even more about the quality and effectiveness of the school's programs than do the output measures currently employed by most school systems.

It takes skilled judgments made by professional educators and others to assess properly the data on the quality of programs. Yet even though ratings of some of the most important school performance factors are subjective, professionals' systematic gathering and reporting of results and interpretations of data on the items just enumerated (plus other relevant items) can usually provide some indication of the quality of programs. Moreover, if comparable data are gathered and reported on a regular basis, then trends can be identified. A more complete discussion of the assessment of performance is provided in Chapter Eleven. The resource section at the end of this book contains a case, "Management Report to Stakeholders," that provides a comprehensive list of performance measures.

Unfortunately, the nature of reporting or the lack of comparable data being reported by individual schools makes it very difficult to compare the performance of one school against another except on standardized test scores (and then only if the schools administer the same tests at the same grade level), and even those comparisons are clouded by the fact that the schools have different student raw material and different curriculum sequencing. Despite the difficulties in obtaining true measurements, a regular and systematic analysis of available data and an objective professional interpretation (if not a full-scale evaluation) can provide some guidance in evaluating the quality of a school's programs—and programs are the school's most important "product."

Quality of the Board. The board of education can be an important asset (or liability) of a school system. Insofar as the board represents the community or the marketplace, it could be viewed as an outside constituency and therefore have been discussed in Chapter Three. Certainly a board's composition and activities reflect some of the trends and circumstances existing in the external environment. I have chosen, however, to include the examination of the school board as part of this discussion of the resources of a school district. In practice, most boards act as part of the executive management of school systems. They set policy, and they oversee and sometimes make management decisions. In a small or middle-sized school district, a board can be an important part of management, even though the theory says, "The board makes policy and the superintendent carries out policy."

The first item to discuss in regard to a school board pertains to the quality of the board members as individuals. Most people elected to a school board are lay citizens. When first elected to the board, they may know little about the school system and its operation. Occasionally, a new board member is elected on a single issue and comes to the board with just that axe to grind. He or she may even have been elected on a platform of getting rid of the current superintendent. The majority of board members, however, are most likely citizens with good intentions and interested in the best education possible for the children in their community. They come to the board with a desire and willingness to devote their time and effort to the pursuit of this goal. Usually they are parents with children currently in, about to enter, or recently graduated from the school system. (I base this conclusion on general observation and reading, especially of administrator and school board journals, not on scientifically gathered data.)

Whether the foregoing description is valid for all your current board members, it is probably useful to use as a starting assumption in dealing with directors and especially when working with those who are newly elected. A new board member's early orientation and "training" can have a very strong influence on his or her future behavior as a school official. Usually this orientation consists of reading a set of manuals from the National School Boards Association, possibly reading some materials and attending workshops offered by the state chapter of the same association, and perhaps reading some local district manuals. A good superintendent supplements these activities with some carefully planned face-to-face conferences and local orientation sessions.

In some cases, of course, board members bring valuable experiences to their school systems, in addition to their knowledge of the local community and its views. They may serve on other boards, act as executives for other organizations, or have some previous experience in education. At a minimum, they bring different views and perspectives to the school administration. Surveys taken and reported by the *American School Board Journal* ("The Typical School Board Member," 1989, p. 21) indicate that well over half of school board members responding hold managerial or professional jobs, and the reported "typical" family income for a school board member in 1988 was between $40,000 and $49,000.

Board-Superintendent Relationship. The relationship between the board of education and the superintendent is a crucial one for the school system. Here are some questions to ask about that relationship:

- What kind of help and training did the superintendent provide to the current board members?
- Who seeks advice from whom? On what?
- Do they meet outside of board meetings?
- Are they in constant contact on key issues?
- Does the superintendent keep the individual board members informed on key issues and upcoming problems?
- Do individual board members keep the board and superintendent informed of issues and concerns in the community?
- Is the relationship cordial, friendly, distant, something else?

Questions about the conduct of the board's meetings should focus on who runs the meetings, who sets the agenda, and what the pattern of interaction is. How often does each member speak? How often does the superintendent speak? How often does each person ask a question, answer a question, lead the discussion to a new topic, express negative views, express positive views? How often are his or her ideas agreed with, built upon, ignored? How often does he or she agree with or build upon someone else's ideas?

A simple interaction analysis can be very revealing, especially as it determines the role and power of the school superintendent, board chairperson, and individual board members. By using the kinds of categories exemplified in the preceding questions and keeping track of the amount and sequencing of comments by each board member at a board meeting, an observer coached on how to record and classify dialogue and interactions can conduct such an analysis. He or she can do this by being present at a meeting or by examining a transcript of the meeting. Just one or a few meetings can be enough to provide interesting and sometimes surprising insights.

Questions about the superintendent's role in board meetings might include the following:

- How well does the superintendent provide data to the board?
- Does the superintendent present one recommendation for approval on important questions, or does she or he present two or more options with analysis of each and a recommendation or just an analysis and no recommendation?
- Does the superintendent attend board committee meetings?
- Does the superintendent determine the charge and provide direction to citizen/board committees?
- Does the superintendent communicate the minutes of the board meetings to the community? If so, how?

The most important act of a board is the selection of the chief executive officer. In analyzing the current board-CEO relationship, as well as the board's performance, it can be very useful to examine the process the board used in appointing this superintendent. If that act was not a recent event, it is useful to examine the status of the current team. Did the present board select this superintendent? If so, with what criteria and job description? If not, how many current board members were on the board that did select the current superintendent? How has the superintendent "trained" the current board? How has the board "trained" the superintendent?

The school board not only hires but also sets the compensation of the superintendent, evaluates his or her performance, and determines how long he or she shall remain in office. In this regard, the school board is quite different from a corporate board. It is not unusual to find school boards terminating or failing to renew employment contracts for their superintendents; this is quite unusual in the corporate world. Occasionally, a school superintendent is fired without obvious cause or warning, though the wording of the contracts that some superintendents negotiate with their boards may put limits on this. In practice, a superintendent usually, but not always, has some warning that he or she might be losing the board's support.

The majority of school boards seem to have a good and amicable working relationship with their superintendents. However, the fact that the composition of the board can change suddenly (in most states school board elections are held every year and at least one-third of the board seats are up for reelection) means that there is an ever-present threat to the superintendent's position. The fact that a superintendent can be fired rather suddenly and without major cause—even though this occurs only rarely—lies quietly (sometimes not so quietly) in the background and must have some impact on the conduct of the board-superintendent relationship. From a managerial point of view, it is important to give some thought to this issue.

(For a more complete discussion of board-superintendent relations, evaluation of the superintendent, and a very useful discussion of the role of the school board, see *The School Board's Responsibility: Effective Schools Through Effective Management,* co-authored by a person with a business and consulting background and a person with experience as a school superintendent, Genck and Klingenberg, 1978; and for some practical suggestions on working with boards, see *The Superintendency: Leadership for Effective Schools,* Davidson, 1987, chaps. 2–3.)

Students: Heredity and Environment. Heredity and congenital factors are really the heritage that the families in a district provide to its student population. This heritage impacts on the intellectual and athletic performance levels that might be expected from a given group of children. While research has shown that the environment, that is, the school and home support system, has a great deal to do with how abilities are developed and with the motivation to use one's abilities, it is believed that heredity sets the parameters or limits of the performance or achievement. (For a brief and cogent discussion of the influences of heredity and environment on IQ and performance, see Weinberg, 1983.)

Recent findings indicate that these parameters are very broad indeed; seldom do any of us come close to achieving a small fraction of our potential. Thus the school system should not look at the level of IQ apparently inherited by its students as being a significantly limiting factor in their achievement. There are many schools in very poor neighborhoods (where presumably the parent IQ level is lower than in middle-class or upper-class suburban systems) where students perform exceedingly well.

Environment, both inside and outside the school, thus becomes a very important contributor to the performance of a school district. A student's environment outside the school—for example, home and family life, the attention and example parents give to the child, particularly as they reflect parental attitudes toward the importance of school, and the emotional support they give the child in his or her efforts at school—can be significant in terms of the results the school can achieve. While many of these factors are outside the formal control of school district management, there are some actions a superintendent can and should take to influence the community's learning support systems. This is especially true in schools where the percentage of children coming from single-parent or broken homes is high, a situation that exists in a large and increasing number of districts. Some possible actions are:

- Inviting people by phone to a meeting for parents on how to encourage children to study
- Visiting homes
- Having parent grade-level parties
- Arranging special courses or meetings where topics of concern to parents—such as AIDS, teenage pregnancies, and drug prevention—can be discussed

Some urban schools have tried with varying degrees of success to institute programs to provide students with some of the outside support needed to encourage their attention to school work and have even been successful in getting poor and working single parents involved in the schools.

Therefore, although it is important to consider the intellectual and other capabilities of the student body when interpreting the meaning of achievement test scores, it is not appropriate to absolve the school system completely for student performance levels that allegedly relate to the socioeconomic status of its student body. Both a low-income district with a high dropout rate and low test scores and a high-income district with above average scores but scores below its average child's ability and past performance level should be held accountable for the level of performance of their students. A school system should be given credit (or blame) for the gains (or losses) in such scores in relation to the starting point of its students and held accountable when scores do not move up as fast as they should given the raw material input.

Physical Facilities. Physical plant and facilities are a self-evident resource, but their uniqueness and importance in making possible many alternative activities and programs are often missed. Almost all school systems are rich in useful physical resources: classrooms, laboratories, gymnasiums, auditoriums, community centers, libraries, offices, desks, chairs, computers, chalkboards, television and other audiovisual equipment, football fields, playgrounds, other athletic facilities, testing rooms, music rooms, musical instruments, cafeterias, and so forth. Obviously, some schools are much more highly endowed with these assets than other schools are. The question for the leadership of a local school to pose continually in a variety of settings is "What other community needs or current school program needs might these facilities serve, either as a public service or on a fee-for-service basis?"

Image, Reputation, and Other Assets. Any assets of a school system may be strong or weak, big or small, in abundance or completely lacking (or even actual liabilities, as in the case of a negative reputation and image). Most of the key assets that can make a difference in a school's performance have already been discussed. Rather than discuss each of the remaining assets enumerated at the beginning of this chapter, I will make a few general statements here about the other assets that should be evaluated as part of the resource audit. I encourage school executives to examine the existence and strength of such important items as reputation of the school (an annual survey sent to a small random sample of parents and nonparents might be helpful in tracking changes), special programs and their perceived value, past student achievement and participation rates, and community support for the school system. Each of these factors can be assessed and utilized as a school system considers new services and new markets.

In the development of a strategy and plan or set of programs to be offered and goals to be pursued, a full examination of the external environment and the opportunities it possesses, as discussed in Chapter Three, and of the resources and limitations, as discussed in this chapter, is an extremely important first step.

Summary and Application to the Golden Valley School System

In 1978 the Golden Valley school system had, as is true of all school systems, many strengths and resources, both potential and in use. The key items are discussed below.

Teaching and Administrative Staff. First were the teachers. They were highly trained, most with master's degrees and some with Ph.D.s. A majority of the fifty-seven certified teachers had at least ten years of teaching experience. The elementary teachers were considered among the best in the area, though they were not all equally popular with parents and students. Most of them were hard-working, caring, diligent people in the classroom, and as a group they seemed to work well together.

The middle school and high school teachers were more independent than the elementary teachers, as one would expect. Curriculum development, teaching, and most academic matters were handled by the faculty. The middle school had some subject areas that were thinly staffed or in which the faculty was considered only average; on balance, however, it was considered to have a superior program, and compared to other junior high schools in the area, it had excellent student discipline and performance. The high school physics and math teachers had excellent reputations with both the student body and parents, and the advanced college-level physics course was especially popular in the high school.

The administrative team comprised the superintendent and three principals—one for each school. All administrative duties, such as bus routing, class scheduling, discipline, instructional supervision (done in only a very limited manner), were shared by the principals, while the superintendent handled budgets, board relationships, personnel matters, and external relations. The administrators seemed to work quite well together.

The elementary school principal had been in his position for the last twelve years, having taught previously in a nearby suburban district. He held periodic faculty meetings, and while he was observed to be quite directive in his leadership style, he was also supportive of and seemed to have good rapport with his staff. He did not have a formal teacher evaluation system in place and was not known to do a great deal of class observation of teaching. He seemed to relate well to and know most of his students. The middle school and high school principals concentrated on matters such as counseling, college placement, extracurricular activities, discipline, athletics, teacher assignments, and scheduling, as was typical of secondary school administrators in those days.

Programs. Like most other schools in Minnesota, Golden Valley was involved with a variety of high-quality programs in addition to its regular academic offerings. In the elementary school, the art program was considered better than most and quite special because of a very talented and inspirational teacher. The elementary school choir and the middle school band were also considered exceptional. Theater arts and orchestra in the high school were good but did not have a particularly outstanding reputation. Exceptional teachers stood out here and there in the school system—for example, the teacher of a Shakespearean English course, teachers involved in the math and physics sequence referred to above, an excellent chemistry teacher, and a sixth-grade multidisciplinary social studies/economics teacher.

For those students who desired a high school vocational program, there was a dearth of opportunity in Golden Valley. In fact, this was considered one of the few weaknesses in the school system's program. Most Golden Valley students went on to college. The college preparatory program was considered among the best in the metropolitan area, though the course offerings were not as varied as those in neighboring schools.

Student participation rates in cocurricular activities were very high, with more than 80 percent of the boys and over 50 percent of the girls involved with at least one varsity sport, and most students involved with some other cocurricular program. The philosophy of the school in athletics was to let every student who really wanted to participate be on and travel with a varsity team.

Board Makeup and Board-Administrator Relationships. Golden Valley's board consisted of two managerial people (one businessman, who was the board chairperson, and one woman with both public-sector and political roles), two professors (of business and of medicine), an attorney, and a nurse. The six board members worked well together, and board-superintendent relations were very good. There was mutual respect among board members and between the board and the administrative team. None of the board members had been elected on a specific issue, their main concern being to continue to provide quality education to the children residing in the district. All members seemed to take their work seriously and were conscientious in the performance of their duties, yet not intrusive on the superintendent and the management practices of the school system.

Board meetings were moderated by the chairperson, who used his position to limit and direct discussion to each point on the agenda. However, he also allowed freedom and flexibility when a board member wanted to discuss a matter not on the agenda or at greater length than planned, provided the member could justify the need for a departure from the planned agenda. Meetings lasted several hours, sometimes not adjourning until close to midnight. The superintendent was very active in taking the lead on each agenda item and in pointing out the needs, policies, and precedents, where relevant, in the discussion. He also helped the chairperson keep the meeting moving and on the agenda.

Student Background. Golden Valley's students were an exceptional group, who scored very high on PSAT and SAT and all standardized tests administered in several lower grades on a regular basis. In general, the students came from homes very supportive of education and were highly motivated. Most of them came from high-achieving and ambitious home environments. In fact, many parents had moved to Golden Valley because of the academic reputation of its schools, combined with its relative smallness and personal feeling.

Physical Facilities. Golden Valley's physical facilities were also impressive, as noted in Chapter Three. There was capacity for over 1,800 students; an excellent new auditorium and an Olympic swimming pool, both of which were used for some community events; and several athletic fields used by the Little League and by the village's park programs, as well as by the schools' athletic departments. The middle school classrooms were a bit small because of the modern design of the space, with generous common areas where special activities and labs were run. The three school buildings sat on a prime piece of real estate near one of the busiest intersections in the metropolitan area. Poised just a few miles from downtown Minneapolis, it was an area of the city passed by thousands of commuters driving into the downtown section from second- and third-ring western suburbs in the well-to-do ''lake'' area.

Image, Reputation, and Other Assets. The Golden Valley school system had an excellent academic reputation and image in and out of its community although there were two or three larger and more famous suburban schools. The village of Golden Valley was considered a nice suburb in which to live (middle- and upper-middle class), but except for the small, quiet, less known segment that constituted the Golden Valley schools' attendance area, it was not an extremely prestigious location. Thus, newcomers to the metropolitan area seeking an upper-income neighborhood would probably not have been directed to the village of Golden Valley.

Among local people in nearby attendance areas, however, the Golden Valley schools had an excellent reputation. As an indication of this, five families from adjoining neighborhoods sent their children to the Golden Valley schools, paying full-cost tuition to the school system. State law allowed schools to accept children from other attendance areas on a negotiated tuition basis, but both school boards had to agree on any adjustments in the state formula for financial aid for the pupil unit. In the absence of any agreement, the school district of residence lost financial aid for any student who attended another district, and thus the state aid was then not available to either district. Similarly, if a student attended a private school, no school district received state aid for that pupil.

In general, the community supported education very well. A large fraction of the residents who did not currently have children in school (this group comprised over 70 percent of the school district's population) had children who had gone through the system earlier and these parents were still supportive. For example, the excess levy referendum probably had more yes than no votes among the nonschool households that voted.

Weakness and Limitations of Golden Valley Schools. For Golden Valley, one major and very serious problem overrode all the others, and thus made it somewhat academic to discuss specific weaknesses in the staff, programs, students, or facilities. That problem was the significant current and future decline in the number of school-age children residing in the Golden Valley attendance area and the related drop in revenues this was causing. Apart from this life-threatening situation, the chief program weakness, as already mentioned, was the lack of high school vocational course offerings.

The financial and enrollment situation in Golden Valley presented the greatest challenge to its school board, administration, and community. Projections of the future were obtained by means of standard cohort survival techniques developed from historical data. At first, the community did not accept the pessimistic conclusions for the district's future to which these data led. Later, a citizens' committee consisting of some capable analysts who resided in the community, including college professors and statisticians, developed its own scenario of the future using sophisticated statistical techniques. Its findings presented an even gloomier forecast. (Its analysis was captured in a teaching case; see *Golden Valley G*, Mauriel, 1979b. This case might prove useful to the reader interested in some of the analytical techniques that one can employ in evaluating and interpreting enrollment and financial futures. It is available from the Bush Public School Executive Fellows Program, 1884 Como Avenue, St. Paul, Minnesota 55108.)

Next Steps

Having reviewed the external and internal environmental factors affecting the Golden Valley school district, what would you do as superintendent to help chart and implement a course of action for the future? Before deciding, what additional available or obtainable information would you like to have? Would you like to know more about the community preferences? If so, what? Before learning any more about such preferences than you already know from the information provided in Chapters Three and Four, would it be your obligation as superintendent to form a preliminary opinion or at least to articulate the chief options and their respective consequences to the board and community?

Chapter Five presents an elaboration of some of the market research techniques that one can use to obtain further information for making some of the key strategic decisions.

5

Discovering What Constituencies Want from Schools

While a school system is in the process of collecting and examining data on the external environment and assessing the resources and capabilities of the district, it is advisable to engage in some studies of the local "market." This chapter addresses the first and perhaps most important element of the marketing function: market research. Other aspects of the marketing function that are relevant to implementation—or pursuing the strategy—are discussed in Chapter Eight.

Market research is really needs analysis, or the assessment of present and future needs of clients and potential clients of the school district. This chapter includes (1) a discussion of the market research tools employed in the early or "discovery" phase of inquiry to examine broad and general needs and the willingness and ability to pay for the provision of services to address these needs and (2) a discussion of surveys used for more specific and narrower questions requiring quantification. The focus in the discovery phase is on identifying issues and concerns related to the general direction, mission, and strategy of the system. Specific survey techniques, usually employed after the discovery phase, are designed to examine questions of consumer choice with respect to programs, schedules, and operations.

Market Research Data-Gathering Methods

A basic list of general data-gathering methods includes telephone surveys, mail surveys, individual in-depth interviews, focus group interviews, and simulations. The choice of any one of these methods depends on the difficulty of the question and the managerial action step being contemplated. The methods are listed more or less in order of complexity, the first two being designed to answer questions of a simple form where the issues and options are well known and clearly defined—for example, in the case of a decision as to whether the school should drop an elective economics course. The last method (simulation) could be used in determining the amount someone might be willing to pay for an as-yet-unavailable service. The depth and focus group interviews are useful in identifying and defining issues; in understanding feelings, attitudes, and relationships; and in general, for dealing with questions that are not easily put into objective, true-false, multiple choice, or yes-no forms, such as questions about underlying motivations, the depth of feelings, or the general values a person employs in determining trade-offs, strength of loyalty and support, and the like.

Telephone Surveys. It is possible to collect a great deal of useful data at a very low cost with a properly prepared telephone survey. A carefully developed set of questions that can be answered very briefly in a three- to five-minute phone call to a small randomly selected sample of a specific population group can help professionals make better million-dollar decisions or prevent actions that could cause much grief. What may come as a surprise to many school executives is how responsive parents can be to a phone inquiry from their child's school. I once witnessed the administration of a phone survey on the Sunday afternoon of a National Football League (NFL) division championship game that got a 98 percent response, with almost the same number of males as females answering and willingly taking extra time to comment and thank the interviewer. And this was in a city where an NFL team is located.

If you are not sure about the popularity of a program or the need for a specific change in schedules or offerings, then design a very simple phone survey and train some volunteers to conduct it for you. It can be almost cost-free and very informative. On the other hand, management should go through a very elaborate thought process and a thorough conceptual analysis before using even a simple survey; that part is not cost-free, at least in terms of administrators' time. Still, it is not something that can be turned over to a consultant, in my opinion. (Although you may wish to use a consultant to help you ask the questions and facilitate some of the processes used in gathering the data, I believe that the key aspects of the conceptualizing process and the interpretation of the data should be accomplished with extensive involvement of line executives.) Strategic marketing surveys, in other words, are not something to be engaged in at the whim of a teacher, department or program head, or committee chairperson. Such surveys require some thought and input from the appropriate managers or decision makers and some advance consideration of changes or actions that could or might result after the data are analyzed. This approach helps to integrate a survey into a well-conceived marketing plan that can then become an important tool for school improvement.

As noted above, an individual teacher or administrator could use a simple telephone survey. But even this survey should be confined to items over which its designer and administrator had some control and some ability to modify. Thus a teacher might design an inquiry to ascertain the appropriateness or acceptability of a given program or sequence in her curriculum. This kind of quick survey must be very brief, be focused on an issue that the individual(s) administering it can do something about, and contain some provision for reporting back to the respondents. Properly conducted, market surveys can have great public relations value, especially when they include fairly direct contact between a service provider and a client, because the client will often feel good about being asked personally about some aspect of the school's service.

Mail Surveys. Almost everything said in the discussion of telephone surveys applies to questionnaires sent out in the mail. Because the respondent has no opportunity to ask for clarification of a question, however, it is even more important that the queries in a written questionnaire be framed clearly and in simple and unambiguous terms.

Depth and Focus Group Interviews. Questionnaires or highly structured interviews in which the answers requested are of the yes or no or a, b, c, d variety are neither useful nor accurate unless the questions posed focus on specific narrowly defined items with a very limited set of possible reply categories and unless they deal with real underlying core issues or concerns. When the options, issues, and alternatives are not clearly identified, then a preliminary qualitative research approach may be called for. This means examining documents, observing actions and events, and conducting depth interviews (an extensive interview with one individual) or focus group interviews (patterned group interviews). Such interviews, though they follow a predetermined schedule, typically include several open-ended questions and an opportunity for both interviewer and interviewee to explain the meaning of vague terms, identify specific examples of desired outcomes, and explain the strength of feelings, priorities, and trade-offs.

Depth and focus group interviews can be used to help the administrator better understand the underlying issues in order to facilitate the design of a better objective survey instrument or as the chief research tool when the issues are too complex and open-ended to be encapsulated in a survey form, as in the case of motivational or value questions. Thus in a question of whether to introduce a new supervised on-site day-care program (assuming there currently is no such program) or the expansion of the language curriculum, the concerned administrator and teachers might discuss the options and issues and develop an interview schedule to administer to a small sample of parents and students.

In the language example, the language teacher and the chairperson of the department might meet to discuss the increased enrollments in foreign languages. They now have six sections of Spanish and two sections of French along with literature courses, and this represents a 2.5 FTE teaching assignment. The community is believed to have an interest in studying some Oriental languages and also in having some opportunity for recent Hmong immigrants to study English as a second language. Next the department chairperson might ask the principal whether the central office is willing to add to the district's community education offering a course in English as a second language and perhaps a section of Spanish or Chinese and to hire someone to teach those courses part-time and also teach part-time in the regular high school program. If the chairperson gets a green light or at least a tentative commitment, the school can elicit the views of members of the community.

The next step might be to conduct a focus group interview with students now in language classes, then perhaps one with those who are not, to see whether there are conditions under which the latter might take a language course. Next the department might conduct a set of interviews with recent Asian immigrants in the community, parents of students now in language classes, and other parents and community members. These interviews would be used to identify issues, concerns, and desires for improvement or change in an attempt to get some understanding of how the wider community feels about the issues and to determine which language options have enough potential interest to warrant a specific survey to determine prospective enrollment.

The interviews must be carefully designed and focused on questions that may uncover actionable issues related to the expansion of the language curriculum. What do children like about it? Not like? Why do they take language courses? Is it to avoid other courses that are not as well taught? What are the new requirements in local colleges? Are the students who will not go to college interested? Why or why not? Could people come to evening classes (and pay money) to take a course in English as a second language or in some other language? Why or why not? Issues such as the location of the school, the dangers of being in the neighborhood of the school at night, the popularity of the Spanish teacher, the unpopularity of the humanities department, the concerns of the two-income families now moving into the school district, the fact that the language club meets after school and keeps children "out of trouble" might all come up in the interviews and help focus questions that could later be fashioned into a mail or telephone survey.

Depth and focus group interviews can also be the final tool in a research process where the issues are such that these methods provide the core of the needed data. They can be used to collect both qualitative and quantitative data. And although they are typically more expensive than mail and telephone surveys for gathering statistical data, they are more versatile and for certain kinds of questions can be very cost-effective. Thus they need not necessarily be followed by mail or telephone surveys.

Even when the issues are well known, depth or focus group interviews can be used to probe a more complex motivational or value question. For example, if a parental demand for band expansion is being considered but involves a decision on whether to drop orchestra or glee club programs to pay for it, you would want to know the underlying motives of the parents who want it. What are the real underlying concerns or motives of those who are now in the orchestra or glee club? How much do parents know about the cultural and developmental benefits of each? How do parents and students feel about alternatives, and do they feel strongly enough to switch?

One strategic purpose of market research at the broad and general "discovery" level is to determine the strength of demands for new and existing programs, present or revised building configurations, innovative new services, or changes in the system's mission and philosophy and direction, and also to determine preferences for methods of funding future needs. (In this context, I use the economist's definition of *demand,* which includes a willingness and ability to pay for the want or need. In the public school setting, such payment may be in the form of direct fees for service or support for additional tax levies.) The first phase of this research is an issue discovery process. Superintendents who involve board members and key citizens in some sort of strategic planning committee as recommended in Chapters Two and Three already have a nucleus of people to help them frame the questions that must be raised in the discovery phase. If a network of clients or stakeholders on whom to rely for help in monitoring the pulse of the school district community does not already exist, a representative group of people from among the various constituents should be identified to provide ideas and assistance in designing the initial inquiry for the discovery phase of the client needs assessment process. This discovery phase entails some open-ended questioning techniques such as individual depth interviews or focus group interviews designed to discover the basic issues and concerns on the minds of people in your client community.

Discovery methods such as depth and focus group interviews are also effective tools in gathering data for strategic decision purposes, that is, for deciding on major shifts in focus or program or in organization or general philosophy, because they can get at underlying motives and causes. They provide qualitative data. Where specific program decisions are to be based on quantitative data, more precise questioning and survey techniques can be used. The discovery methods help identify what specific questions should be employed in a subsequent survey process designed to quantify responses.

Simulations. A simulation is an acted-out situation in which the subjects are asked to participate in an activity that forces them to reveal their preferences and conditional behaviors.

For example, suppose that twelve parents of preschool children are asked to come to the school. They are then given $2,000 (play money, of course) and presented with some alternatives that they can buy, along with the price of each (for example, all-day commercial day care for one year at a well-known local nursery school, day care and an education program at the public elementary school for nine months, part-day day care at school for less cost, and other activities such as field trips, student care in homes on the block, and so on). The parents are given sales presentations by each supplier, allowed to discuss the possibility of pooling resources with other parents in the room, and allowed to keep some money (refundable for prizes) or to keep the certificates they used to ''buy'' the day care (refundable for discounts). The session is followed by a debriefing, which also helps the researchers learn more about motives, interests, and issues in this group in much the same manner as a focus group interview.

The use of simulations in market research is not well developed. Simulations have been used extensively to teach community groups about power relationships and to teach executives decision-making skills, but I think they have great potential as a market research tool for schools as well.

Simple Guidelines for Designing Market Research Instruments. Here are some easy-to-follow rules or guidelines for designing market research instruments. (Unfortunately, they are often ignored by organizations that send out the many consumer satisfaction surveys or other kinds of market research instruments to which we all are asked to respond.)

- Keep them short. Use no more than one page for a written questionnaire, five minutes for a telephone interview, and thirty to forty-five minutes for a depth interview. (Focus group interviews or simulation exercises can last as long as ninety minutes because of the nature of the social interaction involved.)
- Ask only questions whose answers could change your actions, that is, answers that might actually cause you to change some service or policy. (People often not only tell you what they want but expect you to listen to them and act on the information you obtain.)
- Use terms or descriptions that will have consistent and similar interpretations by the respondents.
- Do not ask for information you do not need just because it would be ''nice to know.''
- Try to explain costs or trade-offs or prioritization schemes when asking about people's desires for added services.
- Include at least one open-ended question that allows respon-

dents the freedom to make any comments or request any clarifications they desire.
- Visualize in your own mind the answer table structure and your decision points before you obtain the results.
- Pilot test each instrument on a few random prospects who have characteristics similar to the population being sampled.

Developing a Market Research Program

A market research program begins with the identification of customers' general and specific needs. This includes close contact with current customers—even if they seem to be pleased with the present level and extent of services—and then expands to other potential customer groups. An ongoing assessment of the changing needs and concerns of clients and would-be clients is a vital part of an effective marketing program. The key ingredients are empathy, sensitivity, concern for others, an open mind, and creativity as opposed to salesmanship, promotional skills, persuasive powers, even though the latter activities are those most often associated with the term *marketing*.

In business terms, needs analysis is referred to as market research. Consumer satisfaction surveys are the most commonly used market research vehicles in schools and are probably the simplest to employ. They also tend to be the least useful for reasons discussed later in this section. A more difficult type of research is an inquiry into the kinds of improvement clients would like to see made in existing programs. An even more difficult type of research is the attempt to discover which well-defined and known services that are not now available in a particular school system its client groups would like to have made available and with what quantity or frequency. Finally, the most difficult kind of market research is an attempt to find out what kinds of services that do not presently exist anywhere in a well-defined form the school community would like to have and how much are they willing to sacrifice or trade off in order to take advantage of such services.

Market research questions are noted below in the order of difficulty in answering them:

Level 1. How satisfied are clients with current programs?

Level 2. What improvements in present services would clients like?

Level 3. What known and well-defined additional services would clients want?

Level 4. What new services that are not offered elsewhere or not well known or well defined would current and prospective clients want?

Level 4. What strategic options would the district's constituents wish to pursue from among the following, and what is the strength of their preference: (a) To be the best educational program possible, providing a full range of traditional K–12 public school services required for the community? (b) To specialize in or focus on certain curriculum areas (magnet school idea)? (c) To diversify into new service areas and markets? (Note: Each of these generic options is described in Chapter Six.)

Level 4. Which alternative means for financing strategic options from among the following would constituents prefer and to what extent could each of these options be pursued with favor: (a) Cooperation or consolidation with other districts? (b) Increasing class size to finance technology or employment of more paraprofessionals? (c) Cutting costs in selected programs and activities? (d) Eliminating selected programs? (e) Contributing private funds to a foundation? (f) Increasing local taxes? (Note: These options are also discussed in Chapter Six.)

The chief purpose of market research should be to aid decision making. So a better way to classify research problems is according to the kinds of decisions they are designed to help one make. In other words, information should be collected for a specific purpose in order to influence some future action. Thus before embarking on a consumer survey or for that matter before engaging in any kind of market research, one should ask what will be done with the information. Questions such as ''Why do

I want this information?'' ''What is my objective (immediate objective in gathering the data and ultimate objective in terms of the overall program or goals of the school)?'' and ''Specifically, what will I do differently after getting the information?'' are crucial general questions to be raised again and again as one contemplates the use of a questionnaire survey or interview protocol. The subsequent discussion on market research is organized around some specific decisions in which market research might be of assistance. The decisions used for illustration are roughly arranged according to the four levels of difficulty noted.

> *Level 1.* We feel that there is a need to update our curriculum and program and would like verification from our clients. We would also like to know how satisfied they are with various aspects of the program so that we can decide what elements to change, contract, leave as is, or expand.
>
> *Level 2.* Should we drop auto mechanics from the school program?
>
> *Level 2.* Should we expand our language curriculum?
>
> *Levels 2 and 3.* We have an opportunity to expand the band program in the junior high school, a program for which many parents and students have been asking. To do so, however, we would have to drop the mixed glee club or the junior orchestra, both of which are considered to be less popular than the band. Which program, if either, should we contract or drop?
>
> *Levels 2 and 3.* Which boys' sports should we drop and which girls' sports should we add to comply with Title IX mandates while remaining within our budget?
>
> *Level 3.* Should we add supervised after-school activities to the elementary school program? If so, which and how?
>
> *Levels 3 and 4.* Should we introduce a new program in the elementary school on a fee-for-service basis for day care and special education for preschoolers? If so, what should be its general characteristics and what prices should we charge?
>
> *Level 4.* Should we consider the following new service that

has been offered to us? An educational materials company is trying to sell us a brand new service that has never been offered to a school before. It involves two-way audio-video communication via interactive cable between the teacher and the home and includes software for reporting a child's progress to parents, for providing at-home drills in basic subjects, with graded feedback and support from the school, and many other features available and planned. The service is very expensive but could be a major breakthrough for school performance. Many other schools in the area seem to be considering it, and the company is offering substantial discounts to early adopters. Should we consider pilot testing it with a plan to request extra funding if the pilot is successful?

Level 4. Which of the following methods for financing would constituents accept, for how much, and if both, in what order of preference: (a) making donations on an annual basis to a private foundation whose purpose would be to support the school's program or (b) voting for extra taxes for the school?

Level 4. How large would constituents be willing to allow classes to become?

The first example calls for a consumer satisfaction survey, perhaps the easiest kind of market research to conduct. But it does not stop there because it proceeds to some action questions and some decision guidelines. If it did stop with just a general quest for an answer to the question "How well is the school doing?" then it would suffer the drawback of most consumer surveys that schools now conduct, namely, little advanced thinking on the action changes that might result. A consumer satisfaction survey is not a useful element of a marketing program unless it is part of a plan for potential change or improvement. On the other hand, consumer satisfaction surveys can be an important part of an overall school evaluation process. Surveys used for formative evaluation purposes—that is, evaluation designed to facilitate improvement—are similar to market research.

The level 2 and levels 2 and 3 examples about expanding, contracting, or dropping currently existing programs that are known quantities to most respondents—though more difficult than the first problem on which to conduct research—lead to the posing of research questions that are reasonably easy to limit and define. But even the questions in these examples can get very complex. A school program is a system of interacting parts, and a change in one can affect many other parts of the system, sometimes in unpredictable ways. Also, a number of political questions can be involved in them.

The discussion of data-gathering methods has thus far involved asking questions of people. This is the most visible part of market research. But there are many other sources of data, and one should do some careful thinking about the problem and alternate perspectives and explore information from currently available records before gathering new data from constituents. A diagram taken from Berkowitz, Kerin, and Rudelius (1989) illustrates the kinds and sources of marketing information used in dealing with a marketing problem. From this diagram, reproduced in Figure 2, you can see that questionnaires and interviews—that is, asking stakeholders for information not available from other sources—occupy only *one* of nine marketing information sources.

For example, some of the many questions to be answered from other sources before one considers applying a market study to the band expansion and music program example include the following:

Questions About Current Customers and Their Options

- What alternatives to band or orchestra might students seek?
- Are there other program options that are available now or could be feasibly developed that students would be happy to take if orchestra and glee club were not available? How could these be expanded or improved?
- What outside options are available to students?
- What are the relevant state mandates?
- What does the school feel its obligations are to the small number of children who want orchestra or glee club?

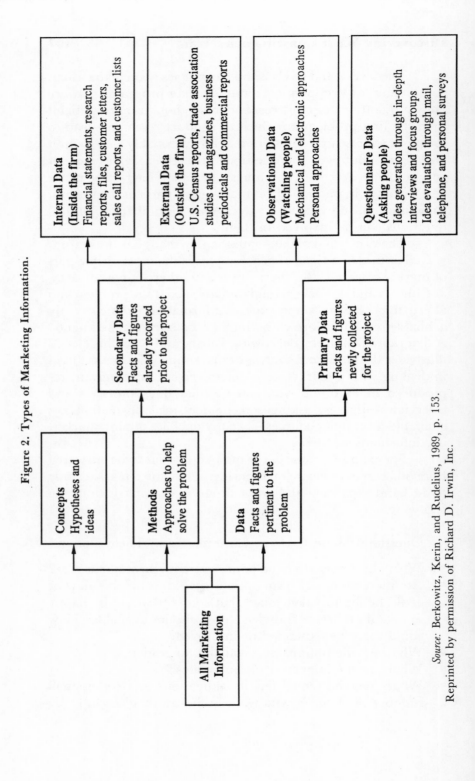

Figure 2. Types of Marketing Information.

Source: Berkowitz, Kerin, and Rudelius, 1989, p. 153.
Reprinted by permission of Richard D. Irwin, Inc.

Questions About Product Developments and Improvements

- Could the school contract with a nearby public or private institution or with an individual for orchestra and glee club services for the limited number of interested students?
- What has been the enrollment history of these programs, and what is known about the reasons for any fluctuations?
- Given current trends, what are enrollments in orchestra and glee club expected to be in the future?
- Is there reason to believe that improvements or changes in the present orchestra and glee club programs might increase enrollments?
- Could some cost reduction measures, such as recruiting volunteer instructors, getting equipment donations, and the like, make the present programs economically feasible despite the expansion of the band?

The school should address these questions before proceeding with an extensive survey. The questions that cannot be answered can at least be sharpened somewhat in preparation for designing a research instrument. As the questions are addressed, the school's administrators should be thinking about the kinds of action steps they could prepare to take if a predetermined level of certain kinds of responses were obtained from the market research. The kinds of questions to consider here are these:

- At what level of interest, satisfaction, or dissatisfaction would the administrators be willing to take some specific action to improve, to partially discontinue, or to expand any of these activities?
- How low must the enrollment fall, or how dissatisfied with the present orchestra and glee club programs must the participants be, or how strong and extensive must the demand for the band be among present and future participants before the administration would actually take the action of dropping one or both of the other programs in order to be able to expand the band?

- Approximately how much would costs have to be reduced in order to maintain the orchestra and glee club at their present levels of enrollment and still expand the band?

After answering the "why" questions, identifying the issues, and discussing the options and prospective action responses and their implications, administrators must take a final step in the process of designing a survey instrument or interview protocol: they must make a table showing the format of the final answers they expect to develop. This does not mean that they have to know what the answers or response frequencies are going to be for each question, but they should carefully think through what the chief response categories are or what the classification system is going to be. Administrators should also try to estimate the potential range of response frequencies they expect to receive on the key questions. In other words, they should determine as thoroughly as possible in advance how the responses are going to be coded and tabulated and have thought about what some of the potential results might mean. Most importantly, administrators should determine the approximate results or ranges of responses they will have to have in order to change anything the school is now doing. Administrators should also decide in advance at least the general nature of the changes they will implement if they receive these answers.

These last steps of attempting to visualize the form of the final answers and to establish trigger points for action are almost never adequately addressed in a market research project. The reason for this may be that doing so is difficult work or that most market research is not done for "action" purposes but merely for information or reinforcement. However, market research should be an integral part of a strategic management decision process. It is important to think in terms of such a process because organizations engage in many more "market" surveys than they do in action plans responding to the findings of the surveys. Market research is a managerial tool that is only used when there is a possibility that real change in policy, program, or procedures will result. This makes market research a top line executive function, as it should be, not a staff technician function, as it is often treated. Therefore, school leaders must be able to specify the action behaviors that will result if the research data read a certain way. In other words, the manager authorizing the research should be able to make in advance the kinds of determinations shown in the examples below.

In the first example, the administrator in the band expansion case (the second level 2 illustration) decides in advance of collecting the survey data that she will drop either the orchestra or mixed glee club, depending on which would lose the fewest students to the overall music program. Therefore, if the number of additional students not now in any music program who say they would join an expanded band exceeds by at least twenty the number of students in the glee club who say they would not join any alternative music activity if either of those were to be discontinued, then expanded band would be offered in place of glee club. Similarly, if at least twenty students more would join an expanded band than would drop orchestra, then the orchestra program would be discontinued.

This example highlights at least three key points. First, significant managerial questions concerning options, alternatives, and decision paths must be explored before one develops the data-gathering instruments. Second, market research is an executive decision-making aid, and the executive responsible for a program must be able to specify in advance (at least in general first-step terms) policy, program, or major procedural decision changes that will result if certain ranges of certain types of responses are obtained. For some situations, this specification might be an intuitive picture held within the responsible executive's mind and not clearly spelled out or perhaps not even openly shared. For other situations, it might involve a clear description of an intended program change. Third, the responsible executive should be able to prepare a skeleton diagram of what the response categories are and how they will be presented and analyzed; in addition, he or she should try to estimate the range of answers before they come in.

The case of the auto mechanics program could be quite simple, particularly if its popularity is extremely low or dropping. However, it also could be very difficult if it involves the possibility of reallocating resources from a program that is basically for vocationally bound students to a program that is used primarily by college-bound students.

The question of whether to expand the language program revolves around the nature, quality, and cost of the expansion. This further complicates the issue because these factors cannot be precisely known until the expansion takes place. But even the language-program question is not as difficult for respondents to answer as are questions about new start-up programs. In the language program, one has a frame of reference against which to judge additions or improvements.

The next sample questions, from the higher of the four levels of difficulty to which administrators can apply market research, are much more difficult than the question of expanding, reducing, or eliminating an existing program. These questions involve people expressing views on issues or program elements that they may not have experienced or observed directly in their own schools. For example, the question regarding girls' and boys' athletics may be more complicated because it involves adding some sport or sports for girls that the school has not had before and also because greater political sensitivity may be involved. In the case of a new supervised after-school program, there are many unknown elements for a survey respondent in a school that has never before had such a program. (What will be the quality of the staff, the logistics and transportation problems, the reaction of the children, the effect on other school programs, the unexpected benefits and costs to parents and children?)

Next the question of how much people would be willing to pay for something on a fee-for-service basis is among the most difficult on which to get an honest answer. So many unknowns, psychic and material, go into a decision to spend money that people have difficulty answering such a question until they are actually faced with the reality of a service offering, know its price, and know which of their neighbors and peers will be using it.

Level 4 questions involving choices from among strategic options are also extremely difficult to research, but they are vital to the success of a school district. Chapter Six discusses approaches to dealing with strategic options.

Despite all the difficulties noted, there are several useful market research techniques for attacking needs analysis problems. Intelligent and careful use of market research can be very rewarding and need not be anywhere near as costly as hiring and giving a consultant carte blanche, failing to follow the guidelines established in this chapter, or not heeding the caveats on citizens' committees or consultant selection discussed below.

Application to Golden Valley

The Golden Valley situation described in Chapters Three and Four is again used as an example in the application of some of the market research ideas described in this chapter. Before we get into the survey research itself, it may be helpful to examine the problems involved in using a citizens' committee. This topic is important at this point because the strategic planning recommendations provided in Chapters Two and Three include the use of such committees and because school districts seem to find it especially helpful to involve a variety of stakeholders in formulating questions of strategic and marketing importance.

Uses and Abuses of a Citizens' Committee. As a result of its impending crisis, the Golden Valley school board appointed a citizens' long-range planning committee, which in turn decided to conduct an extensive community survey to gather data on what realistic options it could consider for the future of the school community and its school organization. First, interviews were conducted with 25 percent of the households, and then a survey questionnaire was mailed to all households in the school community. The interview sample selected included parents and nonparents. Both research tools were designed by the citizens' committee with the help of an outside consultant. The superintendent was present and actively involved in all meetings although he did not chair the committee.

The questionnaire designed by the group was much too long and dealt with too many issues, a number of which were nonactionable and clearly irrelevant to the key decision faced by the school, namely, its survival in the present structure and form. The questionnaire did, however, provide many useful

responses and left the board and the long-range planning committee feeling good about the generally positive statements about
the school and its administration. The board and the committee also felt that the questionnaire responses provided a base
for their future deliberations. The fact that the survey was conducted at all provided the community a feeling of involvement
in the process, which some thought was a political necessity during such difficult times for the school system.

There are pros and cons of heavily involving lay people
in the technical work of questionnaire design. An advantage,
of course, is that the superintendent can get direct input from
the community on the nature of its concerns. This assumes
that the committee represents reasonably well the community
interests and is not a select group of people merely pursuing
their own personal agenda. A second advantage is that the school
can obtain the services of some very knowledgeable citizens at
no cost. In the case of Golden Valley, this included people involved in business marketing, professors, lawyers, and other
professionals.

The disadvantages of involving a lay committee in the
design of a market research program include the members' lack
of expertise, the imposing of their own personal agendas, and
the fact that a group can unduly influence the professional
specialist(s) who is responsible for designing the survey. The
Golden Valley experience illustrated all three of these drawbacks.

It often happens in such a situation that the questionnaire
developed is too long. The high-caliber group appointed by the
Golden Valley board had strong views and a variety of concerns
about their schools and their own children and indeed did steer
the consultant into designing a long and cumbersome research
instrument. Concerns about modular scheduling and the popularity of programs and what was perhaps an undue concern for
verifying the accuracy of the projections of future enrollment
declines (which most people did not wish to accept or believe)
took up much space in the questionnaire.

A typical consequence of surveys designed by committees is that they become overly long by including many "nice-
to-knows" that are at best only slightly relevant and at worst

totally irrelevant to the key action questions for the organization. One temptation is to include questions about clients' satisfaction with the current program. Answers to such questions do not usually provide much guidance to action, unless a particular program turns out to be extremely popular or unpopular. However, in the case of either extreme, the administration of the school probably already knows the level of community satisfaction or dissatisfaction, and the survey data provide little useful additional information. Of course answers often flatter (or deflate) the egos of school executives.

What could Golden Valley have done to improve its questionnaire while still obtaining the needed community views? First, it seems quite appropriate that it used a citizens' committee to discuss and obtain views on the overall objectives of the survey. This is generally a wise idea. At the beginning of this kind of process there should be clear agreement on the role of the committee and the limits of its power and a clear understanding that the research must focus on just a few relevant and actionable items. But a citizens' committee should not be involved in the actual design of the questionnaire. The latter was not clarified in Golden Valley early in the process, perhaps because no such agreement existed. Second, the superintendent should remain very active in the process, keeping before the committee relevant board policies, the current school situation and needs, and projections of future enrollments, programs, and finances, and he or she should provide all the data needed to ensure that the committee is well informed. The Golden Valley superintendent did this.

A problem that often arises with citizens' committees is a disagreement between administration and citizenry or among subgroups on the committee as to what the objectives of the research should be. In the Golden Valley case there was disagreement among various factions within the committee, with the administration generally remaining neutral. The members of one faction wanted to pin down the extent and accuracy of the enrollment forecasts in the hope that they would find out that the situation was not as bad as originally depicted. Another faction wanted to use the survey to document how much people

disliked the new modular scheduling format recently adopted
by the high school. A third faction wanted to ascertain the community's attitude toward various alternatives for dealing with
the future: merger, higher taxes, reduced program, larger class
size, and the like. This, of course, was the real strategic question, the answer to which could help the school system determine which strategic option(s) it should consider pursuing.

Determining the Questions. The Golden Valley questionnaire reflected the wishes of all groups, as one might expect from
a process that was truly participative. However, the group interested in verifying the seriousness of the enrollment shortfall
apparently had more influence than the other factions because
the committee decided to hire a social science researcher whose
subspecialty was demography. Thus questions about people's
intentions to retain residency in the district, sell their homes,
and so on dominated the questionnaire.

The second type of question the committee agreed to include in the survey dealt with client satisfaction with the current school program. "Why not?" the members asked. "It's
a great opportunity to learn what the community likes and does
not like in order to improve the school or at least to verify that
what the school is doing is perceived to be as good as the administration thinks it is." This kind of information is usually high on
administrators' "nice-to-know" lists, and the logic of including
it in a market research project is seductive. Committee members
found this logic hard to resist.

Some information on the perceived quality of and satisfaction with the present program was essential for Golden Valley to
have before proceeding to compare the present situation to future
options. Much of it was already known, however, and some of
what was not known for sure might have been discovered more
simply, as I will explain shortly. Most of the remaining consumer
satisfaction information obtained in the original Golden Valley
survey research was not very relevant, merely "nice to know."

For two reasons, "nice-to-know" questions should normally be omitted from a questionnaire. First, their inclusion
makes the questionnaire too long and reduces not only the

percentage of responses obtained but possibly the accuracy of the answers people give. More importantly, however, such questions divert valuable time and attention—of administrators, committee members, and the community—away from the main issue. These people may then become embroiled in arguments over the wrong issues. Of course, the advantages of consumer satisfaction information are that it is often very reinforcing and good for the spirit, as was the case in Golden Valley, and the act of collecting it has political value because the community is made to feel more involved in the process, as was also the case in Golden Valley.

Perhaps the most important problem with "nice-to-know" questions about consumer satisfaction is the possibility that they might reveal flaws in a school program that the administrators would be unable to deal with because they were absorbed in the bigger issue. This could then lead to the following sequence: increased community expectations (one of the risks of a market survey is that if you ask people what they want, they may expect you to listen to them and act on the information they provide) followed by the administrators' nonresponse, which would be interpreted as lack of interest or competence in running the school in the community's best interest, and finally the citizenry's frustration and reduced support for the schools. (This sequence did not occur in Golden Valley, however.)

In the Golden Valley situation the big issue was the future survival of the school. Thus, the key focus questions on the survey might better have been the following:

- Given the option of supporting an X-mill tax levy or consolidating with an adjoining district and thereby enriching the program or the option of maintaining an independent district with larger classes and a reduced program, which would the majority of citizens select?
- How large would the community allow classes in basic subjects to become before it would prefer consolidation with a neighboring district?
- How large a tax levy would the students' parents be willing to vote for in an excess-levy referendum?

- How large an excess levy would the nonparent voters support?
- Would enough citizens be willing to donate funds to a foundation to keep the school operating?

The Golden Valley school administration needed answers to many other questions, of course, but these seem to have been the most crucial ones to which the community could have provided answers. Other questions might have been better answered by teachers and students or by legislators. Unfortunately, little information bearing on the questions listed above was obtained from the responses to the survey directed by the Golden Valley long-range planning committee. Nevertheless, it was enough for the members to feel comfortable in moving on to the next steps.

Does the scenario just described imply that a school district should not use citizens' committees to deal with important questions that can best be dealt with by "experts"? Of course not. In an institution as central to a community and as public as the school system, it is vital to have client involvement and input. But they must be gained properly. The major flaw in the process at Golden Valley was probably in the fact that the planning committee did not use a discovery technique to gather data to help it understand and frame the issues before it went ahead and designed the detailed questionnaire that was mailed to all the households in the district. The interviews the committee did conduct were designed and administered to supplement the data gathered from the questionnaire rather than to help design the questionnaire. If it had employed a depth interview process first and then conducted a series of three to five focus group interviews before designing the questions for the mail survey, the committee might have ended up with a very different result. The members might have even found a way to keep the school district operating to serve most of the current and future client group well. They would at least have developed some specific wording for the questions above and some indication of which were most important and why. The committee would then have been in a position to design a more focused questionnaire.

Overcoming the Problems of Citizens' Committees. There are ways to involve citizens while still minimizing or avoiding some of the problems described above. Following is some advice to a superintendent on this topic:

- Specify for the board or put in place yourself a committee selection process that has a good probability of yielding a committee that is most likely to meet the objectives of the research. (For example, if you need an accurate reflection of community attitudes, try for a random selection of qualified and interested people; if you are looking for some special expertise, be sure that is identified and adequately searched for among the population of prospective committee members; if you need an accurate reflection of staff concerns, be sure that people who accurately reflect the views of the staff are selected.)
- Closely guide and maintain control over the process by which decisions concerning the general research objectives are made, and oversee the general questions to be addressed.
- Clearly articulate to the committee and your board the general objectives of the research. Do not let an outside consultant control this process.
- Make or approve the final decision on the selection of a consultant or at least describe the specifications for the consultant search process.
- Be sure that your research director or consultant engages in ample discovery and open-ended exploration of issues and concerns before rushing to a conclusion on the need for and design of a mail or telephone survey.
- Try to keep control of committee functions, acting as catalyst and meeting facilitator when important questions and strategic options are discussed.
- Be sure the committee has all the relevant information you think members need, and furnish staff support to provide them with additional information they request and need.

The method the Golden Valley board used for determining the membership of the long-range planning committee involved an application process. Citizens were asked through an ad in the school's newsletter to submit their qualifications. The board members then voted on the forty applications they received,

selecting ten for the original committee. Since most of the newsletter's readers were parents of children currently in school or
of preschoolers, the committee was mainly composed of people
in this group. The board voting process ensured that the final
"winners" would be visible and well-known citizens whose views
were in accord with the board's. In this case it was not crucial
that the committee be a precise mirror of the community's views
since the main goal was to design a process for obtaining these
views. Because the board members were keenly interested in
obtaining intelligent and well-researched answers to their questions about the future of the school, they selected a committee
of interested and talented citizens.

The Golden Valley superintendent did a thorough job of
monitoring the committee and influencing its agenda. He attended all its meetings, actively worked with the chairperson
in shaping the agenda, and provided relevant information about
the district's programs and finances, about state laws and policies, and about the programs of neighboring districts. Even
though the questionnaire got too long, it did provide much information that when later supplemented led to an apparently
effective decision for the school district.

From the very beginning, the superintendent effectively
focused attention on the key issue: the survival of the school
in its present form and its ability to continue, in the face of declining enrollments and reduced funding, to provide the kind of
program that the community deserved and demanded. Although,
as noted earlier, in designing the questionnaire, the committee
did make the classic errors of trying to please too many members
and of including too many "nice-to-knows," it is difficult to
fault the process in Golden Valley, even in hindsight, since the
result that was negotiated seemed to satisfy all parties. (For a
copy of the actual questionnaire used by Golden Valley and a
summary of the responses received, write to the Bush Public
School Executive Fellows Program, 1884 Como Avenue, St.
Paul, Minnesota 55108 and ask for the Golden Valley B and
C cases.)

Managing the Design Process. The Golden Valley planning committee selected an outside consultant, but the same

principles apply when selecting an inside staff person as the consultant. First, the committee put out a request for proposals (RFP). This RFP described the project in general terms, but it may not have had a clearly agreed-upon specific objective (other than to "survey the community"). The committee members were not thinking of the project in market research terms or in terms of identifying and selecting viable alternatives for the community's schooling. Therefore, they did not specify a market research specialist or a community needs assessment specialist. They ended up with a geographer/demographer because his bid was lowest and because some of the committee thought that a key purpose was to find out if the enrollment was really going to drop as much as recent projections had seemed to indicate.

Next, no one exercised the necessary influence to help the committee keep the questionnaire short and focused on the relevant actionable questions. The superintendent might have done something in this regard. But it is probably unfair to place this burden on him since he was in a difficult position politically to deny a committee member's desire, perhaps even that member's right, to know something of interest and importance to the operation of the school. Putting this kind of restraint on a citizens' committee is something that can be done better by the wording of the board's charge to the committee or by the selection of a tough-minded outside consultant.

In this case, however, the consultant could not or did not stand up to the committee members when their demands for additions to the questionnaire became excessive and less relevant to the larger issues. Furthermore, perhaps because the consultant was a demographer, the questionnaire's final design emphasized the demographic issues. Once a consultant is given too much leeway in developing the objectives and goals of a project, the administrator has the same problem as when the community determines the technical aspects of what questions ought to be included in a survey questionnaire. The role and the position do not match.

Appropriate Roles in Market Research Programs. Here are some generally useful suggestions concerning appropriate roles and responsibilities for each person or group in the market research process. Be aware, however, that they should not be applied too rigidly.

- The superintendent usually can best provide direction, frame questions, supply objective data, and provide staff assistance.
- The community/staff committee, with guidance from board policies and the superintendent, can best develop specific objectives for the research, determine the best method for implementing the survey process, and provide guidance on the wording of questions for the survey instruments.
- The consultant can best make the final decision on what questions to include on the questionnaire, determine the overall research design and the method for analyzing the data, and, finally, analyze and report results from the data.

Assessment of Current Service Options. It was useful for Golden Valley to have in its survey some items that provided information on how the community felt about the present program. Whenever there are community concerns that point out problems that can easily be corrected by the reallocation of existing resources (for example, dropping voice and expanding band, changing the timing of English, starting a Parent-Student-Teacher Association (PSTA) in the middle school), then such problems should be corrected, if possible, before a final decision is made to reorganize the school system.

A comparison between Golden Valley as it was operating and Golden Valley as it might have operated if consolidated with another district might have provided a different response than the comparison between the Golden Valley that could have ideally existed with then present resources and Golden Valley as it might have operated if consolidated with another district. The former would have been an unfair comparison on which citizens should not be asked to vote. Yet, how many projects have been sold and bought on the basis of this kind of unfair comparison? (For example, a new computer system working at its peak efficiency is compared to the present manual system, which is being run inefficiently, and so the new computer system is installed; however, this system could be less cost-effective than the manual system would have been if it had been streamlined and run at its peak efficiency.)

Thus, although one may criticize an emphasis on ascertaining community attitudes toward a current program, the need to be sure the problems facing a district are not caused chiefly by the quality of the current program or operation should be addressed. In the case of Golden Valley, the administrators and the survey committee already knew enough about the perceptions of and attitudes toward the present program to obviate the need for survey data to verify that the community was currently satisfied with the schools and their programs. To be sure of this, they could have raised some questions among themselves about the current program beforehand. In the case of Golden Valley, product/service improvement was not an issue. There were some concerns about modular scheduling, but the administration was already aware of this and had made plans to discontinue it even before the development of the questionnaire.

Considering a Consolidation Option. To illustrate the kind of advanced thinking (mentioned earlier) that should be done before a survey is administered, I will focus on a specific but fundamental question the Golden Valley market research process was designed to address: Should the district consolidate with a neighboring suburban district? Assume that in order for the Golden Valley long-range planning committee to have felt that a merger or consolidation alternative was not worth considering as an option, at least 70 percent of the parent population would have had to indicate (1) that they would not object to larger class sizes, (2) that they would be satisfied even if the school had to reduce the number of electives available to high school students, and (3) that they would be willing to support a significantly higher tax levy.

If, on the other hand, the committee believed (through its intuitive feelings) that less than 10 percent of the parents felt this way, the members could have obviated the need for a detailed investigation by using other means to verify that the true percentage of parents feeling that a merger should not be considered was clearly under the 70 percent trigger point. If the committee's hunch about the actual feelings of the community were even close to being accurate, only a small sample would have been needed to prove statistically that the percentage of parents who would be comfortable with larger classes and fewer course options and who would support higher tax levies was definitely less than 70 percent.

Considering New Services or Programs. What kinds of fees for service could Golden Valley have imposed on users of extracurricular educational programs? The committee felt that the district could increase admission charges for athletic contests and introduce a new charge on students participating in high-cost sports (for example, for football and baseball equipment, rink time for the hockey team, and so forth) as long as those who could not pay such fees could easily obtain financial aid. However, there were state-imposed limits on many fees, and the amount of money the district might have been able to collect was insignificant in relation to the school system's impending deficit problem.

The committee also examined the prices that were being charged for school lunches. It determined that a slight increase in price could cause many students to cease patronizing the school lunch program, and thus the school could actually lose money and serve fewer children. Conversely, a decrease in price can sometimes cause an increase in total revenue, depending on the shape of the demand curve. The committee did not believe this was the situation with regard to the school lunch program. Consequently, no price changes were made for school lunches. Even if prices could have been increased successfully, the added revenue to the school would again have been insignificant.

Usually schools do not look for places where they can add services that might not only cover the additional costs of providing them but also contribute additional funds for fixed overhead or salaries of people they might otherwise have to lay off. If Golden Valley had considered some possibilities for adding fee-generating services, then it could have included some items in its community survey to identify these opportunities. In an affluent community like Golden Valley, there may have existed many opportunities to introduce profitable and useful new programs such as the kinds discussed earlier in this chapter and also in Chapter Three. The board might have considered special classes or programs such as day care, preschool, senior lunches, private tutoring or music lessons or tested whether some of these programs combined with some sort of community education sequences might have allowed it to cover costs and keep the critical mass of teachers required to maintain its schools as an independent system. The board did not do this.

Pricing and Costing. In examining the price the community might have been willing to pay for Golden Valley's existing educational programs, the board and the superintendent decided that a six-mill excess levy was about the limit. A levy referendum campaign was run, and the referendum passed by a comfortable but small margin, with many of the yes votes coming from people who did not presently have children in school. Although, by law, such a levy would remain in existence until the voters took a proactive decision to rescind it, the administration felt that it had just two years either to prove the Golden Valley system could keep operating without major restructuring or to provide an alternative plan.

Much can be learned from a thorough analysis of specific program costs and the relationship between costs and the fundamental cost drivers: number of students, square footage, number of buildings, number of courses or programs, and so on. Obvious questions to raise are "Does the school provide any very expensive services (for example, fourth-year Spanish, wood shop, orchestra) that only a very few people would miss if withdrawn? Could these few people be served in another way? Is the service essential and important to them?"

The answers to these questions are not as obvious as the questions themselves. Since schools are not private businesses, they may have to continue some services that are uneconomic. Nevertheless, in some situations the majority can be hurt because a very few are using an expensive service. Dealing with this kind of issue can involve serious ethical policy questions. Such ethical questions are beyond the scope of this book, but it is my belief that school districts should raise and debate such questions, not avoid them.

An even more important project that Golden Valley should have dealt with *before* administering its survey was the development of a range of estimated costs of various present and future options to present to citizens. A survey response is a kind of vote, and adequate information about the options available and their implications should be put in the hands of the "voters" in order for their questionnaire responses to be as meaningful as possible. At the time, such a cost analysis would have entailed answering at least three questions. First, how much money could the schools save if they increased class size by one? By two? Second, how much could the school system save by closing one or more of its buildings and combining grades into the remaining structure(s)? Third, what are the projected financial and program implications of the various future alternatives available to them? For a large school system, it is easy to figure out the answer to the first question. This can almost be done by formula since every class is taught in multiple sections and an increase in class size by even one student can decrease the need for at least one FTE teacher at each required grade level in the elementary school and for each major subject taught in the secondary schools. However, most of the 16,000 school districts in the United States have fewer than 800 students, and for any such district that has fewer than 40 to 50 teachers, this kind of calculation is not so simple. The cost of instruction (the major cost variable in schools) is a step function, going up or down in segments after an accumulation of changes in enrollment, and it does not go up or down evenly with every small shift in enrollment.

Answers to the second question are often overstated. Building closings lead directly only to reductions in utility and maintenance costs. Other savings such as reduction of administration, library, counseling services, and the like are perhaps arguable and more a result of enrollment reductions or existing inefficiencies in the use of classes than of the actual closing of a building. They are often *real*, however, and must be considered.

Answers to the third question, about program and financial implications of various alternatives, involve several complex and extensive calculations.

Golden Valley did do an unusually thorough job of answering all three major questions before making its final decision. The district conducted an extensive study of the financial implications of continuing the same programs it had as an independent school district. It also performed an extensive analysis of the potential impact on its program, tax levy, financial situation, staffing, and busing requirements of consolidating with any one of the three potential adjacent partners. The latter study was funded by a grant from the Minnesota State Department of Education.

These detailed analyses were not provided to the recipients of the extensive mail survey because they were not available at the time. However, they were made available to the community prior to the final series of public meetings held by the board to discuss the alternatives being considered for the school system's future. Though no formal survey was taken at this later time, the input solicited in the large public meetings and the data the board had collected in its studies of alternative future scenarios for the school system, gave the board members enough information to feel comfortable with their decision. In an ideal world the sequence would have been different. That is, the information on the impacts of the various future scenarios would have been presented to the public and then a thorough survey conducted to ascertain the community's reactions and its hopes and desires for the future of its children and the Golden Valley schools.

Designing the Delivery System. Golden Valley had a fairly standard delivery system for its time. It scheduled classes in its buildings from about 8:30 A.M. to 2:45 P.M., bused children who lived more than a mile away from their respective schools, had the usual athletic and other activities in the high school and junior high school, and had several specialists in music, art, and special education in the elementary school. The district had no community education program, believing that it could not launch a successful program that would cover costs given the heavy competition from the programs of larger schools in its adjacent neighborhoods and given the existence of a large university in its metropolitan area. The survey it conducted initially pointed out no particular flaws in the existing delivery system. In fact, the results showed a high amount of community satisfaction with the system. So it seemed to the board at the time that improving the existing delivery system or introducing new programs and services was not a significant issue in the Golden Valley community and that putting energy into these areas was not likely to help it deal with the major survival problem the schools faced.

Market research is a two-way communication process. The more the prospective respondents know about the situation, the more accurately they can communicate their feelings and attitudes. If they know what the cost and price options are, they can better answer questions about program changes. Thus Golden Valley had to tell its community what the added costs per student would probably be to keep the existing program going in the face of declining enrollments, what the future enrollments were projected to be, what the financial and program implications of various future scenarios might be, and the like. The better informed respondents are as to the consequences of pursuing various courses of action, the more valid and useful will be the survey results.

But this is not an ideal world, and the process Golden Valley's school board followed seemed more practical at the time. Board members felt that they needed the initial survey results in order to provide ammunition for their subsequent grant request to the Minnesota Department of Education and also to guide their future efforts. Indeed, they were able to use some of the initial survey responses to guide a number of their actions. The chief problem with the earlier survey was that for the extensive effort it required, it provided only a small amount of useful information on the key questions that needed to be addressed in the short term. To the extent that it gave comfort to the board and the long-range planning committee and made the community feel that a thoughtful investigation was under way and citizens were involved in it, the survey served an additional useful purpose.

The survey was conducted on a very low budget, but the time and effort of many committee members and the extensive time the hundreds of respondents took in filling out the questionnaire or participating in the depth interviews were not included in that budget. When the board decided not to commission another full-scale survey after the data on future options had been analyzed, it was perhaps following the advice presented earlier—don't ask questions when you know the answers or can verify your hunches by interviewing or polling a small sample of the community. The board felt that the data already in hand clearly pointed in a specific direction, and informal discussions with and polling of community members confirmed its decision without a formal vote. The fact that the decision was announced with very little objection from the community indicates that the board had an accurate perception of the community's choice from among the very limited alternatives realistically available to it at the time.

Marketing Communications—Advertising and Promotion. Good marketing communication is especially important in times of impending major change. Thus Golden Valley had to "advertise" its situation to its publics. It had to provide information about the likely impacts—financial, programmatical, and otherwise (in terms of student spirit, and so on)—of maintaining the school system on its present course of operation. This communication was handled well in Golden Valley before a final decision was made on the consolidation issue.

It is also a function of advertising to describe in factual terms what the alternatives are, even if this occasionally means describing a competitive option such as a neighboring public school, a private school, or a consolidated system. For a school to "advertise" alternatives to its continued existence sounds self-defeating on the surface, and it is not usually done. But in the long run, it may be the best course. In the case of Golden Valley, gathering and providing information on "competitive options" led to a very careful and thoughtful analysis of potential merger partners. The classic function of advertising is to provide information so that consumers can make an informed choice. To a great extent, that is what Golden Valley administrators did. Although they did it after the initial and extensive survey was administered, they ultimately provided detailed scenarios for the public to review and discuss: remaining independent or merging with any one of three different adjacent potential partners. (For a description of what the community's futures committee reported concerning the first alternative and for the complete text of what was sent out to the community regarding the second set of alternatives, see Golden Valley G and H cases, which are available from the Bush Public School Executive Fellows Program, 1884 Como Avenue, St. Paul, Minnesota 55108.)

6

Formulating a Strategic Plan

Some of the major trends existing in the Golden Valley external environment and in the environment for schooling in general were discussed in Chapter Three. The process of analyzing the competitive environment was also discussed briefly. A framework for examining the internal strengths and weaknesses of the Golden Valley school system or any other school system was presented in Chapter Four. The combination of activities involving external environmental analysis and internal resource and capabilities assessment is sometimes referred to as a SWOT (strengths, weaknesses, opportunities, and threats) analysis. Chapter Five dealt with the assessment of constituent demands and needs.

Up to this point, then, we have covered five steps of Bryson's eight-step process, though not necessarily in the sequence reported on page 8.

1. Initiating a committee to begin the planning process
2. Identifying the key strategic issues facing public education
3. Assessing external trends affecting school systems
4. Examining strengths and weaknesses of a school system
5. Identifying constituent needs and demands through market research

The next steps in the process of strategic leadership involve pulling together the facts and conclusions drawn from the external environment trend analysis, the district resource examination, and the constituent needs assessment in a way that facilitates the formulation of the district strategy, which includes development of an effective mission statement and/or a vision statement for the school system. This chapter examines the following steps in that process.

1. Clarifying a vision and mission
2. Identifying and examining broad strategic options for fulfilling a school system's mission
3. Reviewing approaches or decision models for strategy formulation

Clarifying the Vision

A vision statement is a very general declaration, as Bunker indicates in Chapter Ten. It represents important personal values, speaks to the heart, and should be short enough so that everyone can state it and remember it. The vision statement should excite people and motivate them to act on behalf of, provide support for, and feel proud to belong to an organization.

Here are a few examples that may stimulate your thinking on some of the possibilities for developing an inspiring statement of vision. The mission of one school district was described to me as "to help our children achieve their full potential and live healthier, happier, and more productive lives." One inner-city school district's vision is, in part, that "our public schools are a place where children of all races and social backgrounds can work and learn together in peace and order and develop skills necessary to pursue successful careers of their choice and to become effective citizens." A part of one suburban school system's mission is to see to it "that every child is nurtured and helped to acquire a positive sense of self-worth." An excerpt from another suburban district's mission states that "children are encouraged to develop the discipline to achieve what their talents will allow, are challenged by a most rigorous academic experience, and are fulfilled by a sense of achievement of important intellectual and personal goals."

Note that these statements are relatively simple, attempt to appeal to widely shared values and beliefs, and articulate obvious but important and noble purposes for schooling. They are statements constructed by ordinary human beings. We used to think that the ability to excite others with a powerful vision resided only in a few "charismatic" leaders. We now know that the ability to create and articulate a motivational vision can be learned and used by a wide variety of managers and executives. One does not have to be a rare individual with an unusually powerful and magnetic personality to develop a vision or mission statement that will enlist the hearts and minds of constituents.

History is replete with famous vision statements (some by well-known leaders) that stirred people to massive action. A few may help bring to your consciousness what you already know about the power to motivate.

Martin Luther King, Jr., expressed his vision in terms of a dream that one day "all of God's children" will be "free at last!" This in effect became the mission statement for the civil rights movement in the 1960s. Our pledge of allegiance to the flag conveys a vision articulating the United States' mission to achieve the noble aim of "one nation, under God, indivisible, with liberty and justice for all." The preamble to the U.S. Constitution and the Declaration of Independence also provide missions for the United States: to "establish justice, insure domestic tranquility, provide for the common defense, promote the general welfare," and envisioning "that all men are created equal, that they are endowed by their Creator with certain unalienable rights, that among these are life, liberty, and the pursuit of happiness." Abraham Lincoln had a specific mission to win a war, and he enlisted support with a mission statement that asked citizens to cooperate in order to preserve the union "our forefathers" established and to see to it "that government of the people, by the people, and for the people shall not perish from the earth."

At an organizational level, it is common to have a motto or slogan that in effect expresses the mission or purpose of an organization. Ford: "Quality is Job 1"; AT&T: "The right choice"; Visa: "It's Everywhere You Want to Be"; and, of course, Virginia Slims: "You've come a long way, baby." For a school system it might be "The school that cares" or "The place where your future is made."

Constructing a Mission Statement for Your District

You do not have to be a Martin Luther King, Abraham Lincoln, or one of the founding fathers to create a vision for a school system. There is controversy, however, over whether the development of a mission statement should involve a wide range of stakeholders in participative discussions, a small group of people at the top of an organization, or be the work of one key person. I would say that the first and last drafts of a mission statement should be completed by just one person, the chief executive officer of the organization, normally the superintendent. In preparing such a statement, however, the superintendent should consult with a variety of people, clearly have a finger on the pulse of his or her constituencies, and be familiar with the dreams and deep-seated beliefs and values of the major stakeholders. As the statement is being developed, the superintendent would be wise to consult with appropriate key people, asking for their comments and testing ideas and phrases on them, but not let the final drafting become a participative exercise.

Inspiring phrases and motivational visions are not put together by committees. Martin Luther King undoubtedly had no mass meeting to find out what elements the majority of his constituents thought ought to be included in his dream for the future. No group, to my knowledge, voted on whether he should have used the word *God* or the phrase ''all of God's children'' when referring to the people who were to be the beneficiaries in his vision. On the other hand, King was in touch with basic American values and reflected a sensitivity to the commonly held aspirations and values of most people, whites as well as minorities. The speech and the motivational words were from his heart, not from a committee's. I am aware of school systems that have spent great amounts of time in public meetings, in staff meetings, and in workshop retreats attempting to agree on a mission statement. In my view, this time could be better spent working on the next level, which is the development of a strategy that defines programs and allocates resources to pursue goals designed to bring the mission closer to reality. That is where the controversy comes in and where group participation, intergroup negotiation, and one-on-one discussions and compromises are needed. The mission statement should not be controversial or specific enough to warrant a great deal of group discussion; on the other hand, the strategy probably should be controversial.

One of the reasons organizations spend so much time working on mission statements is because most specialists on this subject feel that the strategic planning process should start by first developing this statement. This seems appropriate. These "experts" further recommend, and again I agree, that a two- or three-day retreat be held early in the strategic planning process. What often happens is that the entire first day or two of the retreat is spent on developing the mission statement. This activity can be at best exhilarating for the group and at worst frustrating. I do believe, however, that some time must be spent discussing mission and providing visionary goals and statements. Nevertheless, the strategic planning process should begin with the *clarification* of the mission and organizational purpose and a vision for the school system's future, not the *determination* or *development* of precise wording for either. While each superintendent and school board must decide just how to engage in the process of communicating, clarifying, and testing the mission of their organization, I would caution against spending time possibly frustrating large groups of people by raising expectations that they might be able to "participate" directly in the detailed construction of a mission statement.

However, group and committee meetings should be held to discuss elements of the mission statement before the superintendent prepares the final draft to ensure that she or he does truly have a finger on the pulse of the community and also to excite the community about the district's "destiny." Such meetings can give people a feeling of participation in the development of the mission statement, but it should be made clear to them that the discussions are to obtain input and clarification for the person who will prepare the final statement.

Input may be elicited from the strategic planning committee of the district, parent organizations, staff groups, the board of education, and other groups. The input may be obtained as part of an agenda at a regular meeting of the group or it may involve the use of more formalized market research processes such as focus group interviews with samples of people from the community. Once the mission is conceptualized, it is possible to limit the broad strategic options that must be considered in making the final decisions about what should go into the strategic plan. These strategic options are discussed in the next sections.

Broad Generic Strategic Options

The broad and general (generic) strategies or strategic options available to any school system are as follows:

A.   To be the best general educational program possible, providing a full range of K–12 public schooling services required for the community
B.   To specialize in certain curriculum areas ("magnet school" idea)
C.   To diversify or enter new service areas

These three options are, in other words, to do more of the same but do it better (A), to focus efforts on one or a few areas that can be handled exceptionally well (B), or to expand offerings to new service markets (C). The first basic question to ask is which of these general directions should a school system be taking.

Generic Option A. Being the best general educational program possible, providing a full range of K–12 public schooling services required for the community, is the generic strategic option most public school systems in the United States feel obligated to pursue. The strategy then is "Let us continue providing the same general services to the same general clientele, and let us do it as well as we can or better than we have been doing it." Essentially this generic strategy should be identified in the mission statement of the school system. It seems to follow that engaging in such a broad-scoped mission requires significant financial resources, a very diversified and talented staff, and a flexible structure (that is, unless one defines a broad and general education as consisting of a fairly narrow basic and uniform treatment for all clients).

This first generic strategy can be further broken down on the basis of two general methods for pursuing it: through cost-effectiveness or through product or service differentiation. In the cost-effectiveness approach, the school system attempts to provide the most needed general K–12 educational services at the lowest possible costs consistent with the quality of service desired, using volume-efficient scheduling and other means for delivering services at costs lower than neighboring systems might. In the differentiation approach, the school system is not inattentive to cost, but its focus is on demonstrating that there is something unique about its service for which people should be willing to pay a bit more (for example, convenient local community location, an outstanding counseling program, smaller class sizes, the best athletic teams or band or academic performance in the area, an unusually caring staff and administration).

Most school systems that follow processes advocated by the most popular consultants on strategic planning end up adopting some form of generic option A. It is really not a change in strategy, as defined here, but rather an operational improvement in the way the strategy is pursued and a reaffirmation that this is the right general strategy. I call this the "more of the same only do it better" strategy. Strategic planning that is systematized with too organized a process, that has broad participation by several constituent groups, and that attempts to please a wide range of interests tends to drive organizations to this option. When something called "strategic" planning is done on an annual basis, it usually becomes management planning and control, not *strategy formulation,* as I call it.

This is not a criticism of the popular new planning processes schools follow today. Management planning is an important activity, and it can result in significant improvements in cost-effectiveness, efficiency, client satisfaction, and improved overall performance. A problem for school districts with management ("strategic") planning as practiced by most businesses and school organizations only arises if one of two situations exists:

(1) They fail to see the need for major shifts in strategy, significant organizational transformation and restructuring, and the need for new kinds of reward and reporting systems and delivery approaches or some other significant responses to the enormous changes in society and technology that confront educators today. (2) They do see such a need but think they are defining a new strategy that responds to this need when, in fact, they are merely doing "more of the same only better."

Generic Option B. Specializing in certain curriculum areas ("magnet school"), the second generic strategy, is one of focusing on just a few areas in which the school system presumably will develop some special skills and competencies aimed specifically at a selected kind of client group. Examples of specialized schools are a school for the arts, a math and science high school, an elementary "fundamentals" school, an "open" school, and so on. Such schools focus their resources on specific areas, requiring a narrower range but possibly a higher degree of subject matter excellence in their staffs and a more focused marketing approach. They also provide certain logistical and counseling problems and require a more homogeneous structure and staffing process than the more general school system.

Generic Option C. Diversifying or entering new service areas, the final generic option, is equivalent to the business approach known as diversification. It says that the district must enter new markets and provide new kinds of services. Normally, a district chooses this option after an analysis of the trends indicates that the external environment is changing in such a way or the internal resources and limitations of the system are such that the old generic strategy is no longer appropriate. The diversification option involves major new directions for the district, such as launching a new community education venture, undertaking a new preschool program, or starting a summer camp for computer training for all school districts in a region. This option does not include minor program revisions within the current mission, such as introducing a new major in computer science in the high school or adding a concentration in VCR repair in an already existing vocational program.

A school system undertakes diversification when it can fill or can become capable of filling a large demand for service in the community. Diversification may also be called for when the school system's capabilities are such that it can be or become more efficient and effective than current public or private providers at meeting some demand that is important to one of its client groups. Of course, this may mean entering the world of competition and marketing—concepts new to most school systems.

Options for Enhancing Organizational Capability

The next questions of strategic choice concern the method of pursuing any one of the broad generic strategies. Answers to these "how" questions at a broad level are also important strategically because they can describe the nature, character, and kind of school system that is to be. Thus, the action alternatives listed below are also strategic options because they further define a school system in terms of class size, grade structure, expenditure level, and geographic scope. Remember that in this book the definition of strategy formulation includes both the development of long-term goals and the alignment of the organizational capabilities to obtain objectives (Chapter One).

Thus to generic options A, B, and C are added strategic implementation options that define general ways in which a school system might achieve its long-term objectives and an alignment of its capabilities with its environment. These strategic implementation options are as follows:

D.   To consolidate or cooperate with other districts
E.   To cut costs
F.   To eliminate programs
G.   To increase financial support (subsidies, levies, grants)

Option D. Consolidation is usually considered an option when the school district's neighborhood contains too few children for it to continue to mount a broad and rich enough program to satisfy local needs. This might be the result of substantial shifts in housing and living patterns, demands for new programs that are available at nearby locations outside the current district, a physical safety need to update a high school building in an area of economic or population decline, or any other event that reduces the ability of the current school system to provide an adequate program for its community. Cooperation with another education agency, usually another school district, though it could be another kind of local or state government unit or private organization, is considered an option when a solution to these same problems is sought that is not as drastic as consolidation. If it is both financially and administratively viable, cooperation allows a district to solve its problems without losing its local schools and their local autonomy.

Option E. The option to cut costs is used as a means of obviating the need to pursue the option of consolidating or cooperating with another education agency. *If* there is slack in the budget or if more quality or emphasis is given to a program than its benefits warrant, then it is possible to reduce costs without making significant changes in program offerings. While it is usually possible in an organization to find some waste and unnecessary expenditures that can be eliminated, it is uncommon—though not impossible—to find very much budget slack in a school system.

The place to look for potential cost reductions is in the certified staff payroll, the single largest item in almost any school system's budget. Reducing certified staff costs means lowering salaries or reducing people, the former being a matter of collective bargaining and the latter involving a reduction in special services or an increase in class size. Class size and the availability of nonclassroom education specialists are both matters of board policy, and revisions of such policy can be considered as potential alternatives to other cost reduction or revenue enhancement options available to the school district.

Option F. The option to eliminate programs (or narrow the product line) is the opposite of diversification. It involves eliminating programs that are not absolutely essential or mandatory to a full-service public school system. This might mean dropping band and orchestra; reducing special education or vocational education programs; eliminating elementary music, art, or physical education specialists; closing the hot-lunch line; or tuitioning out the high school students. Carried to an extreme, option E becomes generic option B, to focus or specialize.

The preceding options, to consolidate or cooperate, reduce costs, or eliminate programs, in popular education administration language are expanded to four and termed the "four C's": (1) consolidate, (2) cooperate, (3) cut costs, and (4) cut program.

All four of these choices involve some form of cost reduction or improved service per unit of cost. The first two involve working with other districts to reduce costs and perhaps losing the home district's identity. Losing identity, apparently unlike the situation in most small rural communities, is not a major concern for the residents of some suburban communities and of certain neighborhoods in large cities. On the other hand, facing such an alternative is usually a very serious issue and can be an explosive and sensitive one in many communities. The last two options are direct cost reduction approaches involving either cutting out some aspects of a program or eliminating entire programs or reducing the level of some services or reducing costs through improved efficiencies.

Option G. This option looks at the other side of the financial equation—revenues. The questions posed here are: Is it possible to uncover opportunities for increasing revenues by changing strategic directions or program offerings and thereby attracting more customers and funds? Is it possible to remain independent (that is, to avoid consolidation with another district) without making serious cuts in cost and program by taking an aggressive sales- or revenue-generating approach? An analysis of some of the strategies for growth and survival examined from a "business" perspective might help a school board and superintendent identify several opportunities for increasing revenues. It is not typical for a school superintendent to examine revenue enhancement opportunities, but efforts in this regard can offer some helpful solutions to financial problems. Revenue enhancement approaches such as raising private funds, seeking foundation support, asking voters for special levies, and selling new services may well become more prevalent in the decades ahead than they were in the 1970s and 1980s. At least three general kinds of opportunities for attracting additional students or revenue appear possible: (1) marketing new services for a fee, (2) seeking private donations, and (3) attracting additional students.

The first alternative involves using organizational resources to develop and market needed community and educational services on a fee-paying basis. If this takes the school system outside its current service offerings, then it is a product or market diversification and belongs under generic strategy C. Examining the activities that could be considered in the realm of this first alternative forces one to fully mine the data gathered in the external environmental analysis and the internal resource analysis. Yet in a community with many wealthy parents, why shouldn't the school offer some extra educational or personal services for a fee? In a very poor community, might it be possible to obtain subsidies or grants for such services? Preschool child care, special advanced classes, after-school programs, community education, free lunches for grandparent volunteers in the school, special adult education classes on computers, fitness and health programs for the community are just a few of the possibilities to consider. A brainstorming session in any school could yield many more.

A skeptic might look at the foregoing list and say that some of its items cannot be provided by a school for financial gain and others are simply beyond the scope of a particular school system's abilities. To answer such legitimate concerns, one must examine the facts. Most of the above services were considered or at least discussed by a few schools in the 1970s and 1980s. Second, people were paying large fees to obtain many of the same services from private sources with much less credibility than a public school might enjoy.

In addition to introducing fee-for-service activities, a school might consider a second revenue enhancement alternative, namely, a fund-raising (development) effort. Private donations through a nonprofit foundation or some other appropriate medium present a possible opportunity in a well-to-do suburb. They might also present an opportunity in an inner city if the resident business establishments see it in their best interest to have exemplary schools in the neighborhoods where they do business or office their executives. Each state has its own laws concerning the solicitation and use of private gifts in public schools. Certainly such activity was very rare and at best insignificant in the late 1970s, the time of the Golden Valley case, but it has become somewhat more prevalent in recent years.

The third alternative is to attempt to attract new customers to existing programs and services. Thus, another source of revenue and, incidentally, of more students to fill classes to an economic size, could be a program to attract students from other attendance areas. Such an effort would be over and above the normal efforts that many school systems make in working with realtors to try to induce new home buyers to move to their community because of the quality of the schools. (In the Golden Valley case this kind of real estate marketing was not considered very helpful in attracting significant numbers of new students. First, there were fewer young children; second, the reduced number of parents of young children either could not afford to buy a home in Golden Valley or, if they could, had many other schooling options as well.)

An expanded marketing and selling effort such as that implied in the third alternative would have to work around certain state statutes. In Minnesota during the time of the Golden Valley case, a state law prohibited a school system from trying to entice students from other public school systems. In this circumstance, promotion and selling have to be very subtle. A word-of-mouth campaign by parents, announcements of the high quality and small size of the system, and perhaps a campaign to enlist parents whose children are currently attending private schools could be considered.

Such a marketing effort in the late 1970s would have been a rather radical departure from past practice in public schools (as would fund-raising and development) but not necessarily counter to environmental forces in existence at the time. The best-seller *Megatrends* (Naisbett, 1982) included in its list of overall societal trends, a movement toward a multiple-option society with more choice determined at the grass roots level. Why not a public-private option (such as the Golden Valley system attempted) or an appeal to specialized audiences?

Other sources of revenue might include the day-care programs, special classes for a fee, and after-school and preschool programs for profit mentioned above. Such programs would also be tapping new client groups and thus have the potential of attracting these same people or their children to the regular school program. One would have to check the local community to determine what the competition and need for a given service might be. Even after conducting such market analysis, one must consider the resources and limitations of a school district organization, as was done in Chapter Four, to narrow in on what strategic options can feasibly be pursued. After identifying the broad strategic options available, a reexamination of the data gathered in the SWOT analysis (Chapters Three and Four) and the addition of market intelligence data provided by some depth or focus group interviews (Chapter Five) can provide important assistance to the district in assessing the feasibility and attractiveness of each option.

Additional Questions to Raise

Perhaps there are some questions to which you wish you had answers before having to select one or more of the above strategic options for action. For instance, how might enrollment trends change in the future? What about the state financial aid formula? Could your district raise additional tax revenue through an excess levy referendum or some other mechanism available in your locale? Would parents be willing to sustain annual contributions to keep your school going? How important is a rich and varied program to the future of these students (an educational question), and how important is it to parents (a perception or marketing question)?

Some of these questions cannot be answered well at all. Obtaining answers to the others can be very expensive and then may not even produce reliable results. But the process of trying to answer such questions as accurately as possible should begin to provide some insights into the magnitude of the problems facing a district and at least point toward some potential solutions. It is the job of the person responsible for seeing that a strategic analysis is performed to also try to obtain answers to these questions—in my view, that means the superintendent (CEO), working with the board.

Before trying to answer any of the foregoing questions, however, one should know what effect, if any, the answer might have on managerial action. Thinking this through in advance lessens the need for a full analysis of every question and may point to the fact that in some cases complete precision is not essential. An example of such a thought process is provided in the application to the Golden Valley situation later in this chapter.

Examples of surveys administered with no economic or managerial justification abound in schools today; so, too, do surveys with questions that never should have been asked because administrators knew in advance that the answers could not change a major decision. This situation results from some of the problems relating to citizens' committees discussed in Chapter Five and some political concerns identified in Chapter Seven.

Decision-Making Models

The Harvard Policy Model. In Chapters Two, Three, and Four, two of the most often used frameworks or models for strategic planning—the SWOT (strengths, weaknesses, opportunities, threats) model and the competitive analysis model—were presented. Andrews (1987) has expanded the SWOT model to include personal values of managers and their acknowledged responsibilities to society. The expanded model has been named the Harvard policy model (Gilbert, Hartman, Freeman, and Mauriel, 1988). A diagram of this approach to the formulation and implementation of strategy appears in Figure 3. This is the model I employ in completing the strategic analysis.

Personal values and social responsibility are extremely important considerations in the strategy formulation process because most crucial organizational decisions are strongly influenced by values. There is no one provable right answer that all analysis will point toward. Choice, then, is made by including a concern for the personal values of the community and the

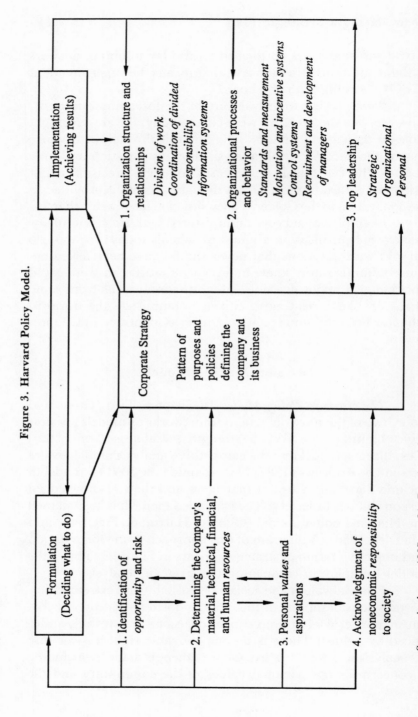

Figure 3. Harvard Policy Model.

Source: Andrews, 1987, p. 21. Reprinted by permission of Richard D. Irwin, Inc.

school executives and by acknowledging the responsibility of the school system to its stakeholders, including outside constituent groups, and the greater society at large.

In fact, school officials typically hold strongly to a personal value that gives high priority to equity and equal access for all students. This strong desire for equity, coupled with a fear that if the school did something extra for "paying" customers, it would be at the expense of the less fortunate, often inhibits school officials from pursuing some of their options for marketing extra services. Before proceeding with a gifted program or a special child-care program, an official holding this value would have to be convinced that the program would not diminish the school's ability to serve all children with all kinds of programs that they need. In this situation, a case might be made for the existence of special programs on the grounds that they help attract better faculty and in general enhance the quality of all the programs in the school.

The Stakeholder Model. Another framework, described by Gilbert, Hartman, Freeman, and Mauriel, is the stakeholder model. Figure 1 on page 13 depicts the stakeholders of a school system as those attempting to influence the allocation of resources or intended direction of the school system. For each school system, the governing body must determine who the major stakeholders are and how they are to be assessed. The stakeholder model is implied within and consistent with the Harvard policy model.

The first outside stakeholders to consider are the owners of the school system. Who owns the schools? In a sense, we all own the schools, for if the schools do not do their jobs, society will not prosper and we will all suffer. A better question might be "Who has what power to influence, enable, or constrain schools in performing appropriate missions?" This requires an analysis of the community power structure, an evaluation of internal power structures (teachers' associations, unions, and so on) and a judgment on how important each potential school system goal is to each of these groups. This kind of political analysis is discussed more fully in Chapter Seven as part of the process of executing the strategy.

In obtaining stakeholder input, one must ascertain what is important to each stakeholder group. To do this, the school executive may use frequent surveys, open meetings, informal discussion groups, focus group interviews, and sensitivity to the needs (both articulated and unarticulated) of the community and staff. Questions should probe how the community feels about richness of program versus retaining its own local school and how much in extra tax dollars the community would be willing to pay to keep the school operating in its area. It requires great skill to pose a series of preference, priority, and trade-off questions and great skill to interpret the answers to such questions.

Before members of the community can give helpful answers to questions about their preferences for options for the future, they have to have some reasonably clear idea of what the alternatives and their implications are. This is where the professional school administrator can provide knowledge and education so that the citizenry can make informed judgments. This knowledge comes through clearly written materials, a series of public meetings and discussions, and a great deal of time and effort on the part of both the school administration and its citizenry.

Assume that you have provided intensive public education on some matter. That is, you have prepared detailed reports, public speeches, and visual aids describing the implications for children, parents, community members, and tax rates of following each of the general feasible options for maintaining the status quo, specializing, diversifying, consolidating, cooperating, cutting costs, and enhancing revenue. What is the next step? How do you then obtain information on your community's preferences and strength of feeling about those preferences? To illustrate one possible approach, we will assume that you have gathered the following market research data from a questionnaire survey of a random sample of 100 parents, with a 60 percent response:

- 75 percent of parents say they are willing to increase class size up to 10 percent to keep the school district from having to consolidate.
- 27 percent of parents say they are willing to cut athletic programs to save the school district.

- 83 percent of parents are willing to vote for a six-mill excess tax levy if you can prove that such a levy is necessary to maintain the school's programs and show that it will save the school for an indefinite but long time.
- 20 percent of parents say they are definitely willing to make a personal contribution of $300 or more per year to keep the school system in operation, 20 percent say they might be willing to do so, and 50 percent say they definitely are not willing to do so.

We will also assume that when nonparents are asked if they would continue to support the six-mill excess levy and would also support an additional six-mill levy, 20 percent say they definitely will, 20 percent say they probably will, 30 percent say they are not sure whether they will, and 30 percent say they will not.

Another piece of information you have is that neighboring schools do not seem eager to consolidate with you except on terms very unfavorable to your district. Let us assume further that you have examined the data available and concluded that on the basis of what you already know, you are going to recommend to the board that the district consider consolidating with a neighboring school system. You are not completely comfortable with that decision, so before you act you decide to collect some additional information. Let us also assume that you are able to obtain additional enrollment projections indicating, with about 70 percent certainty, that the enrollment decline is going to level off at about 900 students (instead of the projected 850) and then begin to rise again very gradually. Would that change your willingness to recommend consolidation?

Do these answers help your decision? Have you changed your mind as a result? If not, what would change your mind? Were there any surprises in the data? If you would not change your decision, then why, if you knew in advance that that was the most optimistic result you could get, would you even waste your time and money trying to collect such data? Maybe 70 percent certainty is not good enough (but you know in advance no enrollment projections are perfect) or maybe even in the face of the most optimistic interpretation possible you are still wary of the school's ability to maintain the richness of program that present and future parents and students will demand. Economically, it is then a futile exercise, though the results might be needed for internal political reasons, to satisfy the board and community that the question has been carefully researched, or just to satisfy someone's curiosity. If there were no surprises in the data and if your analysis of the situation has not led you to a specific decision on a plan of action, then just what kind of information might change your decision?

A most important set of questions from the superintendent's point of view is yet to be raised. What do the board members think? How strongly do they feel? Consider how you would proceed if you were a board member. If you were the superintendent. What options are even possible to convince the board to pursue? Only after you have considered and clarified several options is it time to develop a strategy and plan. But for whom is the plan to be created? Who owns the schools? Who are its stakeholders, and what should be their involvement, if any, in the final decisions? What powers and rights do they have?

The Planning Process Model. The rational planning model says that organizations follow an approach similar to the one described thus far in this book—that is, that planning proceeds roughly in the manner noted in Table 4.

The *planning process model* involves the standard questions raised in planning. What are the mission and objectives of the

Table 4. The Planning Process Approach.

1. Scan the environment for trends.
2. Project future demands and revenues and costs.
3. Analyze one's own internal situation.
4. Establish broad goals.
5. Identify gaps between expected and desired results.
6. Communicate planning assumptions, goals, and strategic options to constituencies.
7. Ask for any needed special studies.
8. Present major strategic alternatives to appropriate constituents for decision.

organization? What alternative goals and strategies will support the mission and help achieve the objectives? What are the pros and cons of each alternative? How is input obtained so that one can decide on the ''best'' alternative? Who must understand and be committed to the goals? How is commitment obtained? How are goals and plans communicated and monitored?

But as Quinn (1980) and others such as Lindblom (1959) have pointed out, planning and decision making in organizations do not proceed that way. Managers attempt to achieve their goals in an incremental step-by-step fashion. A process called logical incrementalism, which is the subject of Quinn's book, seems to better describe how strategies are actually formulated and implemented in organizations. Along the way, logics other than the rational planning approach and other rationalizations are developed. Coalitions are formed, small special-interest groups may assume great strength, an ill-informed majority (or minority) may begin to push through a less-than-optimum option. Forces that set illogical solutions in motion sometimes prevail because of the apathy or inability of the majority to push the right organizational button at the right time to stop the momentum.

Another factor that leads organizations to make occasional irrational decisions is the tendency of most leaders to accept the first convenient alternative that satisfies or exceeds the requirements for achieving a goal. Simon (1976) calls this ''satisficing.'' It is the result of a human limitation that makes it impossible for someone to survey thoroughly all the available options (a phenomenon Simon calls ''bounded rationality''). For an excellent bibliography of works describing the intricacies of organizational decision processes, see Quinn (1980, pp. 60–63).

Application to Golden Valley

Strategic decision making may be better understood when it is applied to a particular school system. Since the strategic circumstance of Golden Valley in 1978 has already been presented, this district is a convenient application vehicle. The objective is to determine what kind of a school system or array of services should be made available and then to determine how those services may best be made available to the various Golden Valley constituencies. The chief stakeholder groups of the Golden Valley school district and of most other districts are listed below. My definition of a stakeholder group is a constituent body that is significantly affected by or can significantly affect the work of the school system and that has different needs than another constituent body.

- Parents of children now attending the schools
- Parents of children who reside in the local community but attend other schools
- Parents of preschoolers and future parents residing in the district
- Children now attending the schools
- The community of home owners living in the attendance area
- The current school system's staff members
- The local business community
- Local government units providing services in the area

Further Background on the District. Golden Valley is an upper-income first-tier suburb whose parent group is largely professional, with both parents living at home with their children and usually with a female spouse who is not employed in a full-time job outside the home. Yet there are also single-parent and lower-income families, as well as a very small group (1 or 2 percent) who receive AFDC payments. There is also a normal percentage of handicapped children, with a very vocal parent group demanding more services in special education.

About 75 percent of the residents do not have children in school and are chiefly middle-aged couples, many of whom have had children in the Golden Valley system and who still feel good about the schools. Many in the nonparent group are supporters of good neighborhood schools if for no other reason than to keep real estate values high. On average, real estate values in that portion of Golden Valley comprising the school district's attendance area are among the highest in the greater Twin Cities metropolitan area.

In earlier years the citizens of Golden Valley had passed an excess levy override of six mills. It was one of the first suburban systems to take advantage of the special provision in the levy limitation law that allowed a community that could get more than 50 percent of those voting in a referendum election for additional taxes to levy such taxes for general operating purposes. However, because of the nature of the promises made when the excess levy was proposed and passed, the administration feels that it has two years to produce a long-range plan for continuing high-quality education for the children in the community at a feasible cost. Projections show that within five years, the schools will have fewer than 850 students and will be running a deficit of $200,000 to $400,000 per year unless something changes the financial situation before that time.

Drawing on earlier descriptions of Golden Valley as a reasonably well-to-do district with a reputation for high academic quality, we may identify options that it might use to increase its revenues. In Minnesota, the law did permit private solicitations by a school district as long as the funds collected were placed under control of the duly elected school board. In other words, individuals or a private foundation collecting money in the name of the school could provide financial support for the school, but not usually for specific programs or teachers.

On the other hand, an outside foundation formed for the purpose of supporting the school could make program-specific grants to the school. Calculations made at the time by two board members showed that in the face of the worst deficits projected for the future, it would take an average contribution of only $500 per family with children in school to balance the district's operating budget. In other years, a smaller amount might suffice. Since this would be a tax-deductible contribution, it would compare very favorably to the $4,000 to $5,000 per year that private independent schools were charging in tuition at that time. Some people viewed the current Golden Valley schools as providing for them a "public-private" option at a fraction of the cost of the tuition of a private independent school.

The Golden Valley superintendent at the time told the board that the difficulty with private contributions was their uncertainty. Even if enough money was collected in one year to keep current programs operating, there was no guarantee that the next year would bring the same. Some programs and staff members needed longer than year-to-year commitments to operate effectively. Furthermore, there was little local history of successful private fund-raising for public schools at the time. In other words, the district did not deem it wise to take the risks involved in starting something relatively new and unfamiliar and fraught with uncertainty, even though it really would not have been a poor option for the system to pursue.

Other sources of revenue in a well-to-do community such as Golden Valley might include day-care programs, special classes for a fee, and the after-school and preschool programs for profit already mentioned. Such activities would also tap new client groups and thus potentially attract these same people or their children to participate in the regular school program. At the time, however, this kind of effort seemed a bit radical to Golden Valley's administration.

The purpose here is not just to develop a strategy for Golden Valley but to apply the strategic analysis process to a specific situation so as to illuminate its power and effectiveness. Performing the same analysis in any school district would help the administration develop a better and stronger long-term strategy. But if you had been superintendent of the Golden Valley school system in 1978, with the information provided to you in this case, what would you have recommended to the board or what other actions would you have taken? Why?

The sense of the board was that the community was willing to consolidate if the terms were carefully worked out to save the elementary school and the older students could attend a nearby secondary school that was perceived to be of high quality. A small group in the community, including two board members, was interested in trying some more radical options for maintaining independent status, but a majority of the board deferred to the superintendent's judgment.

Most board members reacted coolly to radical options such as depending on private donations or counting on attracting enough outside students. Furthermore, they had not been presented with nor had they thought about any great number of fee-for-service programs. Most of their deliberations had been around the "four *C*'s." They spent a number of years discussing and implementing possibilities for cost reduction and cutting programs and also discussed the questions of cooperation and finally of consolidation with other districts.

The politics and structure of the Golden Valley school community, whose attendance area comprises only one-third of the village of Golden Valley, seem to be relatively unimportant in this case relative to the larger problems facing the school system. More could be done with this kind of analysis in the Golden Valley case, but a simplifying assumption existed in that situation that allows one to proceed further without intimate knowledge of the Golden Valley community. That is the impending enrollment-driven financial crisis. Since the issue of school enrollment decline and financial and program problems so overwhelmed other concerns, it is justifiable to focus on them exclusively.

While the administrators of Golden Valley held equal opportunity as an important value and were genuinely concerned for and paid attention to the less fortunate and handicapped in the district, the primary values of the elected school board and the community centered around concerns for academic excellence, opportunity for personal development, and challenge in formal study, athletics, and cocurricular activities. These two groups felt that the needs of the community were best served by providing a rich and challenging program for all, regardless of background and skill level. The board felt its obligation was to serve the average student well, to serve the gifted student also, and to provide a rich array of opportunities for all. The community also supported the existence of high standards and high academic expectations.

Making the Decision. The incremental approach was followed in Golden Valley. Two key decisions were made. First, in 1978 a decision was made to seek a merger partner. Second, in 1980 the decision on which partner to select was made. In 1978, after much analysis and study, the Golden Valley superintendent recommended that the board seek the best merger partner under the best conditions that could be negotiated while the district was still viable. The school board decided to follow the superintendent's recommendation and seek the best possible arrangement for a consolidation or merger with one of its contiguous suburban school districts. Prior to making this decision, the board obtained reports from the citizens' "futures committee," which described what the school enrollment and financial picture would be if no major changes in district organization or finances were made. The report painted a gloomy picture.

In preparation for the next key decision, which partner to select, the board commissioned a study of the implications of merging with each of the three contiguous suburban districts. For each district, this study, financed by a grant from the Minnesota State Department of Education, examined the programs that would be available to the current Golden Valley students, the financial results, the involuntary termination of teaching staff and what that would mean to current Golden Valley teachers as well as to the number of preparations and quality of instruction, the mill rate levies in each taxing authority, and the quality of student life in terms of bus travel time, size of school to be attended, and mix of students. Each of the three resulting impact evaluations was compared on the same measures with the option of maintaining the status quo.

The impact evaluations were presented to the community in a factual, objective manner with no recommendation attached. Printed material describing the implications of each potential merger and of remaining independent was mailed out to community members along with an announcement of a series of public meetings to discuss the issue. During these meetings board members and the superintendent fielded questions. The meetings were reasonably calm, and board members felt that the discussion proceeded smoothly and effectively.

It is interesting to note that no poll was taken of the community. The board "felt" a sort of general consensus and then proceeded to negotiate the best terms it could with each of the three districts so that it could later present a recommendation to the public as to which district Golden Valley should merge with.

Once the decision to consolidate was made, the issue for the Golden Valley board became what conditions should it seek and then what criteria should it use to determine which partner to select. Note that at this stage consideration of all other options ceased. Since none of the potential partners really wanted Golden Valley, the district also needed to educate each of the neighboring districts as to the advantages of taking Golden Valley students. The adjoining districts also had declining enrollments and financial problems and reasoned that if they took on Golden Valley's problems, too, they would then be worse off.

However, an analysis of the Golden Valley district's assets and liabilities according to the approach described in Chapter Three could have demonstrated to another school system the value of joining with this district. As the other school boards began to see the advantages of having the large number of "gifted" students, excellent teachers, and media resources from Golden Valley and also realized that Golden Valley's physical facilities could easily be sold for the amount of its bonded debt and were therefore not a liability, Golden Valley assumed more bargaining power in the negotiations that followed. In fact, just before consolidation talks entered their final phases, the middle and high school complex and grounds were sold for the entire district debt or mortgage value. They were, in fact, sold to a private independent school, which felt that it had made an exceptionally good purchase of a very nice campus. This left the district with an elementary school effectively debt free, and other districts began to find Golden Valley a more attractive acquisition candidate.

The Golden Valley board decided that it wanted any consolidation partner (*acquirer* would be a better word) to agree to the following terms: (1) inclusion of one of the current Golden Valley board members (to be appointed by the Golden Valley board before it was dissolved) on the new joint school board for at least three years; (2) a guarantee that the elementary school in its neighborhood would remain open for the children in its geographic area for at least five years; and (3) protection for all the Golden Valley teachers who would not have lost their jobs had the district remained independent.

Apart from these terms, the second of which was crucial, the board was seeking the best conditions for its present and future students in terms of peer relationships and smallness of high school, maintenance of certain programs felt to be strong in Golden Valley, the best conditions possible for its present teachers, and a board willing to work with the Golden Valley community during the transition period.

One additional consolidation or cooperation alternative not yet discussed was the possibility of merging or forming some sort of cooperative relationship with the city of Minneapolis, which was also a contiguous district on the eastern border of the Golden Valley attendance area. The Minneapolis superintendent had expressed his interest in discussing a possible relationship with Golden Valley and in fact was the only superintendent who took the initiative in trying to begin such negotiations.

The Golden Valley school board feared the possible consequences of such a partnership because at the time Minneapolis was operating under a legal mandate to achieve certain court-ordered desegregation goals and was using some complex busing arrangements. Furthermore, Golden Valley was adjacent to what in its view were very poor and troubled areas of the city. There may also have been an unstated concern that large busloads of Golden Valley children might be taken into largely minority-populated schools to help the city achieve its racial balance, and then the currently upper-middle-class white school in Golden Valley would become populated with poor, low-achieving minorities bused in the opposite direction.

A small minority of white citizens in Golden Valley would have favored the city merger as an enriching experience for the suburb, but the board knew it would not be a popular alternative, and many members honestly believed it would be a very poor choice, whether popular or not.

Golden Valley discussed other cooperation options, but after some consideration dismissed them. The feeling was that Golden Valley as an independent school district in its existing attendance area would eventually become too small to operate and that it was better to "shop" for a merger partner while it was still strong enough to negotiate favorable terms. After another series of public meetings and discussions that chiefly involved the sharing of information and facts from the evaluations of the three potential merger pairings, the Golden Valley board decided in 1980 to merge with the contiguous suburban district to its west.

Several factors led to the board's unanimous decision. First, the district it chose had the smallest high school and the highest socioeconomic profile (and thus the closest match on this measure to Golden Valley), met all the Golden Valley board's stipulations, and perhaps most importantly had the only board of the three that actively pursued Golden Valley after the negotiation process began. Second, this district also promised a great deal of help in the transition and seemed genuinely to look forward to welcoming Golden Valley high school and junior high school students.

Both communities (Golden Valley and its merger partners) accepted the decision, and the merger went smoothly. The Golden Valley community had been well prepared with facts and information and had been heard. It accepted, though with some sadness, what most considered inevitable: the disappearance of their small and personal system. Teachers and students from the soon-to-be-merged districts spent the school year before the actual merger visiting each other's schools and classes, and a great deal of preplanning and extensive involvement by both staffs kept the problems of transition to a minimum.

Was this decision the right decision? There will never be a certain answer to that question. What I can say, some ten years after the merger, is that all seems to be going well in the combined district. Golden Valley's process had some flaws, as we have seen. Would the application of one of our strategic decision models or frameworks have helped make a better decision? I leave the answer to this question for the reader to decide.

If a school system takes seriously the issues identified in Chapter Two and the environmental trends discussed in Chapter Three, develops a similar list of additional issues and trends pertinent to its own state and local situation, and then thoroughly conducts the kind of resource examination called for in Chapter Four and market analysis suggested in Chapter Five, it is hard to imagine that it would not determine that it needs a significantly new and different strategy. Thus strategy formulation in the 1990s should rarely end up with a "more of the same only better" strategy. One would expect that the first time a district follows the strategy formulation decision process recommended herein, it would end up deciding to enter new markets, significantly reduce or expand its service offerings, launch a major system restructuring effort, significantly redesign its curriculum, incorporating major technological changes, or make other significant changes in mission, direction, or goals.

Part Two of this book provides guidance for pursuing a new strategy by means of a three-part approach: politics, marketing, and operations. Part three then explains how to introduce major changes in strategy and how to assess and report performance of the strategy.

PART TWO

Implementing the Strategy

In the second part of this book, Chapters Seven through Nine introduce processes and functions for pursuing, or implementing, school system strategy. Note that the separation of formulation and implementation is artificial and done only to help clarify the principles and the exposition of concepts. In the year-to-year workings of a school system, strategy is being simultaneously and continuously formulated and implemented. It is being revised as it is implemented because the implementation processes constantly influence strategies being formulated.

As you read the next chapters, you will note that each of the managerial and leadership functions discussed—politics, marketing, and operations and instructional leadership—are not only part of an implementation process but also influence the formulation of the content of strategy. The first part of the book focused on long-term analysis and a conceptual framework for engaging in strategic management and planning, with an emphasis on determining the general policies, directions, and overall objectives of the school system. This second part focuses on more specific, shorter-term action processes and techniques, with emphasis on determining how to guide the school system in ways that can facilitate its achieving the desired objectives.

Chapter Seven provides an appropriate transition between Parts One and Two because politics, policies, and political analysis are inherently involved in establishing a strategy for a school district, but the methods for analyzing political power are also very useful for facilitating implementation programs.

7

Gaining Support for Change: The Politics of Strategic Leadership

by B. Dean Bowles

What is politics? What is policy? What are politics and policy in education?

Some Cases About Politics

• At an annual school board budget hearing, the high school athletic director spoke up to oppose 125 people from the local hockey association who wanted to include money in the athletic department budget for a new varsity interscholastic ice hockey program. The athletic director's opposition to the program was on three grounds: (a) it would be too costly, (b) it would cause competition for athletes among winter sports, and (c) the hockey association is a narrow pressure group.

• The publisher of a major newspaper in a large city demanded that the superintendent cut the school budget by 5 percent in order to obtain editorial and political support for changes in the educational program.

• A Republican secretary of education announced from the "bully pulpit" that a more academic curriculum should replace the comprehensive curriculum in American high schools.

- The Republicans on a state legislative committee held up the appropriation for the state adoption of a social studies textbook until the author and publisher agreed to provide a more conservative interpretation of the administrations of Presidents Harding, Coolidge, and Hoover and to downplay the emphasis given to a Joan Baez poem.

- Organized teachers in a midwestern state succeeded in obtaining a statute that provides for binding arbitration and outlaws strikes and lockouts in school board/teacher labor disputes. The practical outcome was that in small, rural school districts school boards are at a disadvantage in labor disputes.

- The parents of elementary school children in a suburban school district refused to support a school bond referendum if the school board persisted in its plan to add the fifth grade to the sixth- through eighth-grade middle school. They believed that the plan would do great harm to their children, physically, emotionally, and educationally.

- A school superintendent announced his retirement three years in advance and then aligned himself with a scant board majority of four to three in order to secure massive school closings without affecting the middle school concept and grade alignment.

- A school superintendent listened to staff arguments that providing basic stimulus-response therapy for a severely mentally retarded and multiply handicapped child is the responsibility of the public schools. Later, the superintendent decided that the child was not the responsibility of the public schools and therefore should be institutionalized.

- During lunchroom and other informal discussions, teachers reached consensus that sex education should be taught in three separate units—one in elementary school, one in middle school, and one in high school—and should not be integrated into the K–12 social studies, science, and physical education curricula.

- A new superintendent who is also the elementary school principal in a small, rural school district demoted a veteran lead-teacher in the elementary school because of philosophical differences. Later the superintendent was reprimanded by the school board, and the teacher was allowed to return to the lead-teacher position.

- A superintendent recommended to the school board that instructional computers should be purchased and assigned to schools without computers to compensate for PTA-purchased computers available in the other schools in the district. This action would ensure that all children in the district have equal access to a computer regardless of whether the computer was purchased with private or public funds. The school board accepted the proposal. Later some of its members were the object of a recall election on grounds that the compensatory policy was unfair to the PTA and other parent and community groups that wanted to augment the computer education program at "their" schools.

- Over 1,500 people jammed an auditorium for a public hearing on (a) removing specified books from the school library, (b) eliminating the United Nations from the social studies curriculum, and (c) balancing the "Darwinian view of evolution" with "scientific creationism." A minority of the seven-member school board sought the proposed changes. The staff and three members of the board were adamant against any change or compromise; two members of the board thought that the request was extreme but were willing to compromise.

- For many years two key legislative leaders blocked state-mandated programs for the gifted and talented because they believed that the state role in education is to ensure equity and the local district role is to promote excellence. Moreover, the legislators believed that any new state-mandated program would lead to a new category of financial aid, which could better go to property tax relief.

- Members of a state task force agreed to exempt school social workers, psychologists, and counselors from the classroom teaching requirement for administrator licenses if their organizations would support other recommended changes in administrator licensure and preparation.

Political Analysis

Political analysis and the skills for political analysis are essential to (a) a knowledge of individual, group, and institutional stakeholders, including their social and political relationships; (b) an analysis of problems and issues, including their resource, value, and power dimensions; and (c) an understanding of stakeholders' sentiments, beliefs, and values about the issues. A knowledge of stakeholders yields information about power, influence, and power structures: the *who* of politics. Issue analysis yields information about the political stakes, including both the explicit and implicit value, resource, and power characteristics: the *what* of politics. Knowledge of stakeholders' sentiments, beliefs, and values yields information necessary for the resolution of conflict: the *why* of politics. Figure 4 illustrates

Figure 4. Analysis of Political Policy.

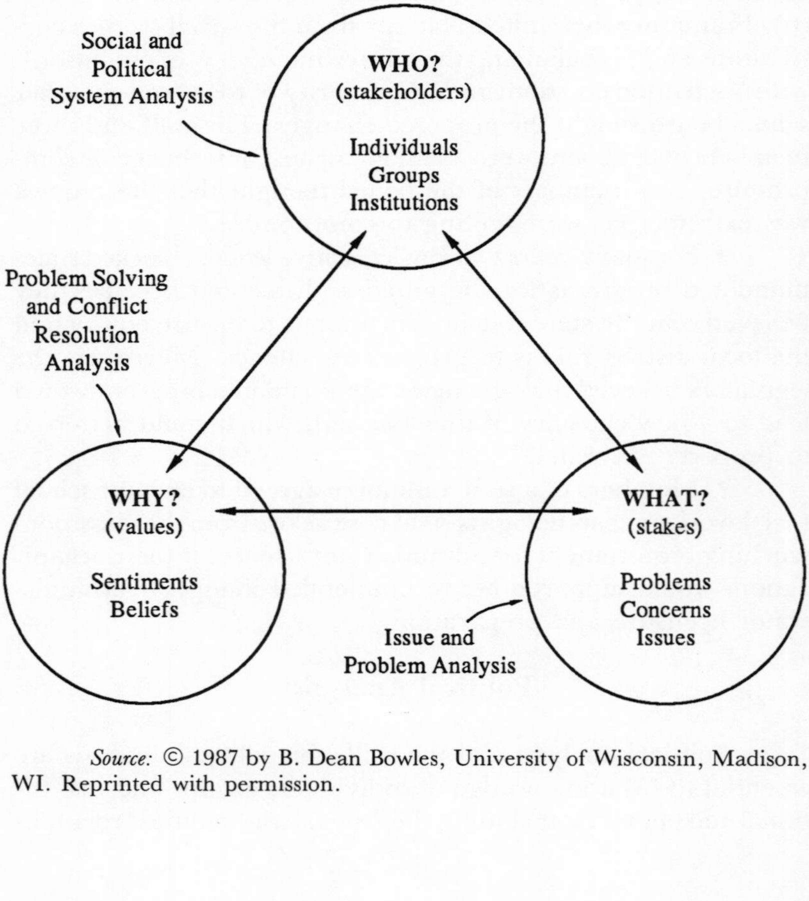

Source: © 1987 by B. Dean Bowles, University of Wisconsin, Madison, WI. Reprinted with permission.

not only the *who, what,* and *why* factors involved in political analysis but also their interrelationship.

The approach to political analysis illustrated in Figure 4 is a political adaptation of the analysis of social relationships by Homans (1950) in *The Human Group.* Homans's framework describes the relationships among people in terms of the frequency, amount, and quality of their interpersonal "interactions." However, Homans found that interaction among people occurs in their common "activities," not at random. Hence, "interaction" is interdependent with "activity." Similarly, the "sentiments" and beliefs people hold are not random but about "activities." Therefore, not only are "interaction" and "activity" interdependent, but so, too, are "interaction" and "sentiment" and "sentiment" and "activity."

When the triangle of interdependence develops "customary" patterns of "interaction," "activity," and "sentiment" among people, groups form around those patterns. Homans's methods of social analysis suggest that the study of groups would be vacuous if they were not studied in relation to both their sentiments and activities. In terms of change and intervention, Homans found that changing the activities of a group affects the patterns not only of sentiments but also of interactions, and changing the interaction patterns affects the activities and sentiments.

Who? What? and Why?

In terms of adapting the Homans schema to political analysis, broader conceptualizations of "interaction," "activity," and "sentiment" are necessary. Therefore, the "interaction" concept is broadened to the *who* and includes individual, group, and institutional stakeholders and their patterns of communication and interaction. The "activities" concept is broadened to the *what* and comprises the problems, concerns, and issues important to stakeholders. The "sentiment" concept is broadened to the *why* (values) and encompasses stakeholders' sentiments and beliefs concerning the issues.

Who: Stakeholders. Stakeholders (as discussed later) are any individuals, groups, or institutions that may have an interest or stake in the resolution of actual or potential conflict over the allocation of resources, values, or power. In the cases cited at the beginning of this chapter, the athletic director, newspaper publisher, school superintendent, and legislators were individual stakeholders. The 125 hockey boosters, Republicans on the legislative committee, organized teachers, and parents of an elementary school's children were group stakeholders. The school board, task force, and PTA were institutional stakeholders.

All of these were actual and explicitly identified stakeholders. However, all potential stakeholders must also be identified. Potential stakeholders include not only those that are currently participating in the political process but also the individuals, groups, and institutions that logically have a stake in the outcome or could be influenced to participate through the use of rewards/inducements and sanctions/contributions. For example, the teachers in the lunchroom who decided about sex education were only one stakeholder group; others not explicitly identified could have been parents, the superintendent, the school board, those against sex education, and Planned Parenthood.

The process of stakeholder identification is one of brainstorming all possible individuals, groups, and institutions. The process can be facilitated by also identifying all of the issues in which each stakeholder could have a stake. Since stakeholders, issues, and beliefs are interdependent, then each issue should generate even more stakeholders associated with the newly identified issues. For example, the 1,500 people in the auditorium were evidently concerned about library books, the UN, and evolution. The explicit stakeholders were (a) the "minority" among the 1,500; (b) the minority's "two allies" on the board; (c) the staff; (d) the staff's "three allies" on the board; and (e) the two "compromise" board members. Brainstorming could yield many other stakeholders, including the students, the superintendent, the majority of the 1,500, and the teachers' union, among others.

By brainstorming about other issues and beliefs associated with this case even more stakeholders can be identified. For example, it is likely that the publishers of library books, who have a stake in both intellectual freedom and book sales, were stakeholders. It might also be assumed that if "staff" were better differentiated, the social studies and science teachers would have had a greater stake in their curriculum and some well-defined and more intense sentiments, beliefs, and values than the kindergarten or mathematics teachers.

What: Stakes. Stakes are any problems, concerns, or issues that allocate resources, values, or power. The subsequent discussion of politics, especially the section on resources, values, and power, will identify many of the explicit stakes, including budget cutting (resource stake), censorship (value stake), and binding arbitration (power stake).

Again, these stakes are actual and explicitly identified, and again, all potential stakes must also be identified. Potential stakes include not only those issues and policies that are explicit but also those that logically could become stakes if new stakeholders were to participate in the political process. For example, the explicit stakes in the bond referendum case appear to have been the middle school and the grade arrangement for fifth-graders. Other stakes not explicitly identified in that case could have been enrollment patterns, cost effectiveness, curriculum, and transportation.

The process of identifying all the stakes involves brainstorming all possible activities, problems, concerns, issues, and politics involving resources, values, or power. The process can be facilitated by also identifying all of the stakeholders and the potential issues for each stakeholder. Since stakeholders, stakes, and beliefs are interdependent, then each new stakeholder should generate even more stakes associated with the newly identified stakeholders. For example, in the PTA computer case the explicit stakes were equalization of resources in all schools and a recall election. Some brainstorming could yield other stakes, including board authority, policies about the use of private funds, fairness, and excellence.

By brainstorming about other stakeholders and beliefs associated with this case even more stakes can be identified. For example, it is likely that the staff in the "equalized schools" and "disequalized schools" would have had different sentiments about the superintendent's recommendation and the board's action. If this had been the case, then other stakes might have been potential staff morale problems and conflict among school faculties. It might also be assumed that if the stake of "equalizing resources" were differentiated, still other stakes would have emerged, such as "equalizing student services," "equalizing maintenance," and "does equality mean sameness?"

Why: Values. Values are any sentiments or beliefs that a stakeholder may have and that influence the resolution of actual or potential conflict over the allocation of resources, values, or power associated with a stake. Values can be observed in terms of both direction (for or against, good or bad, right or wrong) and intensity (very important, important, unimportant; indifference, inclination, preference, demand; changeable, negotiable, not negotiable).

In the minicases the direction of many values was clear. For example, the PTA thought giving computers to their schools was "good"; the Republicans were "for" giving the Harding, Coolidge, and Hoover administrations a different interpretation; a minority of the 1,500 people felt that teaching about the UN was "wrong."

The intensity was also evident. The superintendent in announcing his retirement and aligning himself with the four-to-three board majority clearly articulated that the middle school idea was not negotiable. The secretary of education had a clear "preference" for academic education as opposed to a comprehensive program. Finally, the two legislative leaders thought that property tax relief and equity were "important" enough to block state-mandated programs for the gifted and talented.

Relationship Between the "What" and the "Why." The relationship between the "what" and the "why" of political analysis is facilitated by simultaneously focusing on the value-belief-sentiment and issue-problem-concern aspects of the six *E*'s of educational policy analysis:

1. Equity
2. Excellence
3. Efficiency
4. Election (choice)
5. "Eccountability"
6. Effectiveness

One of the six *E*'s usually dominates the "what" and "why" of policy analysis, and the remainder are customarily present or conspicuous by their absence. The case of the severely and multiply handicapped child is replete with examples. The equity issue certainly dominated the politics and policy of whether to educate the handicapped child in a public school or in an institution. Another value-issue nexus was the matter of the parents' or child's election, or choice, of educational program. More implicit in the value-issue analysis were efficiency, or cost of education for the child, particularly when compared to the cost of education for other children, and effectiveness, or success in educating the child—at least as measured by the criteria and with the standards customarily used for other children.

The legislative stance on programs for the gifted and talented certainly brought equity into sharp contrast with excellence and election. Indeed, the state policy of promoting a floor of equity at the state level and leaving the ceiling of excellence to the local level is an interesting distinction that is typical of state-local differences in educational policy. Also interesting is the fact that in this instance advocates for the gifted and talented were seeking a state mandate to provide a local election (choice), which could be construed as also providing for excellence.

The computer allocation case also exemplified the six *E*'s in that there were elements of equity for all children; excellence in the schools with the PTA purchases; efficiency in the use of scarce resources; "eccountability" to the school board for local school initiatives; election in the sense that the PTA may choose to allocate resources in areas other than computers in the future; and questions of effectiveness in the instructional program relating to computers.

In summary, political analysis involves the broadest analysis of values, beliefs, and sentiments and issues, problems, and concerns. Moreover, the six E's of equity, excellence, efficiency, election, "eccountability," and effectiveness are useful as part of any set of questions or analyses.

The Uses of Political Analysis

Identification of the stakeholders and their customary relationships is essential to a determination of the power structure of any community or political system. The customary patterns of interaction—or the absence of interaction or negative interaction—among stakeholders about the stakes, including shared sentiments, beliefs, and values, yields the stakeholders' power structure. For example, members of the hockey association clearly shared some common sentiments about the value of varsity hockey and the need to allocate tax resources for it, whereas the athletic director and his allies did not. If these groups had persisted and demonstrated a customary pattern of difference over all athletic policies, the power structure would have been *competitive-factional.* On the other hand, if the groups had persisted and demonstrated a customary pattern of agreement over all athletic policy except that pertaining to varsity hockey, then the power structure would have been *plural-rational.* The italicized terms are defined and discussed later in this chapter.

Identification of the stakes is necessary for effective policy analysis, research, development, and implementation. The interrelationship of the stakes and the stakeholders yields politically efficacious policy. For example, in the case of programs for the gifted and talented, policy research could have yielded the finding that gifted and talented children from families below the poverty level are twice as likely not to have access to gifted and talented programs as children from families above the poverty level; policy research would also have shown that school districts that receive a large amount of state aid are less likely to have programs for gifted and talented students than are districts that receive a small amount of state aid. Thus, policy research could have resulted in the development of policy proposals that (a) mandated programs to ensure access for all children because the failure to have mandated programs resulted only in the denial of access to poor children; (b) provided "equalized" categorical aid that would have provided equalization aid and property tax relief; and (c) addressed the specific concerns of the legislators. In short, a thorough identification of the stakes—and stakeholders—can yield policy options that address the problems, are politically salable, and resolve actual or potential conflict.

Identification of values is crucial to conflict resolution. First, knowledge of sentiments, beliefs, and values and their intensity is necessary to make a judgment about whether stakes are different, changeable, negotiable, or not negotiable. Second, such knowledge is the fundamental building block upon which issues are framed, or around which they can be reframed. The anecdotal cases are replete with instances in which values and their intensity can be judged and, as a result, alternative political courses of action can be narrowed and decided upon. Similarly, with an understanding of the sentiments, the problems, issues, and policies can be reframed. For example, shifting the teaching of the United Nations as "an aspect of American foreign policy" rather than "world government" reframed the issue as one of improving curriculum, not one of professional versus public authority. If the issue of programs for the gifted and talented had been reframed as one of excellence or election rather than one of equity, the outcome could have been different. In short, a thorough identification of stakeholders' values, beliefs, and sentiments—and the associated stakes—can yield policy alternatives and conflict resolution options not otherwise available.

Three Perspectives: Program, Policy, and Market

Strategic leadership may be examined from (1) the program or operations perspective, (2) the policy or political perspective, and (3) the market or consumer perspective. These are by no means mutually exclusive; rather, they are inseparable and interdependent factors for effective strategic leadership in public education.

The dominant perspective of most school administrators is on program and operations: how to provide educational services with efficiency, effectiveness, and a degree of accountability. The key question raised by this perspective is "How will (insert new idea, change, opportunity, or threat) impact on current programs and operations?" A program-perspective question about the hockey program case would be "How would this affect the current athletic program, including competition for winter-season athletes?" A program question in the evolution-creationism case would be "How would this change the way that we deliver our current science curriculum?" The program question implicit in the severely multiply handicapped case is "Are we currently teaching children with these severe and multiple handicaps, and how much does (would) it cost?" The program or operations perspective is common to most textbooks on school administration and is the subject of Chapter Nine in this book.

The second perspective, the policy or political perspective, asks how to allocate resources, values, and power in order to resolve actual or potential conflict. The key questions raised by this perspective address problems such as how available resources can be distributed so that there is an equitable distribution among poor and rich children and potential conflict will be resolved. Politics and policy are critical factors in effective strategic leadership. Hence, this chapter will focus on the nature of politics and public policy; the allocation of resources, value, and power; political analysis; community power structure; the resolution of conflict; methods of analysis; and the political and policy skills for strategic leadership.

The least predominant perspective of school administrators, the market perspective, asks how to identify consumer needs and then promote and deliver the educational services consumers want at an acceptable price. The key question raised by this perspective is "Who are the customers, what do they want, and how does the school get it to them at an acceptable price?" A market question in the evolution-creationism case would be "Who are the consumers who want creationism, and how can it be delivered by the public schools?" A market question in the middle school referendum case is "Who wants fifth grade in the middle school and who does not, and how can these two market segments be satisfied by the services provided by the public schools?'' The market questions implicit in the secretary of education's message are ''What market segments want a purely academic high school program, and what market segments want a comprehensive high school? How can these market segments be satisfied by the products and services offered by the public school, and how can the schools promote and deliver the services at a competitive price?'' The market perspective does not simply involve school public relations because public relations is only one feature of promotion in marketing. For a more detailed discussion of the marketing function in schools and the marketing perspective, see Chapter Eight.

The Elements of Politics

All of the real-life cases described in the first section of this chapter have two things in common. First, they involve either the allocation or the reallocation of (a) resources, such as money, jobs, credit, time, materials, expertise, and information; (b) values, such as right or wrong, good or bad, justice, fairness, legitimacy, social norms and myths, beliefs, and sentiments; or (c) power or authority, such as who should decide, who should control, where authority should reside, who should be involved in decisions, and how decisions should be made. Second, each case involves the resolution of actual or potential conflict. Therefore, an easy definition of politics is the resolution of actual or potential conflict in the allocation or reallocation of resources, values, and power.

Allocation of Resources, Values, and Power. The city newspaper publisher's demand for a budget cut is caught up in the obvious issue of allocating resources. Not as readily apparent is the issue of allocating power because in this case the publisher appears to exercise an extraordinary influence over school budgets, how decisions are made, and who are involved in decisions. Even more subtle are the value issues associated with right or wrong, justice, and the legitimacy of the publisher's involvement. Of course, the case cries out for the resolution of the potential conflict because apparently there will be no budget or things could get worse for the district or the superintendent unless the budget is cut.

Similarly, the legislative committee that wanted substantive changes in a social studies textbook in exchange for an appropriation is obviously negotiating a resource allocation issue. The apparent value allocation issue is the treatment of Presidents Harding, Coolidge, and Hoover on the one hand versus Joan Baez on the other. However, an even more subtle value issue is whether legislators should be involved in the editing of textbooks since that is the customary prerogative of authors and publishers. The authority allocation issues are essentially governmental ones: Should states adopt textbooks? Should legislators have authority over editorial content or be able to influence the process at all?

The case of teachers winning statutory binding arbitration is clearly an instance of reallocating authority from school boards to teacher unions and arbitrators. Implicit in this case are issues of community values such as local control, turning over local decisions to outside arbitrators, and the legitimacy of strikes for teachers.

Each one of these cases encompasses a political issue that is primarily a resource, value, or power allocation issue. However, virtually every case has some element of each type of issue. The computer distribution decision is primarily a value reallocation issue involving equity, fairness, and excellence. However, it also has overtones of authority allocation about who should be making decisions on the allocation of instructional resources in the schools. Similarly, the case of the library books, the United Nations, and the science curriculum is essentially a power-authority reallocation issue, but one involving critical questions of beliefs about what should be in a school curriculum. The referendum case is essentially a resources allocation issue with undercurrents of values about what is good or bad in various grade arrangements for children.

Resolution of Conflict. Conflict is another element of the political process that is apparent in each of these cases. Conflict is sometimes actual, as in the case of the superintendent align-

ing himself with the board majority over the issue of school closings and in the case of the 1,500 people confronting the board
about curriculum in a public meeting. However, conflict may
be potential, as in the case of the secretary of education's dictum on public school curriculum and in the case of the newspaper
publisher's demand for a budget cut if the superintendent does
not agree or comply. Conflict can also appear to be resolved,
as in the cases of the teaching of sex education and the apparent
agreement of the social workers, counselors, and psychologists
to support the report if they are not held to the classroom teaching standard. Conflict can also range in intensity. Indeed, the
moribund, low-intensity legislative action on programs for the
gifted and talented contrasts sharply with the high-intensity
drama of an auditorium packed with 1,500 people. Similarly,
the low intensity of the teachers agreeing on the sex education
agenda is different from the personal humiliation faced by the
superintendent who was reprimanded by the board in the teacher
demotion case.

What Politics Is Not. Politics is not necessarily governmental, although virtually all political behavior is directed ultimately toward an authoritative decision by an executive, legislative, or judicial institution. To be sure, the work of elected
and appointed government officials—even the work of civil ser-
vants who claim distance from politics—is almost all political
in nature. Nevertheless, much political activity is frequently that
of groups whose primary interest is social or economic. For example, the athletic director in the hockey case, the parents in
the referendum case, and the teachers in the sex education case
are community groups or professionals who have short-term
political goals and are behaving politically.

Politics is not necessarily partisan. Indeed, virtually none
of the cases cited are partisan events. Effective school leaders
must understand politics as normal, pervasive, and even desir-
able if they expect to accomplish their objectives. Yet popular
notions of politics, which restrict our conception of politics to
partisan figures and governmental institutions, cripple our ability
to understand "things political" and to function effectively
politically.

What Politics Is. Politics can be described as the process by which groups, governments, or societies allocate scarce resources, differing values, and power and authority through the resolution of actual or potential conflict. Politics is normal and pervasive. However, it is important for superintendents to conceptualize politics properly. The essential elements of that conceptualization are as follows:

1. Politics and political behavior are not restricted to governmental institutions or partisan activities but are more or less part of the normal activities of all social groups.
2. Political issues always involve the allocation of resources, values, or power.
3. Actual or potential conflict is always present in the allocation of resources, values, or power.

The successful school superintendent will have skill in (a) analyzing and knowing both the explicit and implicit resource, value, and power allocations at stake; (b) knowing the individuals, groups, or institutions who are the stakeholders; and (c) managing and resolving conflict.

Power and Influence

An understanding of power and influence is essential for the political literacy and effectiveness of a school superintendent. Without such an understanding, managing and resolving conflict are virtually impossible.

Types of Power

The types of power are essentially three: social, economic, and legal. One can use these types of power and their various sources to resolve conflict and influence the decisions affecting the allocation of resources, values, and power in a political system. Therefore, it is important not only to be able to identify the types and sources of power but also to catalogue and inventory the power that individual, group, and institutional stakeholders possess.

Social Power. Some sources of social power include:

Friendship groups	Work groups
Social status	Prestige
Racial identity	Ethnicity
Language	Personal charisma

For example, the power of a consultant who holds a Ph.D. to influence public policy in a local community depends on the social context. More specifically, such a person might conceivably be more influential in a high socioeconomic community that respects university degrees and professional specialization than in a lower socioeconomic community that prizes a "commonsense" approach.

Language is another example of social power. It is frequently said that people with excellent verbal skills are often influential. Then again, it all depends on the social context in which the verbal skills are used. Those whose power and influence come from the use of language are people who can use their communication skills for the benefit of the social group, can manipulate the symbols of language that are important to the group, and are capable of effectively interpreting events and communications for the group. Few individuals have this intergroup and cross-cultural ability. It is unlikely that a silver-tongued school superintendent could be particularly effective with the 1,500 people who want curriculum change if the superintendent is not perceived as a legitimate member of that group. Similarly, the dictum from the secretary of education—a symbol of a Republican administration—for a new high school curriculum may receive plaudits from loyal Republicans but will probably be the object of derision among hardcore Democrats.

Economic Power. Some sources of economic power include:

Money	Credit
Jobs	Expertise
Information	Time
Material	Land

Economic power is anything of value to an individual, group, or institution. In an advanced industrialized economy, money, credit, and land are almost universal sources of power. School budgets are fueled by money and credit that result in assets of land, jobs, and material, which, in turn, translate into instructional time, professional expertise, and institutional information.

The school superintendent who decided not to shift budget dollars from regular education programs to a program for the severely retarded and multiply handicapped influenced the priorities in the school system through the control of budgetary dollars. In this case the superintendent exercised power because the discretionary allocation of dollars was used to impact the organization on a matter in which it had a stake. The local newspaper publisher has power through a monopoly on the mass medium of print and can influence the school budget by exercising that power. The superintendent had power in the control of jobs in the school district in which he demoted the lead teacher, and he exercised that power.

Legal Power. Legal power derives from a number of sources:

Laws	Rules
Policies	Court decisions
Voting	Constitutions
Contracts	Police enforcement

Like economic and social power and their sources, legal power and its sources provide tools that can be used to resolve conflict and influence the decisions affecting the allocation of resources, values, and power in a political system. The power of state legislatures lies in most part in their ability to make laws. The power of governors rests in approving laws, enacting rules, and using police power to enforce the laws and rules. The power of both is constrained by a constitution. Local school boards possess the power to adopt policies and enter into contracts. The ability of teachers to influence school boards rests on state law and local negotiated labor contracts. The 125 people who wanted the hockey program implicitly threatened to vote against the board or the budget if they did not get their way. Parents who did not want the fifth grade in the middle school explicitly threatened to withhold their vote for a school bond referendum if they did not get their way.

Relationship of Power and Influence

There is a difference between power and influence. The best analogy comes from the distinction in physics between potential energy and kinetic (or actual) energy. Potential energy is equal to power, and kinetic energy is equal to influence. In short, power is potential; it is at rest; it is not being used. Influence is actual; it is in action; it is being used. (See Figure 5.) How does power convert to influence? Let's take a look.

In any situation each individual, group, or institutional stakeholder has to be identified, and the social, economic, and legal powers of each must be catalogued as potential political resources. For example, the parents who would not vote for the referendum had legal power in the proportion of their voting strength to the whole. The advocates of an education program for a multiply and severely handicapped child undoubtedly had power in the social cohesion among friends and other advocates who believe as they did, and they certainly had legal power in their ability to use federal and state law, rules, and court decisions to their advantage. The newspaper publisher who threatened to block the school budget if it was not cut certainly had economic power in his ability to editorialize and influence public opinion. To the extent that a social network was a reality and the newspaper could influence public opinion, his power increased.

However, power is subject to stakeholder decisions to commit all or a portion of their political resources. In short, all individuals, groups, and institutions, regardless of their potential power, decide to participate wholeheartedly, half-heartedly, or not at all. For example, the organized teachers in the midwestern state decided to participate and committed political resources, but it is unclear what political resources the stake-

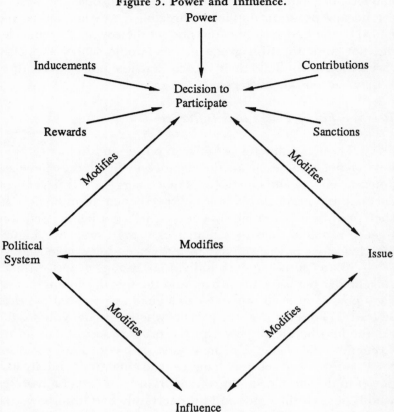

Figure 5. Power and Influence.

holders would commit in the special education case. Decisions by stakeholders not to participate obviously nullify their power because they cannot influence the outcome of events except by creating a power vacuum and thereby enhancing the power and influence of those who do participate.

Let us assume that stakeholders decide to participate and commit some or all of their power. In that case power may be moderated or enhanced by either the nature of the issues or the political system through which the issues will be decided.

Go to the issue variable in the paradigm. For example, if the special education case is framed as a resource allocation "issue" and equal educational opportunity is not raised, then the legal power of the superintendent and board in the budgetary process will be enhanced and the social and legal power of the advocate group will be lessened. Similarly, had the situation in which the superintendent demoted the teacher been defined as one of values ("differences in philosophy") rather than one of authority ("demote a teacher"), the power of the superintendent would have been enhanced, and the social power of the teacher's friendship groups would have been lessened. With 1,500 people jammed in an auditorium, the power of a professional's information and expertise is lessened if the issue is framed as (a) "dirty books," (b) "un-American" ideas, and (c) an "un-Christian" curriculum because the lay public is about as good at recognizing these characteristics as professionals are. On the other hand, if the issues are ones of (a) scope, sequence, and content of curriculum; (b) the role of professional educators in curriculum development; and (c) board procedures and policies, then the expertise of a professional will be enhanced in a group setting.

Now move to the political system variable in the paradigm. In this instance stakeholder power may be enhanced or moderated by the system in which the decision is being made. For example, the power of the athletic director would undoubtedly be enhanced if the decision were confined to influencing the administrative staff rather than a school board that is being cross-pressured in a public meeting of controversy. Advocates of programs for the gifted and talented would obviously fare better if the decision could be shifted to a more favorable forum and away from the legislative committee controlled by the two key legislators. The teachers who informally decided about the sex education curriculum would not have fared as well had sex education been included on the agenda of the public hearing with 1,500 in attendance.

The paradigm, however, is interdependent. Perceptions of the issues influence the stakeholders' decision to participate. For example, if the sense of efficacy is high when the issues are framed favorably, there is a greater chance that stakeholders will decide to participate and commit political resources. Conversely, if the sense of efficacy is low when the issues are framed unfavorably, then there is less chance that stakeholders will decide to participate and commit political resources. Similarly, when the system or political arena is perceived as favorable, there is greater likelihood that resources will be committed than when the system is perceived as unfavorable. Likewise, the definition of the issue influences the political system in which it will be resolved, and the political system influences how the stakeholders define the issues to be resolved.

Every successful superintendent has at one time or another asked for the creation of an advisory committee to study and make recommendations on an issue knowing full well that the committee, if properly appointed and staffed, will be a safer haven for many decisions and the issue will be framed more favorably than if the same issue were left to a broader public arena. The teachers knew that arbitrators provide a better political system for the resolution of their salaries than direct negotiation with a recalcitrant school board, so they worked for a statute on binding arbitration. The superintendent who announced his retirement three years in advance so that the school closing issue would not be contaminated with the issues of the superintendent's personality and contract renegotiation knows how to define an issue and maximize his power for resolution of the issue.

Enhancing Power and Influence

Power can be enhanced in five different ways through the paradigm: (1) by reframing the issues, (2) by changing the system through which decisions are made, (3) by augmenting the base of power, (4) by increasing the awareness of existing power, and (5) by influencing stakeholders' decisions to participate. Reframing issues and changing the system have already been discussed.

Augmenting the base of power is perhaps the most obvious approach. If an individual, group, or institutional stakeholder needs more power, it can acquire more power. Powerless teachers translated their social power base of group cohesion into a legally recognized union, then into concerted political action, and finally into binding arbitration. The social workers, psychologists, and counselors increased their power by allowing themselves to become a part of a coalition of support for issues that were not of immediate self-interest or concern. Many professionals know how power can be enhanced through expanded control, if not a monopoly, on information and expertise.

Individual, group, and institutional stakeholders can also increase their power by becoming aware of power they did not perceive they possessed. They can do this through a simple but systematic inventory of social, economic, and legal sources of power. For example, a thorough research of the laws, regulations, and policies at all levels of government frequently uncovers legal power bases not heretofore known. This certainly should be a recommended course of action before the superintendent takes action in the special education case. Brainstorming among friendship and work groups that links the stakeholder(s) with key, influential decision makers is often a productive exercise. For example, developing social power linkages to the two blocking legislators on the gifted and talented issue may prove to be more effective than trying to convince the blockers of the relative merits of property tax relief and funding programs for the gifted and talented.

Influencing other stakeholder individuals, groups, and institutions to participate—or not to participate—is perhaps the most effective but underutilized way of enhancing stakeholder power and influence. This is done by convincing other stakeholders who are potential allies that the rewards of gaining a favorable allocation of resources, values, or power outweigh the potential sanctions and that the stakeholder inducements are greater than the contributions. Conversely, influence is enhanced by convincing other stakeholders who are potential adversaries that the sanctions for participating in the decision outweigh the resources, values, and power to be gained and that the contributions outstrip the inducements (March and Simon, 1958). For example, had someone with personal access to the athletic director convinced him that opposing the hockey program could possibly result in 125 people not supporting other athletic programs, the athletic director might have thought otherwise about his comments at the meeting or at least tempered his remarks and enthusiasm. The social worker, psychologist, and counselor stakeholders were certainly made aware that failure to support the entire report would result in their losing their exemption from the teaching requirement.

Discretionary Use of Power and Influence

One final note on power and influence. Stakeholders must not only aggregate power and influence; they must also have the discretion to use power and influence and the good judgment to use them well and with some calculated risk. For example, many a superintendent has a budget, which suggests a potent economic power base, but the budget is for naught if circumstances conspire to deny the superintendent the necessary discretion for using the power implicit in it. On the other hand, the textbook adoption case provides not only an example of a legislative committee that had the legal power to deny an appropriation but also an example of a committee that had the discretion to use the power and did.

Community Power Structure

A fundamental characteristic of school districts and the communities in which they are found is that power and influence are not distributed equally and/or randomly. Rather, community power and influence structures can be systematically described as falling into one of four types, and the school boards in each type of community power structure tend to function differently. The power, influence, and political skill demanded of a superintendent in these four kinds of communities depend on the type of community power structure and accompanying school board.

Types of Community Power Structure

The four types of community power structure are:

1. Monolithic-elitist
2. Factional-competitive

3. Plural-rational
4. Inert-latent

McCarty and Ramsey (1968) did considerable research not only on community power structure but also on the relationship of community power structure to the role of the elected school board and the role of the board to the role of the superintendent. (See Table 5.) Their research is essential to an understanding of these interrelationships and is relied on heavily in this section, where each of the four community power structures will be described in terms of (a) distribution of power, (b) structure of power, (c) bases of power, (d) issues, (e) role and function of people in public office, and (f) customary political behavior.

Table 5. The Relationship of Community Power Structures to the Roles of School Board and Superintendent.

Community Power Structure	Structure of School Board	Role of Superintendent
Monolithic-elitist	Dominated	Functionary
Factional-competitive	Factional	Political strategist
Plural-rational	Status congruent	Professional adviser
Inert-latent	Sanctioning	Decision maker

Source: Adapted from McCarty and Ramsey (1968).

Note: McCarty and Ramsey identified the community power structures as dominated (for monolithic-elitist), factional (for factional-competitive), pluralistic (for plural-rational), and inert (for inert-latent).

Monolithic-Elitist. A monolithic-elitist power structure in a community means there is an unequal distribution of power among the populace. One person or a relatively few people are involved in making the fundamental decisions affecting the community. However, the few people who participate in these fundamental decisions are socially and economically linked to a wider network of supporters and others who share a wide range of common opinions about the allocation of resources, values, and power. Those who lead and rule in monolithic-elitist communities tend to have economic power and strong, traditional social power linkages. The monolithic-elitist power structure is concerned about all—not just educational—issues affecting the community. Those who are in elected or appointed public office are customarily not among the few people who make the fundamental decisions about the community but are among the immediate supporters and followers.

Monolithic-elitist communities are usually rather stable and tend to be smaller, more socially homogeneous communities. People among the elite tend to be long-standing members of the community who have "paid their dues," whose values and ideas are well known and predictable, and who are vulnerable to the community's social and economic sanctions. Conflict concerning the allocation of resources, values, and power is not uncommon, but open, public conflict is. In short, monolithic-elitist politics is the politics of a selected priesthood, not the marketplace. The votes of city councils and school boards in these communities tend to be unanimous and reflect the sentiments of the influential in the community power structure. Those who serve in elected public office are usually elected by wide margins in low voter turnout and uncontested elections. Superintendents are expected to be functionaries and to carry out the policies that reflect the prevailing allocation of resources, values, and power.

Factional-Competitive. Communities in which there is a factional-competitive power structure have an unequal distribution of power among their populations. Two or more cliques or coalitions are involved in making the fundamental decisions affecting the community, and these cliques or coalitions have different preferences in terms of the allocation of resources, values, and power. One person or a relatively few people are involved in making the fundamental decisions affecting each clique or coalition. However, the few people at the top who participate in these decisions are socially, economically, or politically linked to a wide network of supporters and others in and out of government who share a wide range of common opinions about the allocation of resources, values, and power. Those who lead and rule in factional-competitive communities tend to have economic, social, and legal power linkages. The factional-competitive power structure is concerned about all issues affecting the community. People who are elected or appointed to public office may be found among those who make the fundamental decisions about the community.

Factional-competitive communities are usually politically unstable and tend to be larger, more socially heterogeneous communities. People among the elite may or may not be long-standing members of the community who have "paid their dues," have values and ideas that are well known and predictable, and are vulnerable to the social and economic as well as political sanctions of the community. The critical characteristic is that two or more cliques, factions, or coalitions are in competition. Therefore, conflict concerning the allocation of resources, values, and power is common, open, and public. In short, factional-competitive politics is the politics of the marketplace, not the priesthood. The votes of city councils and school boards in these communities tend to be split and reflect the sentiments of the vying cliques, factions, and coalitions. Those who serve in elected public office are usually elected by close margins in relatively high voter turnout and contested elections. Superintendents are expected to be political strategists and educational leaders who work to build coalitions of support for the allocation of resources, values, and power.

Plural-Rational. Communities in which there is a plural-rational power structure have an unequal distribution of power among their populations. Two, three, or more cliques or coalitions are organized around clusters of issues (for example, community development, education, recreation, housing) and are involved in making the fundamental decisions affecting the community on those issues. These cliques or coalitions may share different preferences in the allocation of resources, values, and power, but because they are organized around issues, they rarely are in conflict. One person or a relatively few people are involved in making the fundamental decisions affecting the issues of each clique or coalition. However, the few people at the top who participate in these decisions are socially, economically, or politically linked to a wide network of supporters and others in and out of government who share a wide range of common opinions about the allocation of resources, values, and power. Those who lead and rule in plural-rational communities tend to have economic, social, and legal power linkages. People who are in elected or appointed public office can be found among those who make the fundamental decisions about the community.

Plural-rational communities are usually politically stable and tend to be middle-sized, with some social heterogeneity. People among the elite may or may not have been long-standing members of the community. Whether people have or have not "paid their dues" may not be a criterion for membership among the influential. The same is true of having values and ideas that are well known and predictable and being vulnerable to the social and political sanctions of the community. The critical characteristic is that two or more cliques, factions, or coalitions are organized around clusters of issues. Therefore, conflict concerning the allocation of resources, values, and power is rational, criteria/data based, and subdued in public. In short, plural-rational politics is the politics of the corporate boardroom and not of either the marketplace or the priesthood. The votes of city councils and school boards in these communities tend to be unanimous and reflect the resolution of conflict in a subdued, rational, and corporate mode while at the same time reflecting the sentiments of the community power structure. Those who serve in elected public office are usually elected by wide margins in relatively high voter turnout and sometimes contested elections. Superintendents are expected to be educational leaders who study and recommend alternative policies for discussion and consideration by the board of education in the allocation of resources, values, and power in this rather stable political environment.

Inert-Latent. Communities in which there is an inert-latent power structure have no clearly identifiable or discernible distribution of power among their populations. While a relatively few people are involved in making the fundamental decisions affecting the community, there is no appreciable consistency among those who participate and there is no discernible basis of power for political action. Therefore, the few people who participate in the fundamental decisions may not be socially and economically linked to a wide network of supporters and others who share a wide range of common opinions about the allocation of resources, values, and power. Those who lead and rule in inert-latent communities tend to have been encouraged to do so because "someone has to do it." The inert-latent "power structure" is concerned about all issues affecting the community. People who are in elected or appointed public office are customarily coerced into being so and are not necessarily among those who have power. Again, public officeholders are often there because "the job has to be done."

Inert-latent communities tend to be relatively small and are usually stable and socially homogeneous. There tends not to be an elite or a segment of the community that could be described as having "paid its dues," whose values and ideas are well known and predictable, or who are vulnerable to the social and economic sanctions of the community. Conflict concerning the allocation of resources, values, and power is not common, but disinterest is. In short, inert-latent politics is the politics of neither the priesthood nor the marketplace; it is the politics of political lethargy. The votes of city councils and school boards in these communities tend to be unanimous and reflect a mood of "getting along." Those who serve in elected public office are usually elected by wide margins in low voter turnout and uncontested elections. Superintendents are expected to be leaders within a zone of tolerance vaguely outlined in the social context of the community. Unless the superintendent oversteps the bounds of the broader social and political propriety—for example, by adopting "big city" methods of passing a referendum or closing a long-revered school which is a symbol of community stability—the superintendent can expect board recommendations to be customarily rubber-stamped without prolonged debate or conflict.

Methods of Identifying Community Power Structures

A key element in the development of any strategy is the identification of the community power structure. This action

may be the most important ingredient in a school superintendent's successful implementation of a strategic plan. There are
at least four ways to collect information systematically to determine the type of power structure for any given community: (a)
through a positional study, (b) through an event analysis study,
(c) through a reputational study, and (d) through a demographic
study.

Positional Study. A positional study is the quickest and
easiest way to begin the study of community power structure.
This method is directed toward identifying people who have held
formal elected or appointed positions in the community. The
positions identified can be restricted to officeholders surrounding educational issues, such as members of the board of education and the superintendent of schools and other administrators,
or they can be expanded to include elected and appointed officials from other governmental jurisdictions, such as members
of the city council, township and county boards, the mayor, state
and federal legislators, the city manager, the zoning administrator, and finance officers. If the study is restricted to education, there is little chance that it will reveal either an elitist-
monolithic or a factional-competitive power structure because
both of these cut across all issues and jurisdictions, and the links
between the plural-rational structure and the other issue-oriented
groups will be difficult to understand. There is also a need to
go back in time and identify veteran officeholders and to note
periods of contested elections, particularly those involving in-
cumbents. This effort will indicate a continuity, or lack thereof,
and whether those in office have been challenged consistently
over time. It will also help in making the distinction between
factional-competitive and other types of community power
structure.

Event Analysis Study. An event analysis is neither quick
nor easily done. Rather, it requires both "library" research and
depth interviews. This method is initially directed toward identifying critical public and political events in the community's
recent history. Recent may mean as long ago as fifty years but

is more likely to focus on events of the last twenty-five years. Critical events are those the community, not the outside observer, has judged as important and critical. Moreover, they are events that were political watersheds in determining "the kind of community we will be" and sufficiently controversial for one to assume that most of the politically powerful would have participated in the decisions surrounding them. Again, the event analysis should not be restricted to educational events for precisely the same reasons that the positional analysis should go beyond educational positions. A recent community power study involved event analysis in the community of "Prairie River." Case researchers identified several events by scanning back issues of local newspapers, and by conducting a dozen half-hour interviews with identified position holders (see above) and three or four two-hour depth interviews. The interviews, which focused on the community and its political history, identified five important and critical events in the community of Prairie River: (1) building of the bridge over the Prairie River, (2) approval of the clinic and medical center, (3) zoning and construction decisions affecting downtown and suburban retail shopping development, (4) referendum on and building of the "new" high school (almost twenty years earlier), and (5) building of the community ice hockey rink.

Once the important, critical events are identified, additional "library" research and depth interviews are required to identify the people, groups, and institutions that were involved and that exercised influence in determining the outcome of each decision. In Prairie River, a community of about 15,000, this entailed approximately twenty-five two-hour interviews. The initial interview respondents are selected in such a way that the names of people, groups, and institutions are identified. Subsequent interviews are arranged with those nominated in previous interviews. The person conducting the event analysis must be sure to interview people other than officeholders and be sure that the interviews cut across all issues. In the Prairie River case it was discovered that the same twenty-five people who were members of four groups (downtown businessmen, country club members, those in partnership in a business enterprise, and the medical clinic staff) managed to control city and school government without significant contested opposition for more than thirty years. This was clearly an elitist-monolithic community power structure. The prototypic model of event analysis is outlined by Dahl (1961) in his classic study of New Haven, *Who Governs?*

Reputational Study. Like an event analysis, a reputational study is neither quick nor easily done. However, it generally relies on a form of survey research and is directed toward identifying people who are reputed to have power and influence in community affairs—hence the name, reputational. A reputational study customarily begins with a listing of names of people in the community who have participated in community events. This initial list can come from a variety of sources: newspapers, interviews about events, or brainstorming with a group of local citizens. The questions asked of each of these sources are "Who are the people that are knowledgeable and informed about community and educational issues of recent years?" and "Who has power and influences the course of events and their outcomes in the community?" Again, the questions should encourage respondents to identify as many people as possible. The focus is on people. The questions should also get respondents to go back a few years in their recollections— at least as far back as the time of a few of the more recent critical events—but without dealing with the events.

Usually the "library" work, interviews, and brainstorming will yield about 200 names. These nominees should then receive a mailing addressed to a knowledgeable and informed citizen—urging each to participate further by identifying other "knowledgeable, informed, and influential" people in the community by writing in their names and addresses on an attached sheet of paper. Experience has shown that there is about a 70 percent return rate on these letters, with as many as five additional names listed on each. This entire exercise will then yield anywhere from 200 to 400 separate names, usually with 50 or fewer nominated more than once. The reputational study can stop here with a crude approximation of the community power structure based on the frequency of nomination of a "long" list of names. However, if all 200 to 400 people receive a second mailing with only the 50 multiply nominated names listed and are asked to identify the 10 most influential, the reputational study will become even more refined and useful. The outcome should yield anywhere from a few people to perhaps 30 or 40 being nominated with varying frequency as influential. From this data, the researcher can infer the community power structure from frequency of the nominations. The problem with using the reputational method alone is that it ignores issues, and issues are a key determinant in the type of community power structure. In short, what one gets is the names of many people in the community who are reputed to be influential, but one does not know their interrelationship. Seen in another way, one knows who they are but not whether they are arrayed in a factional-competitive, plural-rational, or monolithic-elitist power structure. In the Prairie River case the reputational method identified 30 people involved in influencing decisions in the community, but it did not indicate the types of issues or whether the people were in cooperation or competition. In summary, using the reputational study is the best way to generate many names of people who may be influential, but it needs to be done in conjunction with some event analysis not only to corroborate the outcomes but also to infer the community power structure.

The reputational study is also a check on the event analysis study. If, for example, several of the reputedly influential people are not found in the event analysis study, then perhaps there is a hidden power structure working behind the scenes but not readily visible in the playing out of even the most important events. The reason for using event analysis is to identify events that are likely to reveal the hidden power structure, but sometimes the power structure remains hidden, particularly if it is an elitist-monolithic one. In Prairie River all the influentials were revealed in the event analysis and corroborated in the reputational study. An excellent paper by Powers (1965), "Identifying Community Power Structure," describes the reputational method in much more systematic terms.

Demographic Study. It is essential that one conduct a demographic study to gain a total picture of a community's power structure. Because social and economic changes often precede political ones, it is important to know about changes in the community's socioeconomic character, such as changes in racial, ethnic, labor force, income level, land use, and housing patterns. Communities that change from predominantly agricultural to suburban are due for a change in power structure or different competitors in the existing power structure. Stable communities with elitist-monolithic power structures but a new labor force with different social values and income levels are also due for a change. Moreover, members of these newer, "different" social and economic groups will probably not be identified in positional, event analysis, or reputational studies simply because they have not participated in community affairs. Therefore, while they may not be influential, they do have power and can be considered "slack" political resources. It may be years before these groups recognize common issues and common goals and mobilize for political action—even if it is to run for the school board and lose.

Nevertheless, these slack political resources can exercise passive vetoes of proposals put forth by the power structure such as in voting against school referenda. The skill that a superintendent exercises in anticipating these socioeconomic and political changes and in building coalitions will augur well for her or his political sophistication and success. Yet the involvement of any "slack" resources is usually a threat to the existing power structure and must be approached with caution. The need to create a coalition may be the rational thing to do, but the need to maintain power by those currently in authority may prevail; therefore, the superintendent who enters this territory must do so with political dexterity and know-how. Most of the information for a demographic study can be obtained from existing sources, such as census, regional planning commission, economic development authority, housing authority, and school enrollment data.

The use of all four methods is preferable and complementary. They each serve as a check and balance so there is not a bias toward a particular type of community structure. They also serve to ensure that superintendents go beyond individuals, groups, and institutions that are closely aligned to schools and

get out into the broader community to identify the power structure, especially in monolithic-elitist and factional-competitive
communities. In these communities the dominant individuals,
groups, and institutions are not likely to be closely aligned to
schools or school issues year in and year out.

A demographic study is easily done and probably should
be done first; then a positional study with selected interviews
to identify issues and people is a useful next step. Event analysis
and reputational studies are more time- and resource-consuming
and intrusive into the local community. However, the best and
most useful data come from these methods, and at least one of
them ought to be employed systematically. Much of the information collected for purposes of ''political'' analysis can be part
of a program of school-community relations and, therefore,
become less resource-consuming and intrusive.

Conflict Resolution

As the superintendent's political effectiveness must vary
with the type of community power structure, so too the strategies
for conflict resolution vary, depending on the goals of the stakeholders involved in the political process. Table 6 illustrates the
relationship between the goals of individual, group, and institutional stakeholders and the strategies most suitable for the resolution of conflict.

The conceptualization set forth in Table 6 owes much to
March and Simon's (1958) *Organizations,* wherein the authors set
out the problem-solving/persuasion/bargaining/politics (renamed
power play) and suggest the different-changeable-negotiable parts
of the matrix. However, the remainder of the matrix, dealing with
conflict resolution, and the interpretations given to the matrix
herein are mine. Table 6 (a) asks whether the goals of the stakeholders are different, changeable, or negotiable; (b) suggests the
most effective strategy for the resolution of conflict; (c) describes
the needs for data (information and research), planning, and
power; and (d) predicts the outcomes in terms of rewards and
sanctions for the stakeholders, the prospect for implementation,
and the residual relationship among the individual, group, and
institutional stakeholders.

Table 6. Conflict Resolution.

Process	Are the Goals of the Stakeholders . . .			Need for Data	Need for Strategic Planning	Need for Political Power	Risk of Sanctions	Prospect of Rewards	Prospect for Maximizing Implementation	Residual Relationship Among Stakeholders
	Different?	Changeable?	Negotiable?							
Problem-Solving	No	—	—	Very high	Very low	Very low	Very low	Very low	Very high	Consensus
Persuasion	Yes	Yes	—	High	Low	Low	Low	Low	High	Cooperation
Bargaining	Yes	No	Yes	Low	High	Moderate to high	Moderate to high	Moderate to high	Moderate to low	Compact
Power play	Yes	No	No	Very low	Very high	Very high	Very high	Very high	Low	Conflict

Source: © 1987 by B. Dean Bowles, University of Wisconsin, Madison. Reprinted with permission.

Problem-Solving Process. The problem-solving process can be employed in cases where the fundamental goals of the stakeholders are essentially the same because the questions involving the allocation of resources, values, and power have never involved unresolved conflicts. These may be instances in which essentially different stakeholders have common goals, such as the elementary, middle, and high school teachers did in deciding the sex education curriculum. However, these may also be cases in which different stakeholders work out the details of implementing earlier resolutions of conflict, as the social workers, psychologists, and counselors and the other task force stakeholders did to see that their recommendations became law after they struck a bargain on the teaching requirement.

In the problem-solving process the need for data, information, and research is high. The stakeholders will also use data to identify problems, generate alternative solutions, choose the best alternative, and then evaluate the decisions by means of a feedback process. In short, the problem-solving process fosters the use of classical decision-making models, the reliance on data, information, and research, and self-correcting mechanisms.

There is little need for strategic planning or power since either the stakeholders have common agreement and few differences that require planning or coalition building or the necessary planning and coalitions are already in place as the result of previous resolutions of conflict. For example, the teacher stakeholders in the sex education case did not have any fundamental differences (among themselves) on the goals of the curriculum and therefore had no need for strategic planning or power to achieve the resolution of conflict over the allocation of values. Of course, if other stakeholder groups, such as the 1,500 people who jammed the school auditorium, had sought to participate and had fundamentally different sex education goals, then the political behavior of the teachers would have had to change to other conflict resolution processes, and those processes undoubtedly would have demanded greater strategic planning and political power.

The teachers who participated in the sex education curriculum decision in the lounge were committing few political resources to the process, and the political environment was relatively risk free. However, it would also appear that the rewards are not great either. What is encouraging is that the prospect for implementing the decisions growing out of that problem-solving process are very high since there was consensus among the stakeholders. In short, in the problem-solving process the risk of sanctions is very low, and the prospect for rewards is also very low. The prospect for full implementation of the outcomes and decisions is very high because the residual relationship (the anticipated political relationship among stakeholders after the resolution of conflict) among the stakeholders is essentially one of continuing consensus. The concept of residual relationship in conflict resolution is critical to effective leadership over time in a community.

Persuasion. The persuasion process can be employed in cases where the fundamental goals of the stakeholders are essentially different but changeable on questions involving the allocation of resources, values, and power. These are instances in which sentiment and belief about the allocation of resources, values, and power are not so firmly held that the power and force of evidence, rhetoric, social pressure, or legal sanction may not change the mind of one of the individual, group, or institutional stakeholders to adopt the goals of another. Moreover, these are cases of real, permanent changes in goals that lead to cooperation, not a temporary trade-off or compromise of convenience. For example, when the school superintendent persuaded the board to adopt the policy on the purchase and allocation of instructional computers, the superintendent did it by relying on the rhetoric and moral authority of "equity," which changed the vote of some school board members who either had little basis for decision or relied weakly on "excellence" as a rationale. In the case of the parents who resisted having fifth-grade children placed with older children, those parents successfully persuaded the school board that "efficiency" and the housing of children were more important than the fifth- through eighth-grade "middle school concept." Again, the board was permanently convinced of needed changes in the building plans and was cooperative with parents in effecting that policy. It should be noted that the superintendent and middle school principal (both stakeholders) were not persuaded by the "efficiency" and "housing" arguments; it was left for bargaining to resolve the conflict between the parent stakeholders and the superintendent and principal.

In the persuasion process the need for data, information, and research is still high. However, the stakeholders will use data to identify problems, generate alternative solutions, and argue for a specific (not necessarily best) alternative favored by one of the stakeholders. Data may be used for feedback and evaluation of a decision, but not necessarily. In short, the persuasion process fosters the use of problem identification and alternative generation; some reliance on data, information, and research; and self-correcting feedback and evaluation. However, it is most characterized by rhetoric and argument.

There is some need for strategic planning or power since change among one or more of the stakeholders must occur if conflict is to be resolved. The power may emanate, for example, from one or more of the following: work or friendship relationships, a tradition of trust and reliance, command of the information and research basis of decisions, and perceived legal power. Similarly, the school superintendent who was persuaded to institutionalize the severely mentally retarded and multiply handicapped child did so because of the resource and legal arguments and evidence presented by staff members. At that point the superintendent changed goals and cooperated fully in the implementation of the decision. If the superintendent had not been persuaded and had not, in fact, changed his goal for the handicapped student, then he and other pro-institutionalization stakeholders would have had to employ other conflict resolution processes. And those processes might have demanded greater strategic planning and political power.

The staff members who participated in persuading the superintendent to adopt an institutionalization policy committed some political resources in the process, and the political environment was not entirely risk free. However, it would also appear that the rewards were not great for any stakeholder group

either (at least not for those participating at that point). What
is encouraging about persuasion is the prospect for implementing a decision growing out of the resolution of a conflict because
there is cooperation among the stakeholders. In short, in the
persuasion process the risk of sanctions is low, and the prospect
for rewards is also low. The prospect for full implementation
of the outcomes and decisions is high because the residual relationship among the stakeholders is essentially one of continuing cooperation.

Bargaining. The bargaining process can be employed in
cases where the fundamental goals of the stakeholders are different, are not changeable, but are negotiable on questions involving the allocation of resources, values, and power. These
are instances in which sentiment and belief about the allocation of resources, values, and power are so firmly held that the
power of persuasion cannot change the mind of one individual,
group, or institutional stakeholder to adopt the goals of another.
Moreover, these are cases in which compromise and trade-off
are essential to resolve conflict and create an agreement or compact because there is little prospect of permanent changes in goals
that lead to cooperation. For example, when at the public meeting of 1,500 many insisted on eliminating the United Nations
from the curriculum and could not be persuaded otherwise, the
school superintendent bargained with the 1,500 by stating that
the school board would drop the United Nations from the curriculum in the context of "local-state-national-world government" if the group accepted the United Nations "as an aspect
of American foreign policy."

The 1,500 negotiated with the superintendent, and the
conflict was resolved when both parties accepted the proposed
resolution. However, neither the superintendent nor three school
board members changed their values about the United Nations'
place in the curriculum, and the petitioners among the 1,500
did not change their values about wanting the United Nations
out of the curriculum. The two sides did reach a compact and
resolved conflict on that issue. In the middle school case, the
superintendent and principal negotiated with the concerned

parents and agreed to recommend to the staff and board that the fifth- through eighth-grade middle school concept be dropped if the parents would endorse the remainder of the school building proposal and actively campaign for the referendum. Again, the minds of superintendent and middle school principal (both stakeholders) were not changed, but the two accepted the compromise to resolve the conflict and to attain another goal (which, incidentally, was held by the parents): passing the school bond referendum.

In the bargaining process the need for data, information, and research is low. However, the stakeholders employ the data and research that are used to identify problems in other stakeholders' positions and avoid problems in their own, to generate alternative bargaining positions, options, and solutions, and to argue for one specific stakeholder position versus another. Data may be used for feedback and evaluation of decisions, but the feedback is generally biased toward buttressing previous ideas about the values, resources, and power at stake, not necessarily toward generating the best available alternatives. In short, the bargaining process fosters the use of a form of problem identification and alternative generation, along with some reliance on data and research, to buttress old arguments. However, bargaining mainly involves searching for alternatives to gain advantage, compromise, and the resolution of conflict.

There is considerable need for strategic planning and power since change is not possible and must be negotiated with one or more of the stakeholders before the conflict can be resolved. The power may emanate from virtually all sources and must be exercised or exhibited as influence to enhance the advantage of the stakeholders. For example, the power of the legislative committee to withhold funds unless editorial changes were made in a social studies textbook resulted in a classic trade-off: the text about Presidents Harding, Coolidge, and Hoover was enhanced and the Baez poem downplayed, and the funds were appropriated for the state-adopted textbook. The resolution of conflict resulted in none of the stakeholders' being completely satisfied with the editorial changes or with the "political" interference in state textbook adoptions, but the compact among the stakeholders resolved the conflict. However, bargaining compacts result in stakeholders' complying with the agreement in its narrowest sense and working to seek advantage in the implementation of the compact and, at the next opportunity, in changing the policy that allocated the resources, values, and power. On the other hand, if the textbook conflict had not been resolved through the bargaining process and the anti-change stakeholders—the author and publisher—had persisted in wanting their way, then they would have had an even greater need for strategic planning and political power.

Both stakeholder groups in the textbook case committed considerable political resources in a politically risky environment. However, it would also appear that the rewards were considerable for each group. What is difficult about bargaining is the need for strategic planning in identifying stakeholders, stakes, and various coalitions and options for the resolution of conflict. However, what is discouraging are the needs to provide outcomes that are at least minimally satisfactory to all parties and to police the implementation of the compact. In short, in the bargaining process the risk of sanctions is high, and the prospect for rewards is also high. The prospect for full implementation of the outcomes and decisions is low because the residual relationship among the stakeholders is essentially one of continued suspicion and negotiation.

Power Play. The power play process can be employed in cases where the fundamental goals of the stakeholders are different, are not changeable on questions involving the allocation of resources, values, and power, and also are not negotiable. These are instances in which sentiment and belief about the allocation of resources, values, and power are so firmly held that neither persuasion nor bargaining can change one individual, group, or institutional stakeholder to adopt the goals of another.

Power play is found in cases where negotiation and compromise fail and conflict must be resolved by means of one individual, group, institution, or coalition of stakeholders dominating other stakeholders in the allocation of resources, values, and power. For example, when the superintendent aligned with the four-to-three school board majority to close elementary schools and keep middle schools open, the only alternative offered by opposition stakeholders was the middle school option. The resource and value issues involved with the middle school were so intensely held by the superintendent and school board majority that they were not negotiable. Because the critical issues were not negotiable and the superintendent had a firm, reliable board majority, they prevailed on every point. However, in the power play process neither the superintendent nor the school board majority changed its values about school closings and the middle school concept, and neither did the stakeholder opposition. There was no compact, but the conflict was resolved.

In a similar fashion, the lead teacher who was demoted by the superintendent did not negotiate but used overwhelming social power to persuade the school board to veto the superintendent's action and give back the lead-teacher job. In this case, the superintendent held firm, believing in the rightness of the cause and the plenary legal power of a superintendent in recommending personnel actions. At the same time, the lead teacher held firm, believing that a wrong had been done and in the power of a social network of professional friends, parents, and citizens who would influence the board. There was little persuasion or negotiation in the case; both parties used power play tactics, believing they would prevail. The superintendent guessed wrong; the lead teacher prevailed; conflict was resolved. However, conflict would persist in the implementation of the school board action and in other matters pertaining to both the superintendent and the lead teacher.

In the bargaining process the need for data, information, and research is very low. However, in the power play process the data and research that stakeholders employ is used as an integral part of the strategy to gain advantage and win. Data may be used for feedback and evaluation of decisions, but the feedback is generally biased toward launching the next assault on the previous resource, value, or power decision or preparing for a new attack along different policy lines. In short, the power play process does little to foster problem identification and alternative generation or the use of data and research except to prepare for arguments and counterarguments in the heat of the battle. This process is mainly characterized by a search for power and political resources to gain advantage and a resolution of the conflict by winning and without compromise.

There is great need for strategic planning and power when change is not possible and cannot be negotiated among the stakeholders. The power is seized from virtually all sources and must be exercised or exhibited as influence to enhance the advantage of the stakeholders. For example, the power of the newspaper publisher to block the school budget unless cuts were made is power play at its purest. The eventual resolution of the newspaper publisher–superintendent conflict resulted in the superintendent's not cutting the budget and besting the publisher by getting the budget approved without cuts. Yet the resolution of this conflict resulted in other conflicts between the publisher and the superintendent over the implementation and expenditures in the budget and over other matters related to the superintendent's management.

Both stakeholders in the newspaper publisher–superintendent budget case committed tremendous power and political resources to the process in a very politically risky environment. However, it would also appear that the rewards were considerable for each stakeholder: namely, power over the school budget process and all its value, resource, and power priorities. What is difficult about power play is the need for comprehensive strategic planning in identifying stakeholders, stakes, and various coalitions for the struggle that will resolve the conflict. However, what is discouraging is the continuous need to police the implementation of the outcomes of power play. In short, in the power play process the risk of sanctions is very high, and the prospect for rewards is also very high. The prospect for full implementation of the outcomes and decisions is low because the residual relationship among the stakeholders is essentially one of continued conflict.

Other Conflict Resolution Mechanisms. In addition to withdrawal or avoidance of conflict resolution and decision making, there are two other passive conflict resolution mechanisms: postponement and shifting jurisdiction.

Postponement is a tactic to delay the resolution of conflict through inaction or study. Postponement may be useful when one needs time to gather additional information or research to identify better alternatives, policy options, or proposals. Postponement may also be necessary if one is to understand the community power structure, generate the conflict resolution options, and develop a thorough, strategic analysis of the political environment. What benefits would have accrued to the school district if the school board had put off the consideration of the hockey budget request until another meeting? Would the same 125 people have returned? What difference would it have made in the outcome? In the implementation of any varsity hockey policy?

Shifting jurisdiction is a tactic to change the political system for the resolution of conflict. Shifting jurisdiction may be useful when the political system for the resolution of a conflict is unsuitable for any number of reasons. One reason for shifting jurisdictions is to move the resolution away from the power play/bargaining end of the continuum to the persuasion/problem-solving end in order to increase the prospect of implementation. On the other hand, a reason to shift the jurisdiction away from the persuasion–rational decision end of the continuum to the power play–bargaining end would be to take advantage of overwhelming political power or to maximize policy outcomes in the resolution process. In summary, shifting jurisdiction has utility if it allows for some advantage over the current political system in either the anticipated policy outcome, implementation consideration, or power-influence factor. What might have happened if the school board and superintendent had shifted jurisdiction by creating an advisory committee to resolve the fifth- through eighth-grade middle school issue with the parents rather than negotiating directly with them? What might have happened to the superintendent and school district that decided for institutionalization of the severely and multiply handicapped child if they had shifted jurisdiction and asked the state for a decision? What might have happened to the "equity" principle if the school board had turned over the computer decision to a community group? Something different probably.

Just a word about the idea of consensus and voting as conflict resolution mechanisms. The use of voting as the primary means to resolve conflict tends to escalate the conflict, particularly away from persuasion and bargaining to power play. Reliance on voting tends to coalesce groups into voting blocs, with bargaining for marginal votes, and reduces reliance on rationality, persuasion, bargaining, and the use of data. Voting is often required to give authority to a decision, and in such cases it is useful. However, successful superintendents tend to work toward a consensus model in the resolution of conflict. Consensus encourages the de-escalation of conflict, away from power play and bargaining to persuasion and problem-solving.

Political Leadership for Strategic Planning

As a practical guide to political skills for political leadership in the course of strategic planning, the following information will serve as a summary of the chapter.

Some Assumptions About Politics

• *Politics* is the resolution of actual or potential conflict about the allocation or reallocation of scarce economic resources, different social values, and unequal political power resulting in a legitimate or authoritative decision by a social group or governmental institution.

• *Political behavior* is primarily interpersonal, not inter-institutional. It is also not always benign and rational but frequently hostile and nonrational. Today's opponent is tomorrow's ally: never let your goal be to win 100 percent of the time unless an issue really matters. Learn to compromise.

• *Political change* is almost always incremental, not comprehensive. (For a thorough discussion of incrementalism, see Lindblom, 1959.) Moreover, those in authority have a bias against change, particularly when it affects the allocation or

reallocation of power. Change comes more quickly and completely from the outside than from the inside. Allocation of
resources, values, and power is always easier than reallocation.

• *Political power* is always unequally distributed among
the stakeholders, and it is not random but structured and predictable. Political influence requires political participation. In the
use of political power, timing is nearly everything.

Some Political Skills

Following are five of the skills that one needs for effective political leadership.

1. Knowing and applying the fundamental conceptual and
   theoretical frameworks of politics, power and influence,
   community power structure, conflict resolution, and political analysis.
2. Thinking and planning strategically by

   • Reflecting on the broad social, economic, technological,
     and political contexts of programs, policies, and market
     decisions
   • Developing a vision and sense of mission
   • Focusing on a comprehensive plan of action with mea-
     surable outcomes
   • Implementing the vision, mission, and planning incre-
     mentally and with political sensitivity

3. Building coalitions of support by sharing a vision and stressing a moral, public philosophy based on the symbols of
   equity, excellence, efficiency, election, "eccountability,"
   and effectiveness; broadening the base of support by bringing in "slack" political resources and using a process of
   inclusion. In short, molding a team, not going it alone!
4. Being flexible and adaptable and knowing when and how
   to use collaboration, persuasion, negotiation, and confron-
   tation skills and when and how to be a functionary, profes-

sional adviser, decision maker, and political strategist.
5. Being able to define any problem, issue, or policy according to the three perspectives of programs, policies, and markets and according to the structural, human resource, political, and symbolic frames proposed by Bolman and Deal (1984). These four frames, or perspectives, are discussed more fully in Chapter Ten in the context of the introduction of change.

A knowledge of politics and policy and the acquisition of the suggested political skills discussed in this chapter will satisfy the political leadership component of strategic planning. The school superintendent needs now to turn to the marketing component in Chapter Eight.

8

Developing a Marketing Plan

Politics and marketing are very different disciplines but part of a closely related set of processes for pursuing a strategy. Marketing is the second of our three-part strategy implementation or execution process. Market research was discussed in Chapter Five. This chapter discusses other elements of the marketing activity required for the development of a marketing plan.

Public Officials' Apprehension About Marketing

Most public school officials shun the word *marketing* because they have in their mind an incorrect or misleading definition of what marketing is and what its main functions and activities entail. They consider marketing to be chiefly persuading someone to do something or convincing someone that what a given firm produces is the best of its kind or that what a given organization has done is right—in a public relations sense. When someone talks about ''marketing'' a product or service, many public school officials conjure up visions of a slick Madison Avenue salesperson or an insincere PR person who is not objective and does not tell the full truth.

This is not what marketing is. The popular conception of what marketing entails includes only a small part of its function. Nevertheless, most people, including many business people, use the phrase ''to market'' when they really only mean ''to sell.'' Marketing, practiced in its true professional form, involves a set of activities designed to help one better under-

211

stand and effectively serve client or consumer needs. The first and most important aspect of an overall marketing plan is a thorough identification of the relevant requirements of a client group. Later steps involve identifying and classifying various client groups into ''market segments'' according to their needs or characteristics. Still later steps involve developing or further refining products and services to better satisfy the needs of specific market segments.

Only after taking the above steps, does a professional marketer turn to the selling function and begin advertising and promotion. Thus, selling is only one of the many functions of marketing, often a minor one at that. In fact, if the early steps of needs identification and product/service development are done well and are focused on the appropriate target markets, the necessity to sell or persuade anyone to buy a product or to be convinced of the value of a particular service can be small or nonexistent. The sales function then becomes one of merely informing the relevant publics of the availability and attributes of a given product or service or helping a client or consumer see how that product or service can be designed or used to help solve a problem.

Because the concept of marketing was developed and refined chiefly in the private sector, school officials may have to modify it somewhat when applying it to their organization. In schools, the application is much more complex. The key complications arise from the difficulty in identifying who the customer is and in sorting out the multiple (and sometimes conflicting) roles of client, provider, supplier, funder, beneficiary, and recipient of the educational services provided by the school system.

These role ambiguities and conflicts in the public sector must be recognized and the unique and multifunctional position of the public-sector client must be understood when one applies the marketing concept to public school systems. If the differences between the public and private sectors are not understood, then the marketing concept can, and probably will, become a dangerous tool with a potential for destroying the democratic values of equity, fairness, protection of the culturally deprived, and so on that now seem to permeate our school systems. When applied carefully and with sensitivity to the public-private differences, however, the marketing concept can be a very powerful contributor to better services and better satisfaction of client needs and wants. This chapter first defines marketing and then describes each of its functions and its application to school situations.

Definitions of Marketing

Various definitions of marketing from the business literature involve a number of *P*'s and *C*'s. The *P*'s stand for product, pricing, place, and promotion. The *C*'s stand for consumer, cost, competition, and channels (of distribution). Here is a working definition of public school marketing from Kotler and Fox (1985, p. 7): "Marketing is concerned with the implementation of a process whereby transactions or potential transactions among groups affected by or who can affect a school or school system are created, stimulated, understood, facilitated and valued. The end objective is to put the organization in a better position to serve the educational and education-related needs of the constituents of the school community."

Marketing for a school system means executing the chief functions noted in Table 7. Each of these functions will be discussed in turn. The outline in Table 8 illustrates the process of marketing in a way that is much more descriptive than the typical notion of marketing as chiefly a "selling" activity.

Table 7. Marketing Functions.

Identifying clients
Analyzing needs
Developing and improving product/service options
Analyzing costs and/or pricing
Designing the delivery system
Providing relevant information to the publics
Selling and distributing the product or service

Table 8. The Marketing Process.

I. ASSESSMENT OF NEEDS OF "CUSTOMERS"

I.   ASSESSMENT OF NEEDS OF "CUSTOMERS"
     Students
     Parents
     Employers
     Community
     Society

II. MARKETING PROGRAM
     Product or service
     Price or cost
     Promotion or communications
     Place or delivery

III. RESULTING ACTIONS TO SERVE CUSTOMER NEEDS
     New or improved programs
     Special new services
     Added features, more convenience
     Need delivery services
     Client identification

Who Is the Customer?

One of the most important questions for a private or public organization engaged in producing and delivering a product or service is "Who is the customer, and why does he or she buy?" In the case of public schools, there is no clear-cut answer that is acceptable to everyone. The difficulty in answering this question is one of two key reasons why public-sector marketing differs from private-sector marketing. The other difference relates to the fact that with a public-sector service such as education, the recipients of the service, the groups that benefit most from the service, and those who pay for the service are typically not the same people, whereas in the case of a private-sector product or service, the groups are usually identical.

The primary customer of the school is the family, which means both the student receiving the service and that student's parents. It is the parents who typically make the buying decision for the education of younger children by selecting where the family will live and whether they will seek private schools, alternative schools, a magnet program, or something else. As the student gets older, then he or she begins to assume more influence over this decision, such as perhaps in the selection of a high school, a program, and especially a specific elective course, sport, or activity.

However, we could also consider many other groups to be customers for the basic services of a school, among them the future employers of the graduates, the community at large, and the local and state taxpayers who pay for the services the school provides. These groups are appropriately deemed "the customer" when the primary product of the school is compulsory education for children five to sixteen years of age. For any programs that a school might provide on a fee-for-service basis, the customer could be more specifically defined as the person or persons in the household who make or strongly influence the purchase decision. Most likely, the parents of the child recipient make the decisions in the case of extra services that a school might choose to provide, such as preschool programs, after-school day-care or special programs, and the like.

Other services such as senior citizen lunch programs, evening courses, and the use of facilities are usually paid for directly by the recipient of the service, who is thus the customer in the private business sense. It is possible that agencies of the federal, state, or local government could be customers of the school as in the case of the Head Start Program and hot lunch and drug education programs. Even though in many ways the ultimate customer of the school is society at large, as a practical matter, those more directly involved with the service delivery typically make the buying decisions. These consumer decisions are usually made within parameters prescribed by society at large through legislation and federal, state, and local funding.

Of course, if we define the customer as the one paying the bill, then the relevant taxpayer group is the key customer. In the case of a levy referendum or in the case of a state law giving the local community the power to determine the operating budget, this definition can be very significant because taxpayers who have no children in school make up the substantial majority of most communities. Any superintendent who has been involved in a referendum campaign will attest to the importance of nonparent "customers" and of having had marketing communications with these voters and, if possible, of having had them inside the school building recently. Senior citizens who have lunch at school or who participate in "grandparents" days or volunteer programs often have both the time and the inclination to vote yes on a school bond issue. People who use the school as part of a physical fitness program or for taking computer courses at night (especially if the courses are taught by regular school faculty members) may also be influenced to vote in favor of spending more tax money on the schools when the occasion arises.

In effect, anyone living in the community may be a potential customer to "buy" (that is, fund) part of a new school building or program. Voting yes on an appropriation for a school district provides money to that school system just as surely as buying a television set provides money to the organizations involved in producing and distributing that set—and I realize some may not like the analogy. The "market" for school and school-related services begins with the immediate community. Anything community members need that a school district can potentially provide more appropriately and more competitively than another organization, either public or private, is a potential market offering for the school system.

A specific list of current and potential client groups or market segments may help to stimulate thought about the possible definitions of the school's "customer" groups. Even if one considers only the obvious and realistic possible customers, one will have gone considerably beyond the more traditional definition of school client groups. Table 9 includes some traditional market segments (client groups) first and then other possible segments.

In Chapters Five, Six, and Seven, the most important elements of the marketing function—client identification and needs analysis—were discussed. In the remainder of this chapter, the other elements of the marketing function are identified and discussed and the process for developing a marketing plan is described.

Developing and Improving Product/Service Options

After the clients have been identified and whether or not formal research or needs assessment is undertaken, the next step

Table 9. Market Segments for the School.

Traditional Market Segments
Parents of "normal" children
Parents of bright, college-bound children
Athletics boosters
Parents of children with disabilities
Culturally deprived parents and children
Parents of vocationally directed children
Parents and children with chemical dependencies
Teenage parents
Households with two parents employed outside the home
Parents of preschool children
Childless couples planning to have children
Single parents and their children

Newer or Potential Market Segments
Upper-income working professionals
Moderate-income workers
Senior citizens
Health-conscious adults
Adult learners seeking various types of knowledge
People concerned about AIDS education and testing
Taxpayers without children in school
Parents of children in private or other public schools

is to identify opportunities for improving the level of service and variety of options available to the clients of the school system. Even if administrators feel that there is a high degree of satisfaction with the school system's current service offerings and programs, it is very helpful in our fast-changing world to stay ahead of clients' needs and interests by continuously improving programs on the basis of identified market knowledge.

Some of the improvements that clients might suggest and a school might consider introducing are as follows:

- Making a service easier to procure or more convenient (such as arranging for tutoring in basic skills in neighborhood homes)
- Making interscholastic athletic contests more accessible to the public by holding some of them in neighborhood parks
- Providing special tutoring by high school students to middle school children in selected classes
- Upgrading the speed and capacity of personal computers in the computer lab

- Adding an extracurricular drama performance option to the high school English program
- Changing to a new textbook considered to be better and more versatile than the one now being used
- Providing extra bus service options for cocurricular activities

The main point here is to be on the lookout for ways to improve service, to make programs more convenient and easy to access, to keep programs up-to-date, and to be sensitive to the changing life-style patterns of the community. Two of the best sources of new ideas for program improvement are staff and parents. If staff meetings occasionally include brainstorming sessions and some full discussions in which people are urged to think of new and better ways to serve the community, the results may be surprising—in a positive way. The community can also provide ideas in meetings, school activities and the like.

What is probably going through the minds of many effective school administrators reading these last paragraphs is "We already have many ideas for additions and improvements, but where are we going to get the money to provide new services and program improvements?" Of course, administrators must take care when conducting formal market research, or even when informally eliciting ideas from people, not to raise expectations or imply promises that are beyond their ability to act upon. The same principle enunciated earlier in the discussion of market needs analysis, applies here; namely, when the data generated from answers to marketing questions could indicate the need for a change, then there should be the possibility of a corresponding managerial action or change in policy, practice, or procedure (or at least an acceptable explanation as to why it will not be changed at this time).

Thus, for example, before you ask people whether they want more vocational courses in the high school program, you had better consider the costs, practicality, and program implications of adding any of several kinds of the most popular vocational programs. Ultimately, however, if a service is really needed and wanted, then eventually citizens usually, though not always, find a way to pay for it. One of the functions of well-done market research is to uncover the needs about which people feel strongly enough to find a way to raise the funds for their purchase. Such payment could be in the form of fees paid for the services, new taxes or financial legislation supported by the community, foundation grants, private or corporate donations, or reductions in other less needed programs.

Analyzing Costs and/or Pricing

Schools do not think enough about either pricing or costing. Price is what the consumer, client, or user pays for the service. In a free marketplace, it is the consumer, at least in theory, who decides what the price should be. In a public service, it can be the consumer, that is, the student or the parent, or it can be the provider of funds, that is, the taxpayer. The cost of a product or service is the amount of funds that must ultimately be expended in order to provide a given unit of product or service. The identification and analysis of costs is usually much more complex than the analysis of prices (although the latter can be complicated too). There are incremental costs, total costs, marginal costs, fixed costs, semivariable costs, fully variable costs, and so on.

The prices paid for the major services provided by school systems—general education, special education, vocational education—are set by state legislatures in terms of allowable tax levies and by local governments in terms of actual school tax levies. That is to say, the tax levy is the price paid by the clients or funders of the services. These services must then be provided by the school system at no charge to its residents and in ways that the local board deems appropriate, efficient, and effective. Since the chief ingredient of a school system's product line is basic education for people five to eighteen years of age, and this is provided, once paid for by the taxpayer, at no additional charge to any resident user, why should a person in the school district be interested in pricing policy in schools? The "price," after all, is set by taxing authorities outside the school system, with local school boards exerting only a small influence on the amount. Nevertheless, several reasons still exist for concern about the pricing of school services.

First, more and more of a school system's service line is coming under the category of "add-ons." If a financial emergency or other crisis hits a school system, the only services it really has to provide for the tax dollar are those mandated by law: typically, basic educational course offerings plus perhaps some special educational services, school lunches, health and guidance services, and so forth. But even these programs are not free. Somebody must vote for them. Thus, the voting taxpayer determines the price to be paid for the programs included in the basic school operating budget. Furthermore, since the concept of deregulation has much support, it is not beyond the pale to begin preparing for a circumstance in which we might all be paying for basic school services with vouchers, or at least when lower-income people will have vouchers or financial aid grants for certain educational services. The voucher system provides some possibility, according to its advocates, that the advantages of the market and enterprise system to which the American majority are committed can be had without sacrificing the educators' and policymakers' concern for equity and equal access. If a voucher system is instituted, the role of pricing could become extremely important to schools.

Education administrators must learn to price services to cover full cost, not just incremental cost, and when the market allows, to charge even more so as to earn a "profit" or surplus that can be used to subsidize other worthwhile or start-up services that at a certain time may not be able to cover full costs. This may be a foreign idea to many, though it is a variation on the "Robin Hood" schemes that have been covertly used to help provide equity and equal opportunity and access to all. To price accurately requires an in-depth knowledge of costs. When one is attempting to identify the strength of market demands, it is extremely important to present the client or prospective client with the cost trade-offs. It is hard for clients to say that the school should not offer more of something or do something extra if they do not know the cost, the trade-off, what they will be giving up, or the added price they will have to pay. Thus an accurate portrayal of cost-price relationships and trade-offs among various service offerings is an essential element of a public information program to assist pricing and service delivery decisions.

Designing the Delivery System

In business language, the function of marketing that schools call the delivery system is referred to as "place" and "channels of distribution." For schools, this includes items such as the format, timing, location, and assignment of staff members, materials, and equipment, as well as the logistical support and transportation for the courses, programs, and other services the schools offer. As noted in Chapter Nine, I prefer the term *provision* over *delivery* because it connotes a process rather than a product, but I will use *delivery* in this chapter because it seems to communicate the meaning more clearly. Why is "service delivery" a responsibility of the marketing function? It sounds more like a general management and administration function or an operations function, doesn't it? The reason is that designing the delivery system is concerned with making the product more attractive and easier to access and use. In that sense, it is a form of product development and improvement—that is, marketing. An effective delivery system can also reinforce or assist the sales and promotion functions. Thus, the design of the delivery system is an important part of the marketing process. The delivery system design, like the product development and improvement process, must be included in assessments of the school's program when market research or product improvement operations are conducted.

An example of a delivery system change is the offering of high school algebra on cable TV beamed live to the local community from the school, while the teacher is in her or his normal teaching setting, working with the students in the classroom and possibly answering questions from others by two-way audio. This may not be a practical example for many schools, but it is a possibility for some and is offered as an illustration of the dimensions of a delivery system.

Providing Relevant Information to the Publics

This function of marketing is the most publicly visible and the one that most people believe is all of marketing: promotion and selling, also referred to as marketing communications. When applied to schools, however, it is best described as the process of providing relevant information to a school system's market segments, or publics.

Advertising and Promotion. Advertising and promotion are, in the classic economics sense, the providing of information to consumers so that they can make more intelligent purchase decisions. This may mean clearly describing on the school bulletin board the content and objectives of an elective course so students can make better selections, describing in a newsletter or poster a new series such as senior citizen lunches or dinners, advertising in a newspaper ticket sales for a fund-raiser or an athletic event, or placing ads describing the overall school system and its strengths in order to attract parents away from other private or public schools.

Unfortunately much of television and other mass media advertising has become so base in its attempt to appeal at the emotional level and to aim at the creation and stimulation of desires that often cannot be met that promotion has a negative image for many. The thought of advertising and promoting educational services as though they were soap or deodorant is an appalling notion to most school executives. But is it the nature of the appeal to the emotions as well as the intellect or is it chiefly our perceived worth of the product itself that makes such promotion objectionable?

To test the answer to this question, think about your response to the recent NEA slogan "If you think education is expensive, try ignorance." Or what about an ad that shows an underprivileged child entering the doors of your school, receiving support and encouragement, and then coming out twelve years later, head high, looking self-assured and well-dressed, and heading for college and a successful career? Would you object to these emotional appeals? Should you?

The real trouble with much of the kind of advertising to which we object is that it tends to shade the truth, often trying by implication to connect unusual but unrelated benefits to the use of a product (for example, if you drink a certain kind of soda pop or smoke a certain brand of cigarette, you will be surrounded by beautiful people of the opposite sex). Or perhaps it is just full of emotional appeal and music and color but no real information. That is not what the free-market economists had in mind when they defined the purpose of advertising in our capitalist system.

In a market economy such as ours, advertising can and does play a very important role. The market system only works well when there are several suppliers in competition and when the consumer possesses full information to make intelligent choices from among several viable alternatives. Advertising, in its classic economics description, helps to provide that information. Unfortunately, today we sometimes get more hype than information from advertising. This is ironic because the consumer's ability to make choices in today's complex environment is even more clouded by the dazzling array of product and service alternatives, many with complicated technical specifications. Wouldn't it be helpful if auto manufacturers provided for each car they advertised the kind of information that *Consumer Reports* magazine provides—crash test results, frequency-of-repair records, decibels of sound noise inside the passenger compartment at sixty miles per hour, objective road test results, and dealer cost and price data!

Educational organizations do not have to compromise their principles in order to advertise effectively. Education has much to boast about, promote, and advertise. Yet in the rush of today's thirty-second TV commercials and with the advertising and information overload, it is easy for all of us to lose sight of how important schooling and education are and where they fit in the overall scheme of the fast-track life of success and happiness the advertisers keep telling us about.

Describing the Products of Schooling to the Publics. The question for education administrators is how they can compete for attention and support in the current environment of deregulation. How do they describe to parents or prospective parents and students the various outcomes of good schooling? In the absence of a good marketing communications program, the main information people will get about the schools is the test score gains or losses, the problems with discipline, and how well the athletic teams in major sports are doing. But both educators and parents know that schooling is much more than preparing students to score well on standardized reading and math tests, providing a baby-sitting service for working couples, and training students for athletic events—as important as these functions may be to specific market segments, or publics. Indeed, private competitors can often provide these services more effectively and economically than the public schools. "Competitors" here does not mean just other schools but also competitive methods for achieving the same results—for example, educational television, community athletic programs, day-care centers, videocassettes, and so on.

Another function of advertising in the classic economics sense was to "educate." Who has more right to try to educate than the school system? Some people feel that the school system not only has the right but the obligation to educate parents and children on the importance of education to their future; on the dangers of drug abuse; on how to deal with teenage pregnancy; on the social, physical, health, and economic consequences of sexual activities; on the importance of taking certain courses or completing certain programs.

Being Realistic in Advertising. Should a school advertise the fact that in addition to providing good solid education and preparation for life, it addresses affective and emotional needs, builds confidence and self-concept, treats (if not meets) the physical, emotional, and intellectual needs of a student, and enhances certain skills? How does a system advertise this? Is it ethical to imply that certain student needs are met when we know that students learn in different ways and often unpredictably? There are no easy answers to questions of when and how to advertise, but it is possible that failure to communicate the work and successes of the school to its publics can be damaging to the school's reputation and community support level.

There is a caveat in the decision to advertise how good your school is. That is, it is possible for tax money to be awarded to those institutions that need it most—those that are not providing the best services now. While this might in some cases amount to rewarding the inefficient, the message here is important. Be careful how you boast about your school's services in advertising claims. Taxpayers may think the school is too well funded. It is also clear that you should not promise something your school cannot deliver; so announcements and advertising must be worded carefully to state that a school only provides opportunity. What students actually learn or receive when education services are made available is a function of many things, some of which are not under the school's control. Yet it seems appropriate to speak out about the opportunities and to describe the benefits that past students have actually obtained or believe they have obtained or to use parents to give "testimonials" about the school and its services.

Another function of advertising in business is to create revenue by selling more product. Schools do not have product in inventory and thus cannot "create" revenue by selling more. Furthermore, if more people come to use a school's special services, this actually has a negative impact on the budget in the short run unless the people are asked to pay for those extra services. Indeed, a major complaint of many schools in the 1970s and 1980s was that they were being asked to provide many more services but not given the additional funding needed to perform them adequately. Dealing with problems of chemical dependency, broken homes, teenage pregnancies, increasing calls for special education services for the handicapped, and now concern over AIDS places extra demands on schools.

Why advertise and promote schools when they already have more demands for services than they have resources to meet those demands? That is precisely when it is important to communicate to the public in forceful terms the quality of the services a school can potentially provide, the special nature of the problems people face and how the school can help them, and the need for additional funding. In the final analysis, the public pays for education. While promoting a new special service for which there is no funding can be painful in the short run, if it is an important service that people need, they will usually find a way to provide funds to the school in exchange for the service, as noted in the preceding section—either through donations (maybe the school could help facilitate a citizens' fund-raising campaign), by voting for special legislation or appropriations, or on a fee-for-service basis. Thus in the long run, advertising and communicating with market segments can make the schools stronger and more successful.

Selling and Distribution

The sales and distribution functions occur when the client agrees to purchase or use the service or product and takes delivery. As stated earlier, if the client identification and needs assessment or market research process is done properly and if it is followed by effective product design, by the development of a responsive delivery system, and by proper pricing and costing, then the last two functions of marketing are relatively easily performed. I would add here that if the advertising and promotion work are done well there is almost no need for the selling function.

For the primary school service—educating children—the "purchase" is made when a parent decides to enroll her child in kindergarten or when any new enrollment decision is made by someone coming into or living in the school district. Other "sales" are made when parents, students, and other clients make decisions on the use of school district services. Typically, school district personnel are passive in these transactions. They wait for prospective customers to come to them, much as a sales clerk in a department store usually waits for customers to come to him.

Distribution may involve school districts more actively, especially in the extracurricular aspects of their programs. For example, decisions as to where and when athletic events, school plays, a senior lunch program, or classes on parenting will be held may be distribution decisions requiring active involvement by a school district. In most cases selling and distribution are minor functions for school systems. Their importance may increase, however, as various states adopt laws and policies that give consumers more choice in the selection of schools and programs.

Developing the Marketing Plan

A marketing plan is a key part of executing the strategy. Developing such a plan involves considering each of the relevant customers listed in Table 8 and considering for each market segment each of the functions listed in Table 7. The techniques described in Chapters Seven and Five, respectively, will help you identify your district's customers and assess their power and their needs and wants. One approach for developing a comprehensive and structured plan involves the following steps:

1. Form a citizens' committee to include representatives from staff, board, administration, parents, and other potential clients.
2. Have each member read Chapters Five through Eight of this book.
3. Design a market research process taking care to avoid the abuses of citizens' committees described in Chapter Five.
4. Use a consultant to help the committee analyze and interpret the data.
5. Prepare a segment-by-segment marketing plan, with goals and standards included, according to the processes described in this chapter.

Applying all the functions of marketing and performing all the marketing activities described in this and earlier chapters should help one develop a stronger school system that will serve its clients well and that probably will develop and maintain a relatively high degree of client satisfaction. Such a school system will also have a parent community that is involved in the school and is knowledgeable about the system and its problems and the alternatives available for educating its children.

The activities involved in the functions of marketing should be organized into a marketing plan. Each district will define, assign, and monitor these functions in its own ways. A structure and process, even if they consist only of a checklist developed from Tables 7 and 8, are recommended. An active marketing function and the existence of a marketing plan force an organization to be more responsive to its community and more involved with its clients. Before developing a marketing program, however, the superintendent and board must be well prepared for the consequences of a more open communications system to which this can lead; they must also take care to map out an effective sequence of activities and response processes. For example, it is almost certainly better to work on improving program quality and sharpening the curriculum design and delivery system before soliciting input from the community about what strategic merger alternatives, if any, to pursue.

The process of identifying the relevant client groups and market segments is another key step to be taken early in the development of the marketing plan. Most important, however, is the continuous process of two-way communication engaged in through carefully designed action-directed market research and through open and clear marketing and communications programs, including some honest advertising and promotion and some mechanisms for responding to the market signals obtained. When client groups are properly identified and their needs are understood and discussed through market research and marketing communications, then sales and promotional activities are often unnecessary. What is necessary is a constantly working product development and service delivery improvement process that is responsive to the needs of the client groups. Thus the heart of an effective marketing function is a good research and communication process and the ability to respond well to the service needs articulated by the community and identified by the research activities. This means intelligently conceived research, a communications program aimed at identifying client needs and an ability to react effectively with product development and improvement efforts and enhanced delivery systems much more than it means ''selling'' and ''promoting'' the school system. More importantly, such a process helps ensure that the strategy and overall policies of the district are in line with the current and future needs and demands of its client groups.

9

Instructional Leadership: Providing Quality Educational Services

We might view strategy implementation as a three-legged stool. One leg is *politics,* another *marketing,* and the third *production,* or *operations.* The political and marketing aspects of strategy implementation were dealt with in Chapters Seven and Eight. This chapter deals with the effective production, design, and provision of the education services. (I prefer the term *provision*—rather than *delivery*—to avoid the connotation that there is a "product" that is just "handed over" to its recipients.) Ultimately, a school district exists to *provide* needed education services. Any strategy that is formulated involves, first, a discovery of who the constituents or stakeholders are and what their various interests and power positions are (politics), then an analysis of their needs (marketing), and finally a design and provision of the services to fill those needs. Since instruction is the way in which education is normally provided, the concept of instructional leadership is similar to the concept of operations management as I will define it.

Operations management is a term borrowed from business to describe the management of an organization's process of producing and providing at an appropriate place and in an appropriate manner a product or service. The subfunctions of operations management are quality control, cost, efficiency, and logistics. In education, the product is learning and development, a product typically provided in classrooms in school buildings by means of lectures and exercises directed by teachers. The clients are usually present in the classroom, though there is currently emerging a growing variety of methods and places of delivery. Thus *operations,* according to the definition used here, chiefly involves management and leadership in providing instruction.

In the United States, business has put its emphasis on the marketing and financial functions and usually relegated operations to a low priority. The typical American approach is to start with the market needs and develop a strategy oriented around serving those needs profitably. Operations is considered part of the implementation of marketing strategy rather than part of strategy formulation. The managerial assumption is that "they (the production people) must and will produce whatever we say the strategy calls for." In other words, operations waits for strategy and then implements what the strategy says must be pursued on the basis of market needs. Sounds logical and appropriate, does it not?

As the urge to adopt business methods to schools increases, be aware of this caveat: The Japanese and other foreign competitors have beaten U.S. business in the competitive arena largely because of their superior operations skills (especially in the areas of production efficiency and quality control). The analogy to business will not be extended further except to implore school systems to learn from the mistakes of American business. The Japanese approach in the motorcycle, automobile, and other product industries was to start with the matter of operations. In other words, they framed their strategic management and leadership approach as an operations approach rather than as a financial strategy or marketing one. They said, how can we make a cycle or car with a price and quality combination that the market will demand and need? Their answers led them at times to some new operations methods and strategies. For instance, in motorbikes it meant manufacturing in larger quantities and with more advanced automation than the British, who had led the market, or the Americans, and making them cheaply enough so that many people in less developed countries could afford them (really a Henry Ford strategy). In other words, in Japan operations preceded marketing rather than the reverse. This is not to say that one approach is better than the other but to point out the possible dangers of giving short shrift to the operations function.

Focusing entirely on the selling aspect of "marketing" without dealing with quality is not wise. But even to think only of the total marketing function and market needs without also asking what can be done about building new services and delivery systems that might change the nature of market needs is probably dangerous. When new technologies and radically new services are made feasible and available, then the nature of the public's perception of its needs will change. No market survey will pick up this change in demand before the service is available and its potential is known to the survey respondent. For this reason, operations must at times precede strategy as well as the reverse. This means that one can think of operations as an element of strategy, not just a process of implementing strategy. If operations is an element of strategy, if the operations function includes quality control, and if instructional leadership and management are the operations function of a school district, it follows that quality control of instruction is an element of the district's strategy.

Instructional leadership, as discussed below, is at least in part about quality control and quality improvement. The next section identifies quality improvement processes involved in "instructional leadership," and subsequent sections proceed, in turn, to the building of a culture that fosters educational improvement, the superintendent's involvement in instructional leadership, the setting of goals and expectations for educational improvement, the establishment of evaluation and reward systems for teachers and administrators, and finally quality control.

If instruction is the key purpose of the school system, then leadership of schools involves articulating the general themes of effective instruction, and good management means seeing to it that efficient and effective processes are in place to identify, monitor, and reward instructionally effective behaviors and processes and to continue to improve the quality of instruction. One way to assess the quality control efforts in a school system is to determine the importance it gives to its instructional mission. We do this by examining where on the agenda or list of action priorities of the central administration visions, new directions, and proposals for improved instruction exist. Is there an emphasis on educational results, equal opportunity and access, new teaching and learning strategies, instructional creativity? Or is the focus only on budgets, facilities, public relations processes, and management structures and processes, with an absence of content about the educational and instructional purposes these processes are supposed to facilitate? Is there more concern for inputs and process, or is the focus on outputs, outcomes, and the kinds of results for clients that these inputs and processes are supposed to achieve? How much of the discussion at school board meetings is about instructional processes and curriculum?

What kind of staff development programs does the district make available to teachers for improving subject matter knowledge and instructional skills? What kinds of evaluation for teaching and instruction exist in the schools, and what rewards are given for effective teaching and curriculum development? How many new and creative ideas have been introduced into the curriculum and instructional program in recent years? By what criteria have these new programs been evaluated, and what were the results and follow-up actions of the evaluation process?

Building a Culture That Fosters Educational Improvement

The "culture" of an organization is said to be determined by actions and symbols that convey what that organization values, admires, and rewards. It reflects the deeply held beliefs of prominent members of that organization. It can be judged by knowing what stories and anecdotes about heroes and heroines and successful events are popularly shared in the organization, and by understanding what is rewarded by the respected leaders, both formal and informal, in the organization (Deal and Kennedy, 1982; Lightfoot, 1983). One can sometimes sense the "culture" when walking through the halls of a school and noting the pictures and displays, listening to the conversations, and observing the decorum. In the classroom, it is exemplified by the amount of time spent on worksheets, drills, and objective tests versus writing and speaking or versus creative activities and team projects.

What are some of the ways that a superintendent influences the existing culture?

- By standing before citizen groups, board meetings, staff groups, and others and articulating the instructional and educational values the school stands for and the long-range visions she or he believes in, even at the expense of losing some popularity, and then backing up these statements with policy recommendations and other actions
- By introducing slogans, symbols, and general themes to the staff in speeches, memos, and small group conversations that reflect an interest in quality of instruction and a deep concern for student development
- By rewarding people with public praise, special letters, special assignments, or developmental opportunities when they display unusually effective behaviors or results that are consistent with the educational and instructional values that she or he and the school system are trying to foster
- By relating stories or anecdotes that epitomize the positive actions or idealize the personalities that seem to represent the kinds of activities that the district values
- By spending large amounts of time (and asking board members to spend time) on issues and concerns that exemplify the educational values and results that she or he wishes the school district to exemplify
- By holding the building principals accountable for the kinds of results that reflect the instructional values of the school (for example, which results achieve the greatest praise and rewards for principals: Obtaining higher-than-expected test scores? The kinds of staff development they provide for teachers? Discipline levels in their schools? The creative new programs they try? Showing compassion for "at-risk" students? Having quiet and orderly schools with no discipline problems?)

The Superintendent and Instructional Leadership

How can central office administrators direct their culture-influencing behaviors in ways that facilitate the promotion of better instruction and better teaching and learning strategies and also reward the kinds of activities that improve the school system's ability to fulfill its educational mission and serve its various stakeholders more effectively? First and foremost, superintendents must be really interested in and willing to spend time on instructional matters. They cannot merely delegate them to elementary and secondary directors or to principals and then just forget about them. Unfortunately, very little research has been done on the role and effectiveness of the superintendent in instructional matters; even the extensive amount of research done on principals has often lacked solid observations of behavior and evidence of behavioral results (Cuban, 1984; Pittner, 1988).

Cuban (1988) describes the instructional role of the superintendent as having moved from an original heavy emphasis on supervision and involvement with classrooms and teaching in the late nineteenth and early twentieth centuries to less emphasis in the last three generations and now returning again to more involvement in instruction and curriculum. As he states, the superintendent fills an instructional role on several levels. The superintendent is a teacher of teachers in a smaller district, of principals in a larger district, and of the board and the community in any district. If instruction is to be viewed as important and valued by the system, the informed judgment of reflective practitioners and intuitive logic tell us that the superintendent must spend some time in educating her constituent groups on the central role of instruction and also spend some time in schools and classrooms if only for the latter's symbolic value.

According to the research on "effective schools," the principal is supposed to be a "strong leader" who emphasizes "instruction," maintains discipline, and clearly articulates goals. The specific behaviors that the principal should engage in to improve school performance are not entirely clear from the research, however. Nevertheless, common sense, limited behavioral research evidence, and professional judgment tell us that instructional leadership and operations management ultimately *classroom* come down to the level of the school building where teaching and learning take place. This means that the principal must be the "culture bearer" or transmitter of the philosophy that drives the system and also the implementer of goals and the conveyer of expectations that make educational improvements happen.

Several important scholars armed with significant research findings have in the last few years underscored the importance of the principal in school and educational improvement. According to recent studies, the role of the principal also seems to be moving back toward its original emphasis on instructional leadership. What does this mean for the central office? Does the role of the superintendent or of other members of the central office staff change as the building managers assume more responsibility for instructional leadership? It seems logical to conclude that if principals assume more responsibility for a function, then those to whom they report must adjust some of their own responsibilities. It may even be true that in some districts it is the central office staff that sees to it that the principal assumes a more proactive stance in dealing with instructional leadership and development.

It follows, then, that for the central office executives of a school system to influence the instructional process and truly to influence educational improvement, they must exert leadership in how they manage the selection, development, and rewarding of the principals in their district's schools. What kinds of people do they select? What kinds of staff development do they provide for principals? What behaviors and activities of the principals do they value and reward?

Here are some specific questions that a superintendent might raise:

- Have the principals received some training in the last few years on the subject of instructional supervision, teaching-learning styles, or other processes related to the observation and evaluation of teaching?
- Have the teachers received any recent training on teaching-learning styles, teaching techniques, or other instructional improvement methods?

- Do teachers keep up-to-date in their subject areas?
- How much of the budget is allocated to the foregoing kinds of in-service activities and workshops?
- Do principals have discussions and faculty meetings that address the topic of instruction and its improvement?
- What is the state of knowledge of central office personnel on the latest research on teaching and learning? Do they encourage discussion and experimentation with new (to the school) ideas such as peer coaching, heterogeneous grouping, classroom observation, mentor teachers, evaluation processes for instruction, rewards for good teaching, instructional improvement techniques?

These questions are not all-inclusive; you can probably think of many others. They are designed to help you begin to examine the extent to which the leadership of your school system encourages or emphasizes instruction, good teaching, learner outcomes, and the like as opposed to financial issues, administrative concerns, and items having to do with image and client perceptions. The relative emphasis placed on these kinds of activities also shapes the "culture" of a school, its "ethos," and its climate, as defined earlier. In addition, one can infer what a school district stands for in terms of learning and teaching by examining board agendas, staff development activities, minutes of meetings of the administrators, topics of discussion in the faculty lounge and at faculty meetings, PTSO agendas and activities, and so forth. What percentage of time is spent on curriculum, learning, teaching, and educational delivery?

Unfortunately, there is no clear evidence that doing what is prescribed here necessarily leads to improved productivity and performance. The performance of school systems is affected by a large number of contextual factors, including the history of the school and the neighborhood, the community, staff quality, the parent group, and local resources and opportunities, to name just a few. A superintendent, then, must rely on her experienced judgment and the judgment of others in reflecting on their practices and results or in interpreting the meaning of the limited research available. Never should the existence of outside influences on instructional performance be taken as an excuse for not trying to affect and improve factors the central office might be able to influence.

Establishing Goals and Expectations for Improvement

In order to develop improvement goals, it seems logical that a school system should have some ability to assess where it is in relation to a particular standard or ideal. The logic is as follows: If you fashion an improvement goal, it must relate to something you think can be done better than it is now being done. To know that it is not now being done as well as it might be, you must have some indicators or measures or at least a "gut feeling." Even if it is only an intuitive understanding, this gut feeling must have some basis, and someone should be able to articulate that basis in terms of one or more criteria or indicators. If this is true, then the school district's leadership should be able to obtain some baseline assessment of where it stands now in terms of these criteria or standards of performance. The importance of having this baseline measure is that it allows for the possibility of tracking progress over time to see how well improvement goals are being achieved.

Chapter Eleven identifies much of the kind of information that can be collected for evaluation and general decision making. The extent to which school improvement is occurring must be assessed in terms of at least some of the indicators discussed in that chapter. If the improvement processes employed will not, even in the long run, impact the assessment of the school system on any of the evaluation measures that the superintendent, the board, and other key stakeholders of the education system feel are important, then one of two situations exists. Either the district's improvement processes are not dealing with anything of significance, or the measures are inadequate—that is, the school system's assessment system does not include all the important measures of effective performance—a very common situation.

Assessment of the degree to which school goals are being achieved can and should be tied to both quantitative and qualitative measures. In other words, the administration should introduce the systematic use of some broader judgment factors in addition to the normal test scores and survey results that dominate evaluation reports. For example, an outsider's judgment as to how well the students are developing an improved self-concept as indicated by their demeanor and the level of their class recitations might be included in the assessment reporting of the school. It is feasible to broaden the array of objective measures and indicators usually used by adding to the carefully collected quantitative measures, such as test scores and dropout rates, other less commonly used indicators, such as consumer satisfaction indices and tests on attitudes, values, and cooperative skills. While the latters' validity and reliability might be questioned, the mere fact that they are discussed as part of the school system's delivery processes can send a strong message on what the school values besides SAT scores. Over time, reliable scoring methods can be developed and newer more valid measures should become available. The time to begin experimenting may be at hand, but certain cautions must be applied, and these are also discussed in Chapter Eleven.

How Should Instructional Goals Be Determined? If the determination of what is an appropriate standard or goal involves some judgments as to what *can* be done and how, it seems very important to involve those individuals who are directly responsible for seeing that goals are achieved. If a goal represents a new direction (as opposed merely to doing a little more or a little better), then various kinds of change strategies may need to be employed. If a new superintendent, or an old superintendent with a new idea for making a significant change, decides to make a major shift in educational direction or instructional approach, he or she should be careful not to conduct the all-too-frequent "sham participation" exercise. That occurs when a group is called together to "participate" in a decision that essentially has already been made. The popular wisdom among poorly educated managers (that is, poorly educated in terms of their understanding of leadership processes) is that you try to plant an idea in a group and then hope the members come up with it and think it is theirs. Most business executives I have talked to really think this works, and many proudly boast about their ability to carry it off.

People eventually assess what is happening or has happened to them, however, and they resent it. They then become unwilling to engage in important and meaningful participatory exercises in the future, when their input is honestly sought and needed for success. Perhaps that is one reason why so many American executives are having difficulty competing successfully with Japanese executives. The latter seem to be able to manage better and achieve higher productivity with American workers as well as their own workers than U.S. managers achieve. The Japanese do this, at least in part, by obtaining consensus or input (these are two very different processes) on items on which a decision has not been made. They do not ask workers whether the company should make high-quality cars. They tend to ask workers the "how" questions, while explaining top management's reasons for the decisions already made on the "what" questions. Consequently, if school superintendents have an idea for a major change in strategy that they strongly feel is critical, they should admit it, try to explain why it is important to them and to the future of their district, and then elicit participation only in decisions involving the "hows" of implementation. They should ask for participation only in decisions that they feel can benefit from input—input that they are willing to listen to and act on.

The central office should give a good deal of leeway to teachers and building administrators since they are the experts on how to design and employ curriculum and, specifically, on what curriculum will work best in their classrooms. For meaningful change to occur, teachers must be involved in establishing the assessment criteria and setting the goals for the improvement of instruction. This is true not because the central office wants the teachers to "feel better" but because it must believe in their potential as professionals to identify and influence the factors that produce good teaching and learning and the factors that indicate that learning is taking place. If the ability to identify and influence these factors is a latent skill in the teaching staff, then the central office must help teachers develop and use this skill. If this ability is not even a latent skill in a teacher, then that teacher should be removed from the classroom.

All the preaching about improvement will probably not have a great impact on productivity if the professionals who must make instructional improvement happen do not understand what it is. In short, then, the teachers can and must provide the driving force for shaping the specifics of the instructional improvement process. Given the right leadership and just a few catalytic and facilitating actions from the administration, teachers can be a vital and constructive part of the goal-setting and evaluation processes. For instructional improvement to be most effective, however, the general direction, initial boost, and continued moral, symbolic, political, and financial support should come from the central office.

The Content of Goals. Goals for educational improvement should follow from and be consistent with the mission and strategy determined for the school system in the manner prescribed in Chapter Six, include some understanding of the political and marketing elements discussed in Chapters Seven and Eight, and be tied to assessment processes described in Chapter Eleven. Assuming that the instructional improvement goals are consistent with the school system's overall strategy and that the "corporate culture" reflects a real commitment to their importance and to their achievement, the conventional wisdom of effective practitioners is that these goals must next meet the following criteria: Goal Criteria

1. Be attainable, or realistic
2. Involve some stretching
3. Be broad enough to be significant to the district's future, yet specific enough to be observable and measurable
4. Have specific time parameters and methods for assessing progress
5. Be well communicated, understood, and in general acceptable to those who must carry them out

The foregoing criteria are actually generic principles of good management related to goal setting. One specific criterion I add for school district improvement goals is that they relate either directly or indirectly to enhancing the school system's ability to deliver a better educational product or service, thus improving some sort of benefit-cost ratio for one or more of its major services delivered to one of its major constituents.

Perhaps some examples of school system improvement goals that could, in a given situation, satisfy the above criteria might be helpful at this point.

• A district establishes a peer coaching system designed to facilitate the sharing of knowledge among teachers about effective teaching, with a pilot test in the next academic year and a plan for full implementation in the following year. Success in the first year will be measured by both the number of teachers who volunteer to participate and the degree to which they feel they have been helped by the system. In future years the success will be measured by various indicators of impact on student learning outcomes.

• A school system decides to design a marketing program to better understand and meet the needs of the parent community, with a deadline for completing the design by June 199X and for implementing phase one during the following academic year. Success will be measured by consumer satisfaction surveys before and after the program is begun and by enrollments, transfers, attendance rates, and participation in the PTSO.

• One school district establishes a long-range planning process involving citizens, board and staff members, and parents with the goal of redirecting the school system to better exploit the technology of tomorrow. Success will be measured by the degree of change ultimately achieved in classroom delivery systems in terms of use of paraprofessionals, increases in class size for master teachers, increased use of technology and, finally, improved student performance. First-year success will be measured only by the extent to which people are involved in the process and to which the crucial issues are identified and productively debated and the environmental trends are analyzed and better understood by all stakeholder groups. Goals involving specific curriculum technology installations will be developed for future years.

• A group of adjacent high school districts complete a cooperative agreement for the development and use of an interactive cable system for the delivery of high school electives. Success will be measured by the number of courses on line by the 199X academic year, increases in student course options over what otherwise would have been available, and the achievement of budgeted operational costs per course and per student.

Evaluation and Reward Systems
for Instructional Improvement

For improvement in teaching and learning to take place, there must be highly motivated and competent teachers working in an environment that allows for the free expression of the best in their art and craft. Motivation is a complex phenomenon. Many teachers and school administrators derive satisfaction and motivation from the work itself. In other words, the work, the feelings of accomplishment and competence gained by just doing what the doer feels and recognizes is a good job and the satisfaction one gets from feedback from students, provides the satisfaction and the motivation to continue. This is intrinsic motivation. Lortie (1975), in his classic ethnographic study of teachers and teaching, presents a great deal of evidence of the importance of intrinsic motivation in teaching. While extrinsic rewards are vital to most of us since we must have money to eat and live, evidence suggests that in many situations such rewards while perhaps preventing dissatisfaction do not provide motivation to work harder (Herzberg, 1968). Where intrinsic motivation exists, it can provide a powerful influence on behavior. In this circumstance (that is, where intrinsic motivation becomes active), the administrator's role is to see that relevant goals are being pursued and the conditions are conducive to free expression of task- and goal-related behaviors—that no major obstacles are put in the way of effective teaching performance— then to ensure that appropriate teacher-influenced formative and summative evaluation processes are employed, and finally, to see that there is an effective linkage between effort and results and reward.

To illustrate the difference between extrinsic and intrinsic motivation, two different approaches to attempting to improve teaching effectiveness are described below. The first one flows from a Theory X set of assumptions, and the second approach flows from a Theory Y set of assumptions; both are described as "participative." These assumption sets come from McGregor (1957). The Theory X set of assumptions holds that most people are inherently lazy and in order to work must be "motivated" either through extrinsic rewards or through some other form of inducement or coercion. The Theory Y set of assumptions holds that people like work for its own sake and are inherently motivated by the drive for accomplishment and achievement and by the intrinsic rewards involved.

Example 1: Participative Management and Theory X. The superintendent wants input from teachers and administrators on the question of how instruction in this school system can be improved. He calls a staff meeting, explains the situation, tells the staff about some new ideas he picked up at an "elements of instruction" workshop, and then offers the staff $30,000 (or about $300 for each certified staff member) for staff development. The money is to be spent any way the teachers and principals, as a group, choose as long as it is directed toward improving instruction. This is true participative management. The group then decides by consensus that it would like to reward teachers by giving them each a stipend of $300 to attend workshops on subjects the teachers feel are appropriate for professional development. Part of the stipend, according to this proposal, can be used to pay for substitutes to cover classes. The superintendent responds that this is not what he had in mind. He wants the money spent on seminars on the elements of instruc-

244 Strategic Leadership for Schools

tion. The only recommendations he wants from the staff are which of the many available seminars and workshops should be selected, who from the district should attend them, and how the information obtained could be disseminated and put to use in all the teachers' classrooms over time.

Why did this superintendent fail to reveal his full intention at the outset? It is perfectly appropriate to announce a goal and then to ask for participation in how to achieve that goal. It is, however, important that the ground rules and parameters for participation and the amount of true leeway the group has be clearly stated in advance. If the superintendent had followed the proper approach to participative management and announced the limits up front and then accepted the staff's subsequent recommendations, would he have been truly reflecting Theory Y assumptions? No, he would not!

Participative management, à la Theory Y, involves a deeper philosophy and set of values about people's worth and their potential contribution to decision making. The first factor missing in this example is the fact that the superintendent has not identified the issue or problem in terms of an ultimate goal or strategy. Why is he interested in "elements of instruction" training? What is wrong with instruction in his school? How does he measure the effects of good instruction? If it is by test scores, then what reasons other than the quality of instruction might explain why test scores are not as high as he would like them to be? If his measurement is the number of complaints from parents about teachers, then what are the real causes of those complaints? Most importantly, why does the superintendent not share these data with the principals and teachers? Does he not feel that they could help him identify the problems or issues?

Many executives believe that taking this last approach is "selling out" at worst, and at best runs the danger of eliciting negative reactions and noncooperation from the faculty. The argument from these executives goes something like this: "They (the teachers) might get defensive. Naturally, they are going to say that their teaching currently is satisfactory. They'll tell you all the things wrong with test scores as a true measure of their work and why the parental complaints are unfounded or unfair. Or they might agree with parental concerns and tell you the problem is that the teachers need more prep time or more supply money to buy better teaching materials, or they need a little more freedom from central office rules and constraints.''

The example illustrates a common misconception about participative management. Most people feel that if you have a meeting and obtain input and follow some or all of the advice given by subordinates, you are practicing modern participative management. True participative management employing the Theory Y assumptions about people requires a genuine respect for the opinions of the other participants and a willingness to be challenged while at the same time remaining goal directed and keeping the process moving forward toward some previously agreed upon general directions and mission of the organization. A difficult challenge, but not an impossible feat.

The problem is that participative management is a very difficult job. It is not easy to engage an intelligent group of staff members in a process that uses their creativity, enacts enough of their ideas to keep them interested and involved but not over-worked by the demands of participating, strives for consensus, and keeps teachers motivated to work for the system's goals without risking the possibility of creating unproductive conflict or of losing control of the system's overall strategy, direction, and goals. It can be done, however. Approaches for dealing with the process of introducing major organizational change are discussed in Chapter Ten. These include some, though not all, of the elements that are important in participative management. Although the discussion in Chapter Ten is aimed chiefly at the introduction of organizationwide change, it also describes many processes the knowledge of which is crucial in participative management. For example, the concepts of transition manage-ment, of dealing with loss and death of the old ways, and of the management of the dynamics of power, anxiety, and con-trol, as they are discussed in Chapter Ten, are all relevant to any kind of participative process.

Example 2: Participative Management and Theory Y.
Class size is getting smaller and enrollment is declining to a point that the superintendent does not
feel that her high school can continue to offer the
electives and breadth of program that parents demand and students deserve without running huge
operating deficits. She does not think that taxpayers
will approve an increase in school taxes. She believes that the answer to the problem may lie in
microwave TV technology and larger class size in
basic courses, both of which will be controversial
with teachers and perhaps with parents because of
some necessary grade restructuring. The superintendent decides to present the current picture—
along with the district's educational goals and objectives and budgetary constraints—in meetings
held throughout the fall with various groups.

The superintendent holds a meeting with the
teacher first, explaining the problem and the facts
as she knows them—declining enrollment figures,
budget deficits, reduced ability to offer electives,
student and parent survey data or anecdotal data—
and painting a picture of what the school will be
like in five years if present trends continue with no
significant managerial action.

At a subsequent meeting, the superintendent
describes various microwave systems, how they
have been used by other schools, and what those
schools think of them. She also explains that paraprofessionals and larger classes can be used with these
systems and how much money this can save. And
she is careful to point out how such modifications
might impact the present teaching staff. Throughout this discussion, however, the superintendent remains open to other recommended solutions that
fall within the policy guidelines already established
by the school system (and which must be well known
and accepted by the teachers before this discussion

can take place) and within the local school's budgetary limits (a must). During all her deliberations
with the faculty members, the superintendent seeks
their ideas for change and improvement and tries
to share and clarify the meaning of the data already
collected. In addition, she asks the teachers whether
they would like any other information that has not
yet been collected. If so, and if it is available at a
feasible cost to the district and can contribute to
informed discussion of the issue, she sees that it is
collected (perhaps appointing a teacher or community task force to do so).

During this process, the superintendent also
meets with various community groups, business   *external*
leaders, and other stakeholders, sharing data and
eliciting suggestions and comments. She has no
preconceived answers and is truly open to a variety
of ideas and creative approaches. She has determined, perhaps autocratically, the overall goal and
mission of the school system. That is, "to provide
the highest quality education possible with emphasis
on academics, but combined with a supportive environment and stressing ethics and citizenship."
Although the definitions of some of these terms—
academics, supportive environment, ethics, and *citizenship*—are open to some interpretation, the superintendent has worked on them constantly with parents
and teachers (using speeches, symbolic actions, and
so on) until they have developed a reasonable degree
of consistency in their application. She has also
stated the budgetary limits for any successful proposal and has had to convince the staff and parents
that these limits are both real and realistic.

What is different about this second example is that the
Theory Y manager states the educational goals and objectives
up front and then attempts to get help from professionals and
parents in defining ways to achieve the goals. She shares the data

*Author is confusing Theory Y, X with
concept of participative management*

This is still not true participant movement

with them and tries to identify objectively the consequences of different courses of action. Her (Theory Y) assumption is that if she shares the problem and data with others—that is, if other intelligent and motivated people have the same data that she has about the situation—they will come to more productive and useful conclusions that she alone could. The Theory Y manager must not abdicate, however. He or she must continually guide the discussions, being sure that the overall goal is kept clearly in sight, that key data are properly used and interpreted, and that important implications are not overlooked.

There are risks, of course, with the participative approach. The superintendent and all key administrators involved must be on guard against the possibility that a vocal or powerful few have undue influence on the process. If they do, if the public is not ready to accept the facts and the data, and if the teachers have had a long history of mistrusting management and thus cannot openly share their fears or their suggestions for change and improvement, the process can lead to dysfunctional recommendations. How does a superintendent cope with that? What happens if the answers in a participative process are not functional for improvement? How often can the "boss" overrule the group and still maintain participative management? If the superintendent does not agree with or follow the recommendations, will others withhold their support in implementing the new program or process that does come forth? More importantly, will they withdraw from any future participative activity?

Answers depend on how and why the superintendent disagrees with any group solution. If she disagrees because it is not her favorite answer, then she would have been better off making the decision herself earlier and not subjecting the group to a sham participative process. On the other hand, if she can point out to the others that the solution overlooks some important fact or implication or that it does not satisfy the need to pursue a key goal or mission already agreed upon, then she can overturn the decision and send the group members back to the drawing board, without necessarily losing their support or the positive effects of the participative process. I should quickly point out that Theory Y is a set of assumptions about people and their nature, not a leadership style. While it is likely that people who hold Theory Y assumptions will often employ participative approaches, in certain situations a Theory Y manager can and must be authoritarian.

At this point you may be wondering whether we are still on the original subject of this section: reward and evaluation systems. The discussion of managerial assumptions about people is relevant to this topic because these very assumptions that leaders hold about the people around them set the climate for any system of evaluation and improvement. This climate determines the extent of the contribution of the evaluation process to the organization's overall success.

Evaluation as a Program Management Function

Although a more complete discussion of evaluation is presented in Chapter Eleven, in the context of accountability for overall performance, it is important at this point to raise issues of evaluation as they relate to instructional management and improvement. The chief point here, one that is not always understood and faithfully practiced by school administrators, is that continuous assessment of results or outcomes is a management or leadership process. An effective executive is constantly trying to assess the results or outcomes of his or her instructional programs with a view toward adjusting them to better achieve the goals of the organization. One cannot properly manage an operation without attempting to assess its results and then using the data generated by that assessment to modify or improve the operation. That is what the evaluation system used by the Northfield public schools, which is briefly described later in this chapter, is all about—using assessment data to improve the management and performance of an organization (called "formative" evaluation by specialists in the field of evaluation).

Evaluation specialists have a tendency to wrap us up in statistics and methodology because that is what the universities teach when they teach evaluation. Universities seem to place most emphasis on "rigorous" statistical methodology and "hard" empirical findings and less emphasis on areas where empirical evidence or statistical techniques are not so helpful, such as in addressing the value-laden questions of what ought to be evaluated, why, and by what criteria. School executives, however, must focus on the managerial action aspects of assessment— and provide a "hands on" approach to identifying what is to be evaluated, what the criteria and goals are for the evaluation, and how results are to be used. A good professional evaluator can only be a staff assistant in these matters. Choose one who facilitates a process for framing and answering these kinds of questions but does not give you *the* answers.

In evaluating performance, the same general concept presented in the Chapter Five discussion of market research applies. That is, do not ask questions unless you have some plan in advance for classifying and interpreting the answers and for taking actions based on the kinds of answers you may receive. It is important that one formulate this plan well in advance of obtaining the answers. Assessment of results should be an ongoing and natural process performed as a matter of course in the act of leading and managing. Some of the questions that one might raise in designing a process for assessing outcomes of an instructional program, a new activity, a grade level, a school, or the entire school system are as follows:

- What are the objectives? Who cares about these objectives, and by what criteria will they assess the achievement of these objectives?
- What observable kinds of results will indicate that each criterion is being fulfilled?
- What changes or adjustments in goals, activities, or programs should be made as a result of this assessment?
- Are the school system's current goals and energies being directed toward those activities that seem to have the best chance of helping the system achieve its major purposes for its major stakeholders?
- Have the relevant stakeholders been involved in the design of the assessment process?
- At this stage of development, does one assess the process, the content, or the outcomes of the activity being evaluated?

(Stufflebeam and Shinkfield, 1983, discuss what they call the CIPP model, which breaks down the items to be assessed into *c*ontext, *i*nput, *p*rocess, and *p*roduct and which can provide a framework for evaluation.)
- How and to whom will the results be reported, and how will they be used?

Obviously, management of a program is more than just evaluation and assessment. It also involves the ability to take productive action to see that goals and objectives are being constantly reviewed and revised by the relevant people when appropriate. Performing this task typically includes applying a variety of techniques and skills related to human interpersonal interactions. Finally, good program management means making sure that the concerns and issues identified in the ongoing assessment process are addressed. This involves developing action plans, establishing timetables, and monitoring processes for task completion. It is much easier to accomplish this last crucial management step when those who must see to it that the goals of a program are achieved have a strong commitment to those goals.

Another important function of evaluation is quality control, which can be aided through both formative (improvement-oriented) and summative (oriented to making judgments as to absolute value or adequacy of performance level) processes. Employing the Theory Y assumptions and participative methods, one would tend to use formative evaluation processes such as those used in the Northfield schools example described below. Summative evaluation is the sole focus in an organization that operates with Theory X assumptions. On the other hand, summative evaluation is needed in any kind of an organization to make sure programs and delivery processes are on track in responding to real needs of constituencies and in facilitating the accomplishments of organizational goals and mission.

If a school system is to be effective in controlling quality, someone in the district organization must be conversant with the latest research and methods in teaching and learning and in curriculum and instruction so that appropriate summative evaluation guidelines can be employed. The superintendent, if not so trained, must be willing and able to listen to that person and give quality of instruction a prominent place in the operations strategy of the system. The superintendent is a general manager who must know how to employ, coordinate, and direct the work of specialists.

Evaluation as an Improvement Tool

A great deal is being written about evaluation as an improvement device. For improvement-oriented evaluation to be acceptable to the evaluatee, so that it can be properly used for improvement, there must be a level of trust and communication that is usually associated with Theory Y assumptions operating in something akin to Ouchi's (1981) Theory Z type of organization (that is, one that has a long-run view of its work and achievements). To the extent that people trust that the system will not be "used" on them as a punitive device, they can feel free to discuss their own strengths and weaknesses, successes and failures in an atmosphere that allows them to learn and improve from the knowledge such discussion can provide.

What is being recommended here and in some of the evaluation literature is a process that focuses on learning, growth, and improvement rather than merely on exposing poor performance. To install such a system requires patience and discipline. The data gathered in such a system cannot be used as evidence for someone's dismissal. Alternatively, such data should not be used directly to justify promotion or salary increases for one person over another—certainly not as the sole piece of evidence. School districts that are successful with improvement-oriented evaluation processes maintain a completely separate system and data file for collecting information on probationary teachers or for assessing someone whom they feel should be considered for termination for cause and still another separate system for making salary and promotion decisions.

For example, the Northfield school system in Minnesota has two completely separate processes for evaluating teachers— one improvement oriented and the other judgmental or summative in nature. These are described in a case written for use in the Bush Public School Executive Fellows Program (Schultz and Mauriel, 1981). Most of the teachers in Northfield are evaluated according to the improvement-oriented process. The successful development of this process required a great deal of trust on the part of the administrators that teachers could and would come up with useful ideas for improving teaching and the school system's performance.

The Northfield teachers and the administration developed the criteria for good teaching and then agreed on what observable behavioral indicators evidenced the existence of those criteria in a teacher's performance. Then they developed an observational system that involves for each teacher the use of an administrator and a fellow teacher of the evaluatee's choice who observe and give feedback on that teacher's classroom performance. Subsequent steps involve joint goal setting with the teacher and then further observation. The system was introduced over a three-year period, with a good deal of teacher involvement and as much choice as possible for the teachers on matters such as the selection of observers, times for observation, and goals to be set. One absolute requirement from the start, however, was that each teacher involved in the process had to identify and pursue *at least one instructional improvement goal* per year.

One reason that the improvement-oriented process was accepted by virtually the entire Northfield teaching staff is that in the first year only volunteers were used, and trust and commitment were allowed to build gradually over time. Another factor in the success of the process is that administrators are assessed by their peers and superiors in a similar manner and also required to have at least one of their goals directed to instruction.

Perhaps the three most important factors in Northfield's success are that teachers were heavily involved in determining the criteria and indicators of good teaching performance; the administrator who introduced and guided the process is someone the teachers trust; and the school district uses a second and completely separate process for probationary and summative evaluation.

Tenured teachers who have major deficiencies in performance are first given an opportunity to learn and change by means of the improvement-oriented evaluation process described above. If after several years of establishing improvement goals to correct major deficiencies and if after receiving staff development opportunities such a teacher is still not able to perform up to minimum standards, he or she is moved from the improvement-oriented process to the summative evaluation process.

The most important policy and rule here is that *no data collected in the improvement-oriented process are permitted in the file gathered for dismissal purposes.* Those data are locked up and not available to the superintendent or anyone wishing to use them for punitive purposes. Knowing that the data cannot effectively be used against them makes staff members feel much freer to be open and honest in identifying weaknesses or problems, working to overcome them, and truly focusing on professional improvement. (The reader may obtain more information on the Northfield case by writing to the Bush Public School Executive Fellows Program, 1884 Como Avenue, St. Paul, Minnesota 55108, or writing directly to the Northfield Public Schools, Northfield, Minnesota 55057.)

Operations Management of Quality Control

In essence, when discussing evaluation, I am talking about one means of checking on quality. Quality is very difficult to measure in education. Yet that should not stop administrators from making every effort to assess the quality and atmosphere in every learning station in their school system. In going to the moon, zero defects was the goal. In manufacturing processes, achieving less than a 2 percent rejection rate can be so costly that it makes the difference between a company's profit and loss. Can we afford even a 1 percent rejection rate when it comes to the growth and development of children? A school can say that the raw material is defective or that improper use or care outside of the school system is the cause of most learning failures, but the school system must do everything it can to ensure that it is contributing as much as possible to the growth and development of all children. This puts quite a burden on schools, but society asks the education system to bear that burden.

How is quality assessed? Tests, tests, and more tests? That is only part of the check. Other means of assessment, such as looking at affective measures, the self-concept of children, and the confidence and skill that students display in communicating both orally and in writing, must also be employed. Even though most professionals cannot measure quality exactly, they can recognize good teaching and supportive teachers. In most schools, there is a great deal of agreement on who the better teachers are and who the less than good teachers are. The tougher question is what do we do about it? How do we prevent or minimize poor quality instruction in our schools?

There are no magic answers to this question. We can say that good operations management includes assessment on a regular basis of every work station in the education provision process. We can also suggest that an administrator meet with each teacher at least once a year to discuss the assessment of the quality of the educational outcomes being achieved. For most teachers, some improvement-oriented evaluation process such as that described earlier in the Northfield example can be used. But for teachers who are believed to have really serious deficiencies, alternative approaches may be in order. If extensive help has already been given or offered to such a teacher and major deficiencies persist, then perhaps it is time for the kind of summative evaluation that moves toward transfer or dismissal of the teacher (or the administrator if he or she is the source of the problem).

In order to ascertain whether the administrator is a contributing factor in any deficient teaching performance, it is necessary to have all performance reviews assessed by someone at a higher level in the hierarchy. This means that each review of a teacher performed by a principal should be examined or questioned by the principal's supervisor. If goals are clearly stated and evaluation and improvement processes are in place, then quality control can take place in the manner described, even though this is not an easy activity. Like performance appraisal, quality control is a job that administrators too often avoid.

Evaluation as a Change Device

The chief way that a person at the top of an organization can effect change is by understanding and influencing the culture. Culture is shaped by and reflected in the symbols and stories that are passed around in the organization, the deeply held beliefs that express the personal values of the organization's leaders, both informal and formal leaders, and by the value placed on and the rewards given to the actions and results most esteemed by the organization's influential members. In providing leadership for the operations or instructional function, the superintendent must be aware of the key role the principal plays in instruction and its management. Working through the principal, the superintendent can raise a number of questions about the staff development activities and about each school's teaching staff with respect to instructional methods and processes. Further, the superintendent can support activities that seem to enhance the ability of the school to improve its instructional delivery processes. The superintendent can do this by supporting appropriate staff development programs and also introducing improvement-oriented staff evaluation processes and encouraging their use in guiding changes in instructional methods. The superintendent uses speeches and symbolic gestures that reflect the worth and value the school system places on effective instruction.

In establishing goals for instructional improvement, one must consider both process and content issues. Parents, administrators, and teachers must be carefully involved. Adopting Theory Y assumptions about people and their motivation will be helpful to a superintendent who wishes to follow this advice. The superintendent who holds Theory Y beliefs finds it natural to involve building administrators, teachers, and parents and to give them the information they need to be effective contributors to the process of establishing overall educational goals for the school system. Where appropriate, administrators, teachers, and parents will then work together to develop programs for achieving instructional objectives. Administrators must see that the goals and the monitoring systems for assessing performance against those goals are established. But the goals should be set jointly with relevant key actors—those who must achieve the goals involved—with improvement as the focus and with the school system's mission and purposes as the direction. The role of the superintendent is constantly to remind all groups of the desired overall direction for the school system and the implications of various alternative courses of action and to see to it that the process is adaptable but that the progress is continuous and directed.

The superintendent must also be concerned with the content. One cannot assume that just because a good process is in place, good content or substance will follow. The content of goals should include some effort at increasing the attainment of more broadly defined educational outcomes than mere standardized test scores. (See Chapter Eleven for a discussion of other measures for assessing the overall performance of the school system.) Moreover, the superintendent must insist that the final goals have attainment deadlines, be realistic, be challenging, and incorporate the latest in educational knowledge and technology and client needs.

Evaluation and reward systems are an integral part of the management process. They must be ongoing and responsive to the changing circumstances in which the school system finds itself. The ideal to strive for is intrinsic motivation and reward. Realistically, however, extrinsic signs and symbols must also be a part of the overall system. In the case of evaluation and assessment, various constituents must also be involved in shaping the criteria and indicators and providing data on the proper functioning of the system.

In short, the superintendent must thoughtfully and in a variety of ways involve each constituency in the process of instructional improvement, educational delivery, and program management (for example, information giving, information seeking, input for decision making, joint decision making) and be clear about which of these ways he or she is using. The superintendent must know when and to what degree to involve each group and be able to guide several kinds of processes for assessment, goal setting, and problem solving without stifling those processes. If the focus is on improvement rather than punitive judgment, then there is a higher probability that success will ensue.

This chapter, rather than dealing with the technical aspects of instructional management and supervision, has dealt briefly with how the superintendent can effectively influence the process of instructional delivery and improvement. Chapter Ten deals with the leadership processes for introducing overall organizational *change*. One obvious change is the kind needed in a system that wants to significantly alter the quality of its teaching, learning, and instructional efforts.

PART THREE

Evaluating and Revising the Strategy

The final part of this book deals with examining, assessing, and changing the strategy. The leadership skills required for introducing change are vital components in the toolbox of a strategic manager. How to understand and influence change is the subject of Chapter Ten. The discussion in that chapter examines the kinds of leadership methods and approaches that are critical when there is a need for major strategic change—times such as many school districts may face today. While some schools may not see the need to move beyond the generic option A noted in Chapter Six—continuing to provide the same general services to the same general populations but finding ways to do it better—others may want to examine this chapter carefully as their strategy formulation efforts point them to option B or C or toward a major restructuring possibility such as described by option D, E, F, or G.

One cannot know whether the status quo or a major change provides the better strategic direction for tomorrow until one has some data on present performance. Whether a major strategic change is called for or fine-tuning the present strategy is the goal, all school systems need to carefully assess the performance results of their strategic pursuits. Chapter Eleven discusses accountability, assessment, and the reporting of results. Chapter Twelve—the last chapter of this final section—delineates the next steps in the continuous process of strategy formulation and implementation.

The formulation, pursuit, assessment, and adjustment of the strategy are ongoing and interactive processes.

10

Leading School Systems Through Transitions

by Barbara Benedict Bunker

Change and change management are lively topics for today's school administrators. When we talk about changing the direction or culture of large organizations such as school systems, the situation becomes more complex. Not only are individuals involved but so, too, are groups and systems. Not only is internal motivation involved, but external forces also create internal pressures for the organization to change.

There is an emerging consensus that effective change begins with a clear vision of where the organization is going, what kind of place it wants to be, what business it is really in. Schools are places where, historically, change has emerged in reaction to forces in the environment. Now school systems face the challenge of learning to become proactive, of planning and creating their own future.

Missions, Visions, Goals, Strategies, and Tactics

As noted in Chapter One, a difficulty in the planning world of today stems from the way terms are used to mean many different things. This is particularly true of words such as *mission, strategic vision, goals* and *purpose*. Are these things the same, or do they have two very different conceptual meanings?

261

While it might be helpful for each person to define carefully what he or she means by *vision* or *mission*, it may not solve the problem. It is useful to describe these terms as indicating that we are working at one of several different levels of both abstraction and practicality (see Figure 6).

Figure 6. A Personal Strategic Plan.

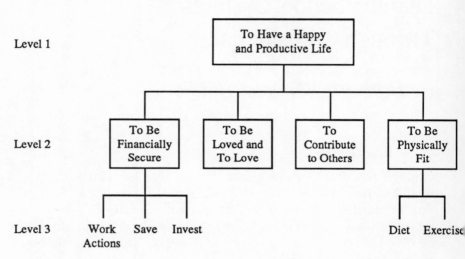

Let us take, for example, our own aspirations for the future and agree that our desire is to have a happy and productive life. "To have a happy and productive life" is a very general statement. It could apply to almost anyone. It represents values about what is important. It speaks to the heart as well as the head and is at level 1 in Figure 6. It is what many call "vision." Some people believe that a vision statement should be crisp, so short and pithy that everyone can state and remember it. It is a *future that we are excited about creating.* The values in the vision statement itself have the capacity to *enroll* people! "If your vision statement sounds like motherhood and apple pie and is somewhat embarrassing, you are on the right track," says Peter Block (1987) in *The Empowered Manager.*

Many organizations also want to express their preferred future in relation to their own business. For example, "Hallmark: When You Care Enough to Send the Very Best," "The Final Word in Vodka," and "The Best Little Whorehouse in Texas" are all statements of organizational missions (visions translated into the organizations' framework), statements of what business each organization is in and how each expects to be viewed in its marketplace.

The previous illustration of strategic planning in Golden Valley described a process that rationally considers both external threats and opportunities and internal resources and deficits. This clearly is essential. However, in recent years organizations have been including an additional step: considering what stakeholders want their schools to be like three to five years (or some other period of time) in the future. This picture of a "preferred future" is influenced by the environmental trend analysis, but it often contains other ideas and values as well. It provides positive energy for change along with rational analysis.

In order to realize future aspirations, people develop more concrete purposes that will move them in that direction. At the second level (see Figure 6), then, we may decide that the way to have a happy and productive life is to become financially secure, to love and be loved, to contribute to others, and to be physically fit. In other words, we develop a series of goals or purposes specific to each of us that can guide our behavior.

Organizations also define purposes for realizing their future. For example, many of Peters and Waterman's (1982) eight characteristics of excellent organizations could easily be used as purposes for organizations that aspire to being excellent. "Close to the customer," "productivity through people," and "a bias for action" could all be purpose statements. In the Golden Valley case, providing a safe neighborhood school for its K–6 students could be defined as such a purpose.

At the third level are the specific activities that we believe will help us achieve our goals. These are often called strategies. They are the "what," the "how," and the "when" of strategic planning or strategy implementation. Thus, in order to be financially secure, we work, we save, we invest. In order to be fit, we may adopt an eating program and an exercise regime. When our preferred future is several years away, our specific activities represent the annual plan for the ways we will work toward our mission in the current year. In this way, it is possible to "plan backward" from a target year, say, 1993, and identify activities that need to occur in each of the intervening years in order to achieve our mission in 1993. These activities constitute the strategy for each year.

Goals or purposes (the two are used interchangeably here) are action targets for the outcomes that we want. One useful device for moving from purpose to strategy is to state the purpose, for example, "to be close to our customers," and then add, "and that means . . . ." What comes next are action steps that we will use to achieve the purpose. At some level, all of this is common sense, but the verbal battles that break out over these terms waste energy and time. What is important is to establish some agreement about the various levels and to be clear about which level is being worked on at any particular time.

The major purpose of this chapter is to discuss the management of school systems that are in the process of changing direction, or purposes, or culture. These are major undertakings that do not occur in a single year. The manager of the change process has to think in longer-range terms. The principles that govern the management of change are very similar whether at the individual, group, or organizational level. In large-scale change efforts, change must occur at all these levels.

Systems Change and the Need for Transition Management

One of the most common mistakes leaders of change efforts make is not managing the transitional state between the current reality and the future that is planned and envisioned. The task of leadership should be to spearhead this transition (see Figure 7). Leading a change effort means understanding where the organization is right now (A)—for example, by means of an internal audit, problem identification process, or something else. It also means developing a clear description of where the organization wants to be (C), as just described in the discussion of mission and vision. In order to get from the present reality to the future state, the organization must pass through a transition state (B) (Beckhard and Harris, 1977).

Figure 7. Organizational Change as a Transition State.

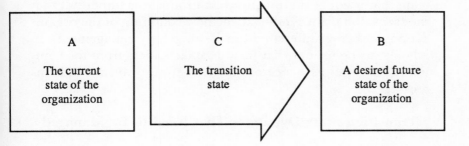

Source: Adapted from Beckhard and Harris, 1977.

In the transition state, people know that change is planned, future goals gradually become clear, and plans are made for how to achieve those goals. This period is not a stable one in the life of the organization or its people. However exciting the opportunities the future may hold, moving away from the known toward the unknown makes people anxious and concerned. The nature of the problems in a transition period, along with some recommendations for how to deal with them, are discussed in the next section. Here it is enough to underline the need to manage this period of time in different ways, not as business as usual.

Managing the transition state first means understanding that it is a state in itself that needs a particular strategy. Second, it means creating an appropriate structure to pay attention and do the managing. This often involves setting up some type of steering committee or task force comprised of representatives of all parts of the system. If the group is broadly representative, it can monitor how things are going, move to deal with problems, and create ways to facilitate the change. In the transition state, transition managers need a free flow of information about what is going on. They also need to share information with the system about what is planned and what is happening.

Sometimes the transition team is the top management of the organization, the superintendent's cabinet, for example. Where this is the choice, special care must be given to creating and monitoring linkages with the entire organization. In any case, it is helpful to the realization of the distinctive task of this team that it not be an intact system group. It is important that the transition team symbolize the new condition of the organization by being different from its ongoing management. In schools, using groups that include stakeholders from the community as well as educators might be one way to send this message.

Transition State Dynamics That Need to Be Managed

In times of transition, three key issues need to be managed: power, anxiety, and control (Nadler, 1987).

Power. When change is imminent, jokes about the amount of time organizational chiefs spend politicking versus conducting their real work are often told and retold. This is symptomatic of the destabilization that change causes in organizations. Coalitions and centers of power are threatened. Individuals may be concerned about their jobs or their own power bases. One superintendent who had a reputation for being politically wise used to show up at local gatherings and community events, especially when the schools were about to embark on major new projects. His intimates kidded him about it, saying that his showing up was an indication that something new was brewing.

Politics is always part of organizational life, but when change occurs, it may overwhelm work and even the change effort itself. Therefore, the intelligent and experienced leader pays attention to political realities as part of the strategy of transition management. The first level of political leadership is to identify key players and stakeholders and get their support. One way to do this is to identify three levels of political clout: (1) those who can make the change happen, (2) those who can help it happen, and (3) those who can prevent it from happening. These individuals or groups then become the key targets for influence attempts.

Another useful approach is to ask (1) who has the power, (2) what their position is, and (3) how important the issue is to them. We know that people who have extreme positions are difficult to influence. We know that people to whom the issue is important are susceptible to influence. Thus, people who are interested in the issue and who have less than extreme positions predictably are the most likely targets of influence. Strategies for influencing these power holders are diverse. Some of the individuals may be influenced by being included in planning and decision making. Some may respond to negotiating and bargaining, to a form of quid pro quo, to cutting a deal. With others (particularly those who can block), the strategy might be to isolate or remove them from influence.

A second level of political leadership is to demonstrate and promote the change. That is, people must see the leaders themselves, the top group in the system, actively promoting and supporting the change. Leaders do this by articulating the vision in persuasive ways, by rewarding support, and by visibly, consistently, and energetically being in favor of the change. Bennis and Nanus (1985) studied leaders' behavior and found that those who displayed such characteristics were highly effective.

Leadership can be projected verbally in everything from inspirational addresses to casual conversation. It can be displayed nonverbally by behavioral example. And it can be demonstrated by consistency between what is said and done. Superintendents who say that schools should be advocates for young people, for example, and then consistently make decisions on the side of parents or teachers in disputes involving student rights will be read by their actions rather than their words. However important congruency is, even more important is the use of all available opportunities to be in touch with and influence people in the direction of the organization's vision and mission. Just showing up sends a message about what a leader considers important. What many leaders fail to mobilize is the power of symbols in the service of increasing their impact and emotional commitment to the project. Some examples may be helpful.

Metaphors can capture people's interest in the change. "Small is beautiful" is one example. An elementary school principal talked about his school as "the enchanted cottage," creating an image of a special place and time in which to create a special dream. When teachers arrived in September, they found the front hall painted with lovely murals and a school logo that elaborated the theme. Superintendents are frequently called upon to articulate the vision and mission of the organization. As stated earlier, it is popular to regard the gift of charismatic public speaking as inherited rather than learned. While this ability undeniably comes more easily for some than for others, the capacity to affect and engage people's emotions through public speaking can be cultivated. One does not have to be either religious or a black American to appreciate and learn from Martin Luther King's "I have a dream" speech. An analysis of that moving address reveals that King used images that are part of the fabric of America's history and wove traditional values with the situation of blacks and other oppressed people in the United States in the 1960s.

Anxiety. Ambiguity can create political uncertainty in transition periods. The anxiety that is released by change can be contagious. Rumors flourish and reach out to include everything and everyone unless concrete information is available. This is a time for leaders to be generous with information and even to risk being seen as repetitive. When people are anxious, they do not hear well.

What information is useful? People want to know what is going on, what is planned to change, and particularly what is not going to change. Any reassurance that leaders can give about job security is especially important. We all know of situations in which people believed erroneous information because it was the only thing they had heard on a subject. Core groups are frequently surprised and upset by what they hear about their efforts. The way to counter these tendencies is to plan and implement a comprehensive dissemination of information campaign, to provide multiple opportunities for discussions and questions in a supportive and open atmosphere.

With change comes uncertainty, with uncertainty comes anxiety. Anxiety can give rise to inaction, to constructive action, or to destructive action. Leaders of the change effort want to see that this emotional force works for them, not against them. What can they do?

Change is disruptive. It means that comfortable routines may be interrupted, and people feel anxious. Therefore, leaders should expect resistance to change. On the other hand, when people believe that something better will be the outcome of the temporary disruption, they usually control their resistance and cooperate with the change. The anxiety that is a natural part of change can work for or against the change. A leader's job is to channel it into positive motivation.

One theory of change requires that three elements be present if people are to respond constructively. First, there must be a clear vision or goal that sets the direction. Second, there must be dissatisfaction with the present situation so that motivation to change is present. Third, first action steps in the direction of the goal must be clear and available. That is, people must be able to do something that moves them toward the goal. These three critical factors must all be present and must outweigh the cost of change as people experience it (Beer, 1980).

Let us suppose, however, that everyone in the school district seems quite comfortable, if not happy, with the way things are. How can one lead a change effort? The first step must be to create tension and even dissatisfaction. There are a variety of ways to do this. The most traditional method is to ask people how they feel about their jobs, the school system, the working conditions. Surveys or interviews with school personnel can almost always be counted upon to produce issues and problems that need attention. When members of the district look over such data together, they will see the dissatisfaction of others, (if not their own), and the "problems" will become evident. Then task forces can be formed to address the problems and propose solutions for implementation. Social scientists call this process survey feedback. It is a common and effective change technology (see Nadler, 1977, for a step-by-step description).

Recently, it has become evident that dissatisfaction can also arise because there is tension between one's experience of the current situation and one's ideal or hoped for future reality. Teachers, for example, may be quite satisfied with their school until they visit an innovative school where values they cherish are being realized more fully. Social comparison processes begin to work and teachers begin to ask, "Why can't we do that?"

This means that their own aspirations have been raised and are creating a tension with their current state. Creating tension between the now and a preferred future is a positive motivational force toward change (Fritz, 1984). Whether one selects the problem-oriented or the future-oriented strategy, dissatisfaction is aroused to produce motivation for change. We now know that change is also a process that involves loss. Even positive changes such as a job promotion may involve loss. Think of the teachers who move into administration. How many try to maintain some classroom involvement? If teaching is one of their strongly held values, the promotion may involve grief over the loss of teaching as well as the pleasure of being recognized and promoted.

Peter Marris (1974), in his elegant book *Loss and Change*, describes the change process as one of value loss. He proposes that our values are realized in concrete attachments in life. Thus, we value close relationships and realize that value in friendships and marriage. He points out than when change occurs, we experience a loss of value when what we are really losing is the attachment or way the value is realized in the world (the value is still within us). Thus, when change occurs, we need time not only to grieve but also to regroup and reenergize ourselves to seek the realization of this value in other settings. For example, some school administrators continue to teach in voluntary community settings when their jobs no longer permit them to realize this value in the classroom.

Anyone who has closed a school building knows about the process of loss that comes with change. It has only been with the work of Elisabeth Kübler-Ross (1969) and her description of the stages of reaction to the process of dying that we have come to understand that change can in itself be a small death. Kübler-Ross notes that participants in the change may go through all of the stages of dealing with loss: denial, anger, bargaining, and acceptance. Any change effort must allow time and the psychological space for these processes to occur.

Understanding these processes can prompt school leaders who have to close a building, for example, to plan meaningful ceremonies that celebrate what occurred in the building and allow teachers to express and deal with their feelings of loss.

In one elementary school that closed after fifty years, the board told teachers that they could take from the building something they would like to have as a remembrance. Teachers took objects that had special meaning to them and symbolized their lives in that building. When this does not happen, readjustment takes much longer. When plants close abruptly, large parts of the work force have been known to show up for work for as long as a month after the official closing. The workers just stand around talking. Intellectually they know that the plant is closed, but psychologically they have not taken it in; they have not worked through the grieving process and come out the other side. In other cases, plants have created groups in which workers can talk about and deal with an impending closure. In these groups, people are helped to take next steps, such as putting together a résumé and planning a job search. In this kind of supportive environment, a positive transition is much more likely.

Control. Helping people manage their anxiety productively assists in reducing their resistance to change, but one must also tap their positive energy, which provides the motivation to move the process forward. To get people engaged and on board, leaders must make them feel that they have some control over the process, that they can influence it, that in part it is their show. This means that those who are affected by the change need to participate in creating the vision and managing the process. They need to own it, not feel like victims of a process that is beyond their control.

Participation is a tricky process. It is not always possible to throw open the doors and invite the general populace to determine its own fate. Leaders tend, however, to err in the direction of being too conservative, of consulting with and involving others too little and too late. Some fear that they will lose control of the direction. Whatever the situation, it is important to realize that one can still be in control while allowing others to actively participate and engage the issues.

The rationale presented here is for situations of major organizational change in which it is natural for people to be anxious. The general literature on participation in decision making, especially in education settings, has concerned itself with participation in a variety of different formats (for example, mandated versus voluntary, formal versus informal, and direct versus indirect) and with different qualities of the process, such as the content, degree, and scope of the participation (see Conway, 1984). Thus, this literature covers a much broader spectrum of participative events than concerns us here. In this broader literature, there appears to be an underlying set of assumptions based on a human relations hypothesis that runs something like this: If people are involved in decisions, they will be happier. If they are happier, they will be more motivated to work productively. If they work more productively, they will produce more results—that is, participation leads to satisfaction and satisfaction leads to productivity and productivity leads to results that the system values (Miller, 1980). But research on participation is more complex than this. It appears, for example, that having clear goals may be equally important to participation in bringing about change. Furthermore, satisfaction has a great deal to do with the content of the decision that one is asked to be part of as well as with how involved one is in the decision.

One way to think about this is suggested in Vroom and Yetton's (1978) decision-making model. The authors describe three major types of decision-making processes. Authoritarian decisions are made by the decision maker without consultation that others are aware of. Consultative decisions are made by the decision maker but with a great deal of input and the opportunity to influence either in one-on-one situations or in group meetings with the decision maker. Consensual decisions are made by groups, with every member having an equal say. In this form of decision making, leaders essentially give away their power to the group of trusted agents (or participate with them on an equal footing). The group then attempts to make plans and decisions that meet the members' requirements. Rather than trying to persuade each other of the rightness of their own views, members of consensus-seeking groups search for a solution that is acceptable to all members. The work of the group is to find or create that solution.

Both consultative and consensual methods involve participation. Both can successfully meet needs for control and influence. The secret is to select the appropriate method and to use it well. Consensus is used when one has time, when the decision is very important, and when people's collaboration and support are needed. Creating a vision, for example, takes time and is often done through an iterative consensual process. (However, this is certainly not the only way to create a vision. Under circumstances of very low morale, for example, the leader may need to put forth a vision that enrolls people enough to generate their energy for becoming involved.) Planning and implementing activities often go very well when they are worked on in a consultative way.

Another way to think about participation is to ask, "At what point(s) in the change process do we want participation?" An old laboratory training exercise called the hollow square exercise illustrates the central issue here. Two teams, the planners and the operators, are assigned tasks. The planners are asked to plan how an eighteen-piece puzzle in the shape of a square with a hollow center should be assembled by the operating team. The operators each receive some of the pieces but do not see the diagram of the puzzle, which only the planners have. The operators' job is to assemble the puzzle as fast as possible and beat other teams working on the same task.

The planners are told that they can involve the operators at any time, but they may not show them the diagram. Planners meet in one room; operators wait in another. Usually, the planners wait until the last minute to invite the operators in. They are so busy trying to figure out what to do and how to do it that it never occurs to them to involve the operators in the early stages. Then when they do get ready to hand over the process, there are usually difficulties that would never have occurred with more time and communication.

Sometimes leaders may want everyone's involvement from the beginning. At other times in change projects, environmental constraints, legal requirements, organizational morale, or other factors may cause leaders to involve people after the initial steps or the parameters have been set. In one early and classic study (Coch and French, 1948), the management of a factory determined that there would be a change in the technology of manufacturing, but the workers were given the opportunity to determine how the change would be instituted, the order in which it would occur, the time schedule, and so on.

Notice that there are opportunities for participation at every new stage in the change process: in the early stages of diagnosis, in goal setting, in the search for solutions, in planning and implementation, and in evaluation. One caveat: Participation is not a gimmick. Inviting participation when one has already decided or when the issues are not open to change can only lead to anger and mistrust. Genuine collaboration, on the other hand, can be the force that makes the change take hold and live. It leads to better decisions and solutions through the utilization of the full resources of the organization.

School executives today often do involve a variety of groups in policy issues that affect them and the schools. However, if the reason is just to make people feel better because they have had a chance to talk about the issues, this behavior over time will not lower resistance to change and sustain feelings of motivation to enact the changes. Customers are very sensitive to whether they are really being taken seriously and their input used. There is a danger in many school settings of automatically creating groups to discuss issues without clearly formulating their role or determining how their input will be used. Participation under such circumstances may backfire. Working in groups takes energy, and even though more extroverted people may be stimulated by working with others, feelings of saturation that occur with too much participation are documented in research.

Different types of problems also require different approaches. When an issue has general support and acceptance, one may question the necessity of much participation in the decision. This may be an opportunity for the superintendent to provide leadership by making the decision. Implementation issues, however, may well be managed participatively.

Forces That Promote or Inhibit Change

Kurt Lewin's (1951) seminal work on change, *Field Theory in Social Science*, provides the theory base for much of today's thinking about change processes. His notion of the force field analysis that he borrowed from physics is helpful in thinking about how to get leverage and produce change. Lewin believed that people work in a setting that is a field of forces. Within that field, they are most comfortable when a balance or equilibrium or the status quo exists. When people try to create change, they disturb the equilibrium and release forces that strive for a new balance (this is true for individuals, groups, and organizations). In this situation, two types of forces are in operation. Driving forces help bring about change, and restraining forces inhibit action. Lewin believed that it is more effective to try to decrease the restraining forces because doing so will permit the natural driving forces to have more sway. (See Weisbord, 1987, for more information.) Force field analysis is often employed during a problem-solving sequence to generate action strategies. Here it is used to indicate two ways of thinking about action. There are actions that drive change, and there are actions that reduce restraining forces.

Creating the Momentum for Change

Bolman and Deal (1984) identify four different lenses or perspectives through which to view organizations—structural, human resource, political, and symbolic. These same four perspectives can be used to generate ideas about creating momentum for organizational change.

As individuals, leaders are apt to have a preference for one perspective. However, it is the world views with which they are least comfortable that they should work with most actively. These are the areas where they are likely to stumble. Although leaders may already know of these perspectives, they do not naturally think about them as they plan. The four models are a useful tool for reminding leaders of what they already know but are likely to forget.

The Structural Perspective. The structural perspective looks first at the mission and goals of the organization. In major organizational transformations, these may change. The first task is to be very clear about the organization's mission and goals. Then the structuralist asks whether the current structure supports the new mission and goals, how well the structure can do the job, and what needs to change. The structuralist views this structure (roles, rules, procedures, technology, information flows, and control systems) as the primary barrier to change. It must be thoroughly reviewed and a new structure that is congruent with the new direction must be devised and implemented.

The Human Resource Perspective. The focus of change in the human resource model is the fit between people and the organization. Change is hindered when people in the organization do not support it, do not understand it, or lack the skills to implement it. Therefore, from this perspective, once the change goals are clear, the first step is to specify the human resources required for effective implementation. Then it is necessary to test the fit between the new direction and existing human systems. This is done through extensive communication that seeks reactions and suggestions from those currently in place. The change strategy is developed participatively, under the assumption that those who must support and implement must be involved in the decisions. In addition, training must be provided for new roles or requirements created by the change.

The Political Perspective. The focus of change in the political model is any shift in the distribution of power that signals a new coalition or new set of values dominating the organizational agenda. From the political perspective, the biggest danger is that change agents may overestimate their own power and underestimate the power of the potential opposition. The strategy, therefore, is to be realistic and make an assessment of who the stakeholders are and what power they have as compared with one's own. The process is to build alliances and coalitions with those who can be persuaded to give support and to minimize the opposition of those who may not be immediately convinced. A rule of thumb in this model is to persuade first, negotiate second, and coerce only if necessary. This is very well articulated in Davidson's (1987) treatment of the superintendency, especially his advice on dealing with boards, the media, and the community.

The Symbolic Perspective. From the symbolic perspective, organizational life is a drama in which all are actors. Change, then, is a rewrite of the script that underlies this drama. As in all drama, a decent script, competent actors, and the audience's willingness to believe are necessary. Attention must be directed to creating a credible script that updates old symbols into a new vision that creates belief and hope for those inside and outside the organization.

The change strategy is to create a vision that attracts energy and enthusiasm and that links the organization's past, present, and future. This vision and the actions needed to achieve it are most effectively communicated through symbols—for example, by telling stories or using logos, graphics, slogans, and signs. Taking visible actions that dramatize the new direction is especially effective. Visibility is created by appearing where one is least expected, rewarding heroes of the revolution, and conspicuously violating outdated traditions.

Creating ceremonies to communicate the new direction and rally the troops is also symbolically important. Leaders need to show up often at meetings, seminars, and pep rallies that promote the new vision and its implementation. They also need to reward those who are making a similar effort in ways that make clear in which direction the parade is going.

Providing Support for Letting Go

Robert Tannenbaum (Tannenbaum, Margulies, Massarik, and Associates, 1985) suggests that the internal personal experience of dealing with change is like the experience of being a trapeze artist. There you are up at the top of the circus tent holding on to your trapeze and swinging back and forth in wider and wider arcs. This is your present, and it is known and familiar. But soon you will be expected to let go of your present and familiar bar and sail out into the future, trusting that another bar will be there for you to grab and hold. The spotlight is on you. You cannot see the new bar to which you are going until you let go of the one you are now holding. The problem of resistance to change is the problem of holding on and letting go. Particularly, it is the problem of letting go of the present before you can see what the future will be like.

We have already discussed in some depth two strategies that help individuals let go and move into a new future. The first is participation that increases the sense of control people feel they have over what is about to happen. The second is taking seriously the sense of loss that people experience when life changes and they leave behind attachments that represent important values. A third way of helping people cope with change is to reduce the stress they feel by attending to their need for social support. People with strong support networks are less affected by and better able to cope with stress in their lives than those without such networks.

Support comes in many forms. When a teacher takes a job in a new school, for example, he may need support from social isolation. That is, he may need people to talk to, to have lunch with, to ask questions of. When a district staff member is overloaded because of the illness of a co-worker, she may need someone to offer an extra pair of hands to help out with work she cannot finish alone. When a superintendent has a difficult dilemma to confront, he may need a close personal friend outside the district to use as a sounding board to listen to his thinking. When a superintendent is applying to a new district for the top job, she may need to know how she stacks up against the other candidates, where they are seen as strong and where she believes her own weaknesses lie. This kind of support can only be given by someone who has the competence to assess work at that level, a senior person in the field. The kinds of needs people have determine the kind of support that is effective. People's needs are different at different times in their lives. Their support system should be relevant to their current needs.

When planning for change in a school system, leaders must diagnose the kinds of support people are apt to need. One way to do this is to ask people what they are experiencing. Sometimes just having a group with whom they can talk openly about what they are experiencing makes a huge difference. At other times, people may be facing a future in which what they know how to do is inadequate. In this situation, leaders can give support by directing them to retraining sources. In any event, the steering committee or core group managing the change can give careful attention to people's different needs for support during transitional times. Creating networks, providing for extra services, and giving emotional support can be crucially effective in dealing with the normal resistance that change creates.

Practical Guides for Working with Transition Structures

As indicated earlier, steering committees, task forces, and ad hoc groups of all kinds are characteristic of transitional periods. Elementary staff, secondary staff, district administrators, curricular departments, building administrators, and department heads are all concerned in any major change in a school system, and they may or may not have different interests. Much of the participation in planning the new while maintaining the old happens in these teams and groups.

How does one create and build an effective work team, whether just for the transition period or for some permanent function? Common wisdom says that success rests in finding the right people. This is true to a point, but it is not the whole story. What is needed first is the district's own model of effective team functioning. Hackman (1987) calls this a normative model, that is, a model of the conditions that lead to effective group functioning. His normative model of group effectiveness provides a guide for creating new groups and working with old ones.

Hackman's model (see Figure 8) proposes that an effective work group is a function of (1) the level of effort that the members exert in doing their task, (2) the amount of knowledge and skill that they bring to bear on their task, and (3) the selection of appropriate ways to do their task. Leaders who think about these factors before they create committees and task forces can help to ensure a naturally developing effectiveness. Specifically, there are issues under each assumption that deserve attention.

Conditions That Support Effort. Norms (the unspoken rules that govern group behavior) about how hard a group works

Figure 8. Overview of the Normative Model of Group Effectiveness.

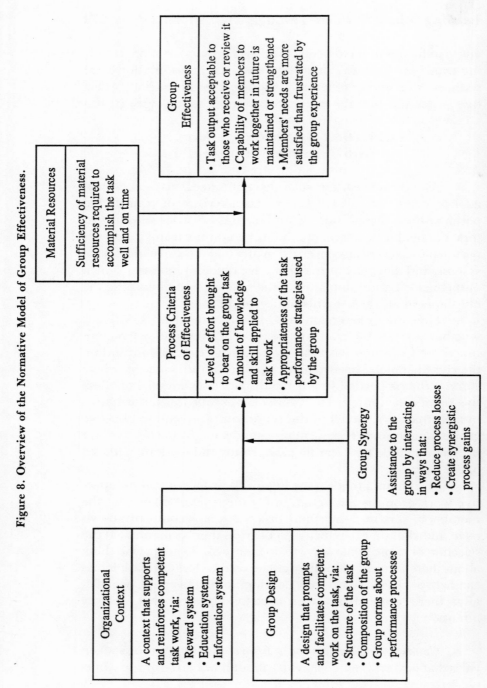

Source: J. Richard Hackman, "The Design of Work Teams," in Jay W. Lorsch, editor, HANDBOOK OF ORGANIZATIONAL BEHAVIOR, © 1987, p. 331. Reprinted by permission of Prentice-Hall, Inc., Englewood Cliffs, New Jersey.

are usually a response to the group task and the work situation. Therefore, whole and meaningful tasks with visible outcomes that have real consequences for real people, including group members, are apt to be motivating. Furthermore, when the organization itself rewards the work that is being done and when the group knows how it is progressing on its task (that is, it gets good feedback), motivation will be enhanced. Leaders should give careful thought to what they are charging groups to do and create tasks that have the kind of properties that will engage members. When a school is trying to make changes in the organizational climate, for example, a steering committee whose task is to manage the change process has a challenging whole task with high potential payoff.

On the other hand, having a long-range planning committee design a questionnaire, as was done in the Golden Valley case, is a poor task for a group. Some tasks are better done by individuals and then reacted to by the accountable body. Anyone who has tried to write documents in committee knows that people's style preferences clash and soon the group becomes frustrated because of individual differences either in what content should be included or in how it should be expressed. *Process loss* is a term used to describe the dysfunction that can sometimes occur in groups when they do not function well. Interpersonal conflict, poor leader initiative, and social versus work norms are examples of processes that detract from rather than enhance the primary task of the group.

In creating new groups, the aim is to minimize process losses. Groups that are too large for everyone to have a responsible part of the action often experience what has been called "social loafing" (Latane, Williams, and Harkins, 1979). This occurs when there is diffusion of responsibility as groups get larger and members reduce their individual efforts. Deciding the right size of a group to carry out the task is important. Generally, when one asks a group to work on a task because one wants to bring a variety of resources to it, five people is the smallest-size group that one should consider. With fewer than five, the dynamics become quite different, with special coalition problems that can be difficult (two against one or two against two). A number between five and nine is optimal because it is not too large for creative face-to-face interaction, yet it is also not so small that it is poor in resources. How big a job the actual task is should determine the size. It is better to start small and add subgroups to do delegated work than to let the group itself become too large.

Groups are also potentially synergistic; they can create process gains. When we talk about a sports team being "on a roll," for example, we are describing the synergy that creates process gains, that makes a group more than the sum of its members. Another example of this phenomenon is the musical group that "takes off" in performance, and both the performers and the audience know that something special is happening. Project teams can also experience this kind of excitement, an experience of being in high gear, of giving their all for an important mission, of having endless energy, of doing hard work that looks effortless. While we do not know how to make this "magic" happen, we do know that attention to the way the group is structured and to the organizational context creates the most promising conditions.

Conditions That Support Knowledge and Skill. In designing groups, choosing the right members in the right numbers is very important. Political considerations often lead to the creation of representative committees that do not have enough gifted members to perform the task successfully. These same considerations also result in groups that are too large (in order not to leave out any stakeholder). While political concerns may be satisfied, the optimal functioning of the group is jeopardized. In looking again at the Golden Valley long-range planning committee, one can ask whether it had too many people with too many different interests to create a functional working group. While the committee did, after several years, finally get its job done, what saved the process for Golden Valley was that the final decision and its implementation were undertaken by the superintendent and the board, a seven-person group that contained a good blend of talents and skills and was perceived by the community as being competent and representative.

The optimal group includes people with enough diversity to be stimulating to each other but not so much that they cannot understand each other. It is also important to consider members' ability to work collaboratively. Group tasks are facilitated when members have interpersonal competence as well as task competence. As the group comes to appreciate the different knowledge and skill of each member, it can resourcefully encourage members to contribute their expertise and the members can learn from each other synergistically.

Conditions That Support Appropriate Performance Strategies. The issue here is to set up a way of working that maximizes getting the job done well. Hackman believes that three factors increase the probability that this will be the case. First, within the group itself, there need to be norms that allow the group to regulate member behavior. If there is anarchy, it is improbable that tasks will be accomplished effectively. In addition, the group must have norms that support strategic planning. Most groups just plunge into their task and somehow work out ways to do it. The best task forces step back and spend some time considering and debating how they will proceed. They plan the process they will use, often considering and weighing several alternative ways of proceeding. For the more action oriented group members, this early failure to jump into action is frustrating, and they rail against it. However, if the group can tolerate the frustration and control member behavior, the results of taking time to plan are usually very productive. Leaders who structure a process for planning how to proceed into a group's early work help the group do its work more effectively.

Second, the group needs an information system that provides plenty of data from and about the organization so that it can judge the situation and evaluate possible solutions. It is common to assume that if a school building has a representative on a committee, for example, all the information needed about that building will be present. Because of this assumption, people tend to select committees according to representation by area, or building, or role in the system. But this assumption should be questioned because much of the work in school systems is performed by professionals operating independently. Committees must think seriously about the data they need and how to get it in "loosely coupled" systems such as schools. In schools there is a low degree of interdependence, mutual influence, and relationship intensity (Weick, 1976). Consequently, a variety of views about issues in the organization are likely within any one unit. A new perspective may be provided when someone who is not part of a building or area seeks out information about that setting. At the symbolic level, a committee may not appear adequate unless it has a person from every building, but the issue of good data is not necessarily addressed by this condition.

Third, group interaction permits effective implementation. This interaction allows members to accept assignments, coordinate with each other, and be accountable for results. One special problem with accountability in school systems is the amount of time that members have to fulfill their responsibilities. Schools are organizations in which people's time is fully occupied, and it is difficult to find the slack periods needed to meet special assignments. Leaders of change efforts must give serious attention to this issue if they wish to have effective groups. Asking personnel to do work that is critical to the system on their own time will lead to a decrease in motivation and process losses. A clear solution to this issue must be worked out when the committee is constituted.

Stages in Creating a Work Team. Hackman (1987) also provides a very useful description of the stages in the development of an effective work team as an outgrowth of his model. The four stages are (1) prework, (2) creating performance conditions, (3) forming and building the team, and (4) providing ongoing assistance (see Figure 9). Across the stages there are nine key considerations to be addressed by those who are leading the effort and chartering the group. These matters provide useful diagnostic help in increasing the probability that effective and synergistic task groups will result. A detailed discussion of the key considerations goes beyond the scope of this chapter, but the interested reader is urged to pursue it.

Hackman's model of group development in task settings is important because everyone who leads organizational groups

Figure 9. Stages of Managerial Work in Creating an Effective Group.

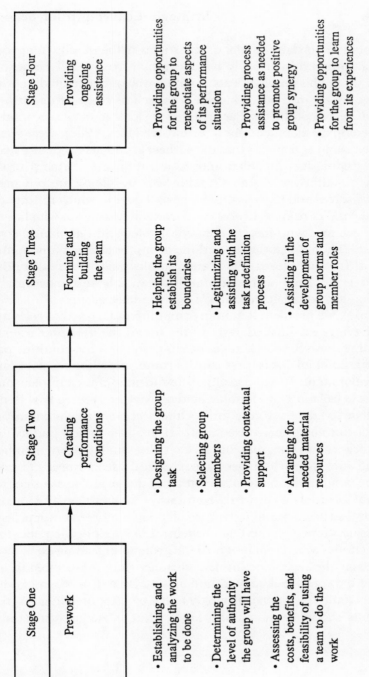

Stage One	Stage Two	Stage Three	Stage Four
Prework	Creating performance conditions	Forming and building the team	Providing ongoing assistance

- Establishing and analyzing the work to be done

- Determining the level of authority the group will have

- Assessing the costs, benefits, and feasibility of using a team to do the work

- Designing the group task

- Selecting group members

- Providing contextual support

- Arranging for needed material resources

- Helping the group establish its boundaries

- Legitimizing and assisting with the task redefinition process

- Assisting in the development of group norms and member roles

- Providing opportunities for the group to renegotiate aspects of its performance situation

- Providing process assistance as needed to promote positive group synergy

- Providing opportunities for the group to learn from its experiences

Source: J. Richard Hackman, "The Design of Work Teams," in Jay W. Lorsch, editor, HANDBOOK OF ORGANIZATIONAL BEHAVIOR, © 1987, p. 338. Reprinted by permission of Prentice-Hall, Inc., Englewood Cliffs, New Jersey.

should have some model of the stages through which a group must proceed in order to become a mature and fully functioning unit. This provides leaders with a way of understanding what is going on in their task groups as well as some ideas for how to deal with problems that arise. As we look across all the models of group development (for a review, see Hare, 1982), there seems to be some agreement that the earliest group task is that of helping people feel included and establishing membership in the group. After the group is established, people begin to express themselves and there is often a period during which differences and conflict may be expressed. Gradually, issues of who has influence and who has power and of roles and decision-making processes get negotiated, and the group becomes a functioning unit. In other words, the group establishes its ways of working and its informal norms of what is acceptable and unacceptable behavior before it becomes a mature task group.

One problem that many committees face is that roles and behaviors established early in the life of the group as ways of dealing with the early stages of group functioning continue past their point of usefulness and become impediments to group development. When a group is first formed, for example, some people feel most comfortable holding back and seeing how things will go, so they say very little. Others who are also anxious talk a lot to reduce their discomfort. If this interaction pattern becomes set and the group has its big talkers and its silent members long after the early stages have passed, the leader needs to work on changing the pattern so that all of the group's resources are available to it. There are several ways to intervene and change group structures and norms. Skilled facilitators can use process consultation to intervene (Schein, 1969). Collecting meeting reactions from all members of the group and feeding back those data at the next meeting is a strategy that is available to all. The data feedback should be followed by a discussion of what one would like to do differently to have better meetings. Agreements should be noted and followed at subsequent meetings.

11

Accountability: Determining How Much Performance Is Improving

The superintendent is accountable for wise and effective use of the school system's resources in pursuit of the mission, purpose, and goals of the district. To determine whether the superintendent and the school system are meeting their responsibilities requires a carefully worked out evaluation and reporting process.

There is no single simple indicator or set of measures that can tell us whether the superintendent is fulfilling her obligations to stakeholders in a satisfactory, let alone optimum, manner. Yet the difficulty of the task should not be used, as it often is, to avoid making a regular and systematic effort to identify the pertinent indicators and criteria of effective school district performance, to gather and analyze relevant data, and then to report results in a clear and systematic fashion on a regular basis to various stakeholders. States sometimes mandate the kinds of reports that must be made to the public. They also require school districts to send detailed reports to their departments of education, typically asking for attendance figures, program enrollments, compliance confirmations, and so forth. In general, we do not find that the mandated reports and statistics gathered to comply with regulations answer many questions for the school system's constituents. Some questions are answered, to be sure, but crucial issues are often glossed over. There is a major difference between *compliance* with a mandate and *commitment* to a

287

result. The latter energizes more focus onto a problem and leads to more effective and reliable outcomes (Marcus, 1989).

What Is Superintendent Accountability?

Accountability is the responsibility and obligation that the superintendent and the school system have to multiple stakeholder groups, including the obligation to use resources entrusted to them in the manner prescribed by law and regulation, to pursue the goals and mission and purposes of the school system and its stakeholders as approved by the school board, and to report in a clear, concise, and comprehensive manner at regular intervals to different stakeholder groups on the state of and strategic plans for the school system. This definition recognizes an obligation to report results in a variety of ways and to explain their meaning in terms of both short- and long-run impacts to key relevant stakeholder groups or market segments. Such reports should not only discuss the many kinds of results achieved in the past period but also describe programs planned for the future and their potential benefits. The kinds of explanations that most people ask for typically go beyond the letter of any law or mandate, though perhaps not beyond the spirit of some state regulations.

When an organization is accountable to other individuals or groups, it must perform certain functions that it is contracted to perform (the contract may be written or unwritten). The people to whom the entity is accountable can only ascertain whether the accountability has been met after evaluative information has been gathered and provided to them. Such information is used to paint a picture of whether and how well the function has been performed. The essence of accountability, then, includes the identification, gathering, analyzing, and reporting of relevant information to appropriate groups in order to facilitate evaluation and decision making.

Why should a superintendent be interested in accountability? First, a superintendent might view accountability as a way of protecting his job or "covering" himself. Rarely, however, is a superintendent's contract not renewed by a school board because the board feels that the district's test scores are too low or because some other performance goal is not being met. While on occasion one of these reasons may be given for asking for a superintendent's resignation, typically, so many other factors contribute to test score gains or goal achievement and district goals are so vaguely specified and achievement so difficult to measure that such a rationale is not considered useful. Thus, the reasons for termination of a superintendent's contract usually relate to his "style," to personnel matters, to a single issue that elects new board members to "get" the superintendent, to a popularized theme or topic that becomes a rallying cry for change but is often beyond the superintendent's control, or to poor "communication" between board and superintendent, the last being a broad and popular catchall reason.

It is possible that good accountability reporting can improve board-superintendent communication and lessen the likelihood that some of the other potential sources of trouble just mentioned will cause a superintendent's contract not to be renewed. But this is not the sole or even chief reason for a superintendent to be interested in accountability. For we cannot say that having excellent accountability and reporting processes and fulfilling all the goals and mandates that the system requires will guarantee the superintendent a renewed contract and a good performance evaluation by the board and community. Some of the other reasons for having a carefully developed accountability system include the following:

- To fulfill a professional ethical obligation to the school system's constituents
- To evaluate the staff and administrative team
- To enhance school-community relations
- To monitor and influence results
- To make better decisions about resource allocation

These purposes can be applied to an evaluation system, and indeed evaluation in its broadest sense is a major part of accountability. Accountability can take many forms, depending on which of the above purposes is most important at a given time. One comprehensive data base may be used to serve several purposes, but different data and different configurations of the data must be assembled to serve each purpose. To present different accountability reports depending on their purpose sounds almost deceitful to many school administrators, but it is perfectly appropriate. In fact, presenting the same report to every audience might actually be more deceitful and certainly would be dysfunctional and inappropriate.

Although each group to which a superintendent is accountable may require the same core information about a project, different groups often require different analyses or additional facts about the same project, depending on their own particular needs. For example, assume that one of the elementary schools in a district introduced a new reading program last year. The superintendent must now report on this program. If her purpose is to improve communication with the school board, the report might include such data as the schedule of implementation, the problems and costs involved in introducing the program, the changes in the same group's reading scores from last year's to this year's tests, and how this program helps the school system fulfill one of the board's key academic goals better than alternatives might have. On the other hand, if the superintendent's purpose is to report to parents, then the data would center more on the gains in test scores, how these gains compare with gains in other schools, and how these scores compare with scores in similar kinds of schools. Yet again, if the purpose is to report to taxpayers or the state department of education, the focus might be on the cost of the program, that cost compared to costs for the same program in other districts, and the gains obtained. If the information is to be used for decision making—such as for deciding whether to introduce the program into a second elementary school—then data about the other schools' past performance on reading tests (to ascertain whether it needs this change as much and for the same reasons that the first adopting school needed it) would be in order. If the chief purpose is monitoring and influencing results, then perhaps a specific item analysis of the reading score data might be examined and reported to staff and outside reading consultants.

A Framework for Accountability

When discussing accountability, it is useful to have a framework for the evaluation process. We refer here to the CIPP (context, input, process, product) model (Stufflebeam and Shinkfield, 1983) mentioned earlier. By modifying this model slightly and treating context as a given, we can divide the accountability process into three parts: accountability for input (wise use of the school system's finances, personnel, and facilities in terms of careful controls on costs and expenditures); accountability for the process (such as teaching and learning methods employed, technology and programs adopted, and values and ethics modeled); and accountability for output (product or result). In other words, accountability has more than one dimension. The superintendent is charged with seeing to it that certain benefits are realized for constituents and also with obtaining these benefits within appropriate cost limits, using appropriate means or processes. Table 10 depicts this framework and lists the kinds of factors to be examined in each area.

Input

In discussing various kinds of input, the concern is with the efficient and proper use of assets at the disposal of the super-

Table 10. A Framework for Accountability.

C	INPUT	PROCESS	OUTPUT
O	Finances	Teaching methods	Test scores
N	Staff	Values modeled	Affective measures
T	Facilities	Peer culture	Participation rates
E	Equipment	Programs provided	Dropout rates
X		Discipline policies	Percentage accepted by top colleges
T		Other policies and practices	Discipline levels Goal attainment
		Class size	Consumer satisfaction Student self-esteem

intendent and the school system. Are assets being used efficiently? Are laws, regulations, and board policies pertaining to their use being followed? Finally, are assets being employed solely for the purpose of pursuing school district goals? The key assets entrusted to the stewardship of the school executive are *finances, staff, facilities,* and *equipment.* These are discussed in turn below.

Finances. Financial accountability relates to how well money is handled in purchasing the items or services the superintendent is responsible for providing. A school district's money is used to purchase people's services as well as facilities, supplies, and equipment. Each school system faces a unique and changing environment that can substantially affect the kinds of results it may be able to achieve, especially as compared to another school system or even to its own performance in previous years. Therefore, some common denominators and frames of reference are needed for making comparisons and judgments in the imprecise art of evaluation. One of several denominators is money.

Most people focus on the legal aspect of fiscal accountability. That is, does the district adhere to laws and board policies? Within the parameters of the legal and board limits, however, a budget usually forces the school system to be more specific about the allocation of financial resources. The superintendent is accountable for an appropriate budget preparation process. In most situations this means obtaining board input at least from the school board and often from citizens' committees and staff members in developing budget allocations and priorities. The next accountability step is to control spending in accordance with the budget specifications and then to report the actual expenditures at the end of the period and the significant variances, if any, from the budget plan and the reasons therefor. Fiscal controls should be in place to ensure that money is spent specifically for the purposes intended and that it is not overspent in any category without good reason and full explanation.

Ensuring that money is spent for appropriate school district purposes and then meeting the budget targets is still not enough, however. At least three important additional kinds of analysis should be performed in establishing good fiscal accountability: cost efficiency, cost-effectiveness, and cost-benefit analysis. These are three very different concepts, and each presents an additional level of analytical complexity. It is very useful for superintendents and boards to understand these concepts and to be able to explain to the public, without using excessive technical jargon, the school system's performance in each area.

The first concept, cost efficiency, involves an analysis of whether the district is obtaining the best possible prices for the goods and services it purchases. That is, are goods and services being purchased at the lowest feasible cost to the district? At this level of analysis, only the cost of the quality or item being purchased is considered, not the differential benefits that might be obtained from using alternate sources. In other words, once the school system has decided that it needs a certain kind of teacher, the question becomes "Is it paying more than the market salary or more than it should pay?" In the case of a piece of equipment or a supply, the question is "Is the district paying the lowest competitive price for the quality level needed?" The superintendent is responsible for seeing that systems and procedures that come as close as possible to achieving this ideal are in place.

The next level of analysis, cost-effectiveness, is more complex because the district must consider the educational results it is trying to achieve with the goods or services it plans to purchase and then examine alternate ways of achieving those results. For example, if the objective is to raise math test scores in one of the elementary schools, the administration must consider whether it is best to add another teacher (thereby reducing class size), to hire a math specialist to work with the present classroom teachers, to hire additional teacher aides, or to introduce computer-assisted instruction. The assumption in this cost-effectiveness analysis is that the school does want to raise math scores as opposed to achieving some other goal.

To decide which kind of educational result would be more (most) productive from a value or benefit point of view, the district must employ cost-benefit analysis. This means using a common denominator such as dollars to value each benefit being considered. However, although economists use cost-benefit analysis to study the overall social benefits to be obtained from various courses of action, cost-benefit analysis is not added in school district work to the cost-effectiveness analysis described above. A school system would not typically apply economic analysis to consider the benefit side of the equation, for example, whether it is better to use a given amount of money to try to raise math scores, raise reading scores, or enhance thinking skills. The additional complication in moving to cost-benefit analysis comes from the need to estimate the dollar value of the benefits so that the district can compare different educational results to the costs of each and calculate a benefit-cost ratio. Such a calculation would be extremely difficult, subjective, value-laden, and certainly controversial.

A superintendent is responsible for educating people and for leading a large-scale education organization (the school district) toward the achievement of its highest goals. Handling the fiscal side of education is a means to the educational end (just as it is in any organization, private or public), not the end itself. Yet one of the superintendent's responsibilities is to see that value is received for money spent. Obviously, not every superintendent has the same amount of money with which to work. Shouldn't the suburban superintendent who has $5,000 per pupil be held to a different standard than the inner-city superintendent who has but $2,000 per student? It is therefore useful to examine cost per unit of output.

Theoretically, the ultimate objective is to calculate and report to the district some sort of "value added" per dollar spent, a concept that is rarely if ever used in reporting school district results. This would mean adjusting test scores for the native ability and past performance of the student group attending the reporting schools. Thus, for example, a community composed chiefly of college-educated parents whose school-age children score in the 80th percentile on average on a given normed test might not be adding as much value (let alone value per dollar spent) as a community with a much lower socioeconomic status (SES) population whose children score in the 45th percentile. Although we do not currently have any national SES group averages for identifying what the test score gains should be for a given age cohort on a given set of tests, it is not unrealistic to anticipate some movement in this direction. Reactions to the U.S. Department of Education's wall chart may well facilitate such movement.

Is debate really shifting from a discussion of "whether state-by-state comparisons should be provided to how we can improve these comparisons," as the authors of one article contend (Ginsburg, Noell, and Plisko, 1988)? If so, it seems only a matter of time before the demands for making the data comparable and usefully tied to statewide and National Assessment of Educational Progress (NAEP) assessments will force the kinds of changes that could make a comparative value-added analysis feasible and even necessary. The next step would be to obtain an average dollar cost for raising the level of an average second-quartile SES student with average previous grades and to compare cost-effectiveness on a total organizational level among schools and school systems.

We are a long way from having the kind of data needed to conduct this kind of analysis. According to Levin (1988), one of the reasons that few cost-effectiveness studies have been done in education is because educators and evaluators have not been trained to do the kind of cost studies required for this kind of analysis. It is probable that the current fiscal environment will lead to a situation in which more attention to and therefore training in cost analysis will be required of educational administrators and evaluators.

The flip side of every outflow of dollars is the benefit or good purchased with the dollars spent. Thus it seems to follow logically that the services rendered by the people, facilities, supplies, and equipment of a district must be assessed and that the superintendent is accountable for receiving appropriate results for the expenditure of funds on those services. Because of this and because the wall chart has apparently stimulated some of the kinds of analysis that may ultimately lead to our being able to make more school-to-school comparisons of both costs and results, it is very possible that superintendents in the 1990s will have to become much more facile with cost-effectiveness analysis and may even be asked to attempt some crude cost-benefit analysis.

Staff. In focusing on the question of accountability for obtaining good value for the dollar spent, one should turn first to the chief expenditure of any school district: teachers' salaries. Over 80 percent of the typical school budget is for the staff, and most of this is for certified classroom teachers and specialists. Thus one of the most important accountability questions to raise with a superintendent is how well the certified staff is performing. And that means a good staff performance appraisal process is a vital component of a superintendent's accountability. The superintendent can assess the effectiveness of a teaching staff not only by attempting to evaluate what the members do (input) and how well they do it (process) but also by examining the results of their work in terms of learner outcomes (output). Just what should the superintendent hold teachers accountable for?

First, in terms of input, teachers should be accountable for the number of hours they are in the classroom and the number of students they teach. Next, in terms of process or how they do it, teachers should be accountable for the number of discipline cases they send to the principal, the amount of cooperation they exhibit for school functions, their manner and style, and the example they set for all students. Such process accountability also involves the trouble or problems their students cause in moving about the building or behaving in an unruly manner, as well as the teachers' intensity and quality of effort and their teaching methods and techniques. Finally, in terms of output, teachers should be accountable for the performance of their students on tests, the number of parental complaints on their classes and the number of student complaints from their classrooms, and certainly the number of positive comments they received about their teaching or how well they score on consumer satisfaction surveys.

Input measures involve relatively objective and easily obtainable numbers, but their value is at best questionable. They can be important assessment vehicles for the teachers' immediate supervisor (the principal) when used with other indicators of performance, but they may have only marginal value to an outside consumer more interested in results than in input. The process measures are subjective, and in the hands of an uninformed observer, they can be misleading. However, if they are gathered in a consistent manner over time and aggregated by building or subject or grade level, trends in these indicators can provide useful data to the superintendent. These data can also have much value to principals as part of an overall assessment of a teacher. Coupled with an attempt by education professionals to provide reasonably objective interpretations, these data can also be used to give helpful information to outside stakeholders.

Output measures or learner outcomes raise the questions of which outputs should be examined and how valid the measures are. Most outside users of the data on teacher effectiveness would probably agree that the best single set of criteria for assessing the performance of teaching staff members is to observe the results they achieve in terms of student outcomes but in the same breath warn us that the longer-term impacts and results are what are important, not the immediate test results.

How should student outcomes be assessed? This question ultimately leads to a discussion of test scores and other measures of student growth, achievement, maturity, and attitude. Before getting into the controversy over the narrowness of standardized reading and math test scores and the dangers of their overuse (clearly when used as the exclusive external reporting device, they provide much too narrow a view to the public of what schools are achieving), we must ask what we really want tests to measure or, more broadly, what learner outcomes we are truly interested in. This discussion is about the teaching staff as an input for which the superintendent is accountable. One way to measure the efficient use of the staff as an input to the school system is to examine the kinds of output obtained from its work. This examination continues in the later section on output measures.

Facilities and Equipment. It would not be especially productive to try to come up with measures such as output per square foot of building or output per dollar's worth of equipment owned by the school district. It might be very useful, however, to ask and answer some basic questions about the use of these resources. Again, every school system is blessed (or cursed) with a different configuration of physical assets.

Here are some questions the superintendent might try to answer for the school system's stakeholders: Is the district using its buildings as well as it might? Are facilities used on nights or weekends? Do community groups have access to facilities? Could some of the equipment be used in additional ways? Can the district learn from other school systems about additional uses for its physical assets?

Process

It is not important to know how some products are produced. It is enough to know that they are produced well and efficiently and that they serve important needs (as long as their manufacture does not pollute the environment or do damage to other people or property). In the case of education, however, in the course of providing a service, schools can have profound long-term effects on the values and functioning of tomorrow's adults, especially the shapers of society. Therefore, it is appropriate to raise some "how" questions. It is not enough for a school system to say that it enhanced the knowledge and skills of the children entrusted to it. The district must explain how the provision of that enhanced knowledge and skill took place and what potential side effects the instructional processes and mechanisms may have had. Did the district's teachers raise test scores by teaching children to be insensitive to others around them? Did the teachers inhibit creativity, enthusiasm, and spontaneity in order to finish the work sheet manual to help the children do better on the math and reading exams?

What about discipline policies? Do they reflect the desires and needs of the community? Are they supportive of local parental norms? What about the peer group culture? What is being done to shape it in a positive form? What values do teachers model? Are these values appropriate for this community and consistent with the best ethical standards and highest values in the local population? Attempts to answer such questions will not provide precise quantitative statistics; they should, however, trigger important discussion about the character and nature of the school system. The most comprehensive measurement of output cannot reveal the entire story of what school systems do to and for their students. Therefore, each school system needs the kind of local scrutiny involved in grappling with these questions. Most educators are used to thinking about such questions even if they are not used to talking about them with the lay public or reporting on them in a systematic manner.

Although ultimate results or outcomes obtained are crucially important, they can never be the total measure of a school system. Today, even for the physician, it is not enough to say that he or she kept the patient alive. Educators, too, are asking the "how" questions. We want to know what the hidden human cost is in providing a given benefit. Just as people are interested in the side effects of prescription drugs, they are also interested in the effect on their children's psyche, love of learning, attitudes, motivation, and value systems of a given teaching methodology.

Output

Finally, the superintendent must address the output or results portion of the accountability framework. Any or all of the following can be results for which the superintendent is responsible and accountable.

- Meeting the goals established by the school board
- Educating all children in the community to the fullest extent possible
- Raising SAT scores
- Maintaining discipline
- Building students' character and self-esteem
- "Educating" the community on the latest and best in curriculum and learning technologies
- Providing programs that meet the researched needs of constituencies and fall within the service capability of the school system

Yardsticks or criteria to measure the attainment of some of these results are simple to develop. However, it is almost impossible to judge whether others have been adequately achieved. For example, "educating all children . . . to the fullest extent possible" sounds more like a mission statement than a measurable goal or result (see Chapter Six).

It is tempting for outsiders and even school board members to trivialize the output of a school system by trying to reduce it to a few simple measures such as SAT scores, dropout rates, or percentage of graduates going on to college. The "bottom line" syndrome pervades our society. It came from the business sector, and it persists despite the fact that the search for short-term profits to which that syndrome leads may be a major factor in America's economic decline in international markets. The problem is that most people do not accept the idea that the purpose of a business is to create and serve a customer, not to maximize profits for the shareholder (Drucker, 1954). To conceive of business's purpose so narrowly as to say it is merely to make maximum profits for shareholders is just as erroneous as to conceive of schools' sole purpose as "maximizing test scores."

Such statements of the purpose of business may provide some ammunition to superintendents who must answer those who ask why they cannot run their districts "more like a business." A thoughtful business executive will recognize the fallacy of judging an organization by one or two short-term results. Yet a poorly thought through and oversimplified school district accountability effort can result in a very narrow and dysfunctional short-term, "bottom line" focus.

On the other hand, concerns about the limitations on current measures should not be used, as they often are, to excuse the school system from systematically reporting results and trying to interpret their meaning to the public. It is tempting for superintendents to withdraw from the responsibility of reporting results on the grounds that the most important ones are "impossible to measure." A variation on the avoidance technique is the practice of bombarding the lay public with such a huge number of statistics as to weaken their meaning and obfuscate the real issues or glossing over discussion about the probable long- and short-term impacts that the results imply.

Learner Outcomes. When people think of result measures, standardized test scores usually come to mind first. However, some would say that such scores tell us more about students' parents (heredity) and life circumstances (environment) than about the school's effectiveness. A better alternative might be to measure year-to-year gains in a given student group rather than to rank school systems on an absolute scale based on the average test scores. Although this measure seems somewhat fairer because each school system starts out with a relatively even chance, it, too, is suspect in that the gains made during the year are also influenced by the family and home situation. Another alternative would be to adjust scores for the socioeconomic level of the student body and then to compare them to the scores in other systems whose students have a similar socioeconomic background.

Still, the most crucial limitation of standardized tests as a measure of school effectiveness is that the tests typically used by most school systems are believed to measure only a small fraction of the learning that schools can and do provide. A response to that criticism might be to identify and use other tests and assessment processes that are considered to provide some measure of the other kinds of learning. The introduction of the wall chart by the U.S. Department of Education has stimulated some state interest in the development and use of a broader array of subject matter tests and in making comparisons among similar kinds of districts. For example, in California, scores are now displayed on a wide range of tests for comparison groups of schools that serve similar populations (Ginsburg, Noell, and Plisko, 1988, p. 7).

But why don't schools use more tests that employ assessment tools designed to measure students' ability to work well in groups, instruments that assess attitudes, interests, and motivation levels? Analysts of these kinds of tests usually question the validity of their measures (Levy and Goldstein, 1986). (Validity means that the score obtained by a test taker on the attribute the test purports to measure does reflect the actual existence of that attribute in the person. For example, if the children who score high on a test of interest in learning are really interested in learning, then that test is said to be a valid measure of that attribute.) However, some tests when used and interpreted carefully do have some degree of usefulness. Experimenting with these tests and carefully employing professional judgments and subjective assessments can help one get a clearer picture of the total school.

The kinds of standardized tests most often used tend to measure how well students learn to complete worksheets, memorize answers, and develop cognitive skills. If those are the only results that schools produce, then we are not getting our money's worth. Computer programs and private businesses that provide

relevant services on a contract basis could probably get the same
test score results much more cheaply than public schools do now.
If the kind of cost-effectiveness work recommended by Levin
(1988) is seriously pursued, we may find that current schooling
methods are in need of great overhaul to achieve results most
efficiently.

Schools produce much more than cognitive skill results.
In order to demonstrate their effectiveness in affective and
motivational areas, however, schools are going to have to develop
new forms of output measures in this age of "bottom line" accountability. Other kinds of assessments, including observation
of a school by trained experts who are not part of the school
system, can be useful. Many people have confidence in such
subjective assessments when they are done systematically, according to certain specified guidelines.

Perhaps a couple of examples would be helpful at this
point. First, suppose one of the goals of your district is to increase junior high school students' interest in self-directed learning, in their desire to explore and to learn. You could use a test
at the beginning and the end of a given year to identify the
students' interest in various topics. In addition, you could report
annually on the results of interviews with a selected sample of
students asked similar questions designed to ascertain their
motivation levels. Such interviews might have to be conducted
by outside consultants or university people.

Now suppose one of your district's goals is to involve
students in meaningful community service work. You might ask
volunteers who direct or hold managerial positions in human
service agencies, nursing homes, and the like to observe and
assess the quality and intensity of your students' work in other
(not the volunteers' own) community agencies.

Another important aspect of schooling, at least according
to most teachers and many parents, is the development of self-
concept. Schools can use psychological tests designed to shed
light on a student's self-image and confidence and report overall
averages and the gains in these averages achieved in a given
year. Why don't more schools do such reporting?

When relevant stakeholder groups are involved in setting
school goals, then the achievement of results against goals can

be reported, discussed, and analyzed with those same stakeholder groups. For example, criterion-referenced test results can be reported, and their meaning can be assessed by the community (with some help from testing specialists who must verify that the district is using tests that are reasonably rigorous and really test what they say they test).

Client Satisfaction Measures. In Chapter Five on market research, I discussed the use and misuse of consumer satisfaction surveys and stated that they are often part of a virtually useless but harmless exercise, at least insofar as providing helpful market data. One legitimate use of such surveys, however, is to provide data that the central office and community groups can assess with a view toward taking actions implied in the responses. Year-to-year changes in some measure can be early indicators of a basic change or deterioration in a program or a change in a stakeholder need. Statistics on such matters can be included in an annual report to stakeholders. It seems logical to a business person to have an annual report that includes some indication of consumers' satisfaction with an organization's products and services. Although a school system cannot use an annual revenue figure to indicate consumer acceptance of its products and services, it can collect other kinds of client satisfaction measures. Why not provide an annual survey, a five- and a ten-year history and graph of the level of consumer satisfaction with the school district's performance?

Other Important Performance Indicators. It should be (and often is) mandatory for schools to publish statistics such as attendance rates, dropout rates, and other compilations that tell something about the level of interest and motivation generated by the activities of the school system and its student population. Another measure of how well the school is doing for its students can be found in student participation rates in a variety of cocurricular activities. The number and variety of such activities available to students can also be an important measure of the effectiveness of the school in serving its publics. These statistics can be reported inaccurately, be difficult to standardize across schools, and even be heavily biased or distorted by a reporting school's method of collecting, interpreting, and presenting the data. Nevertheless, these problems should not prevent a school system or a state department of education, perhaps encouraged by the state chapter of the American Association of School Administrators (AASA) from insisting on collecting and reporting these data to its publics and on overcoming the problems associated with their collection and use. Again, we should note the wall chart's beginning and current efforts to deal with the legitimate concerns associated with this kind of accountability reporting rather than trying to defeat its purpose and use (Ginsburg, Noell, and Plisko, 1988).

Finally, outside evaluations, as evidenced by special awards for excellence, the number of National Merit scholars, or the winning of regional, state, or national competitions in academic or cocurricular areas (such as debate, band, sports), can be reported in the school's accountability to the public.

At this point, it is important to note that I am recommending a great many measures and assessments that are not now formally made or if made are almost never reported in a systematic manner to the public. Where will the school system find the time and expertise to collect, interpret, and report these outcomes? Some school systems are already providing data for the assessments noted above. School district constituencies are performing intuitive assessments or making judgments (often with incomplete or inaccurate information). So why not provide some or all of them to your constituents? Why shouldn't each stakeholder group receive from the school district an annual accountability report written in lay terms and summarized with key items highlighted rather than have to piece together data from a variety of other (perhaps less accurate) sources? If the school system does not provide useful reports for the public, what will be the long-term consequences for our education system in this age of accountability?

To Whom Are the Schools Accountable?

As stated earlier, the tough question to answer concerning test scores is "Which among a myriad of potential measures of the outcome of education should one choose to assess and report?'' To answer this, one must consider the mission, purpose, and objectives of the school system. This then leads to questions about the ownership and control of the local school and to questions about the market demands and needs for education and schooling. This in turn leads back to some very basic questions about the reasons for the existence of schools. The question of what schools are for or why schools exist can perhaps be better dealt with after answering some other questions addressed to the marketplace:

Why does society require children to receive schooling?

What does society expect from its schools?

What does the state want from its schools?

What does the local neighborhood community want from its schools?

What do employers want from schools?

What do parents want from their schools?

What do students want from their schools?

What are the expectations and needs of the schools' staffs and administrations?

Questions of this breadth and depth do not, of course, have simple answers. Not only are the answers difficult to obtain, but they may differ for each major stakeholder group. While some may consider it presumptuous even to try to answer these questions, it is necessary to attempt to develop some general, if only tentative, responses in order to address the key question: What measures of outcomes of schooling best indicate whether the needs for schooling are being met?

Attempting to identify the specific stakeholder groups for whom answers to the foregoing questions are important and relevant takes us full circle, back to some of the questions raised in Chapter Two: Who owns the schools? Who should control the schools? For whose benefit do the schools exist?

If we think that schools belong to society, then questions of social policy and the kind of society we want become relevant. Do we want a society that achieves the highest economic benefit? Do we want a society of highly intelligent technicians, of kind and gentle people, of people who respect authority and

follow orders, or of people who lead? If we as a society want all
of these "good things," then we must consider another crucial
question: What are the respective roles and responsibilities of
the schools, parents, the government, the media, businesses,
and so on in trying to provide them? I will not attempt to answer
this last question, but it is one that must be discussed in the
larger community during the process of establishing the mission, goals, and objectives for the local school system. The remainder of this section focuses on what the various key stakeholders seem to expect from their schools and thus what they
hold the schools accountable for. This approach is based on the
belief that the schools are accountable to stakeholders. Each
stakeholder group is therefore discussed in turn.

Society and the State as Stakeholders. At the broadest national level, the first stakeholder to consider is society at large.
The public demands that the education system see to it that future
adult citizens are literate, employable, cooperative, and contributing members of society. To become literate and employable, students must receive from their schooling a minimum level of skill in
reading, writing, communicating, and computing. These needs
then give us some bases for the first outcome measurements.

There are many usable tests to assess performance in
reading, writing, communicating, and computing. The accountability requirement should therefore be relatively easy to describe
and develop. Some agency, typically the state department of
education, can define minimum skill requirements and designate
tests that assess whether the student has met those requirements.
In some situations, the school system is allowed to select which
of several possible testing instruments and methods best provide such information.

As for the public's second demand, that students become
cooperative and contributing members of society, the outcomes
sought are much more difficult to define and measure. The
testing process for assessing respect for and ability to work with
others is difficult but not impossible to identify and use; there
are tests and simulations that students can be put through that
give a great deal of information on their ability to cooperate
and contribute to group or organizational efforts (Levy and

Goldstein, 1986). On the other hand, it may be easier to assess the matter of motivation level by using existing records of grades, attendance rates, and other teacher-observed actions.

At the state level, the demands would probably include the same measures and accountability requirements the society as a whole demands (presumably, state government reflects in its actions the demands of society) plus a few others. First, the state can (and should) hold schools accountable for learning gains. This involves either adjusting test scores in some way for the ability level of the attending student group (perhaps by using socioeconomic level as a proxy measure) or by taking periodic "before" and "after" measures. Current interest in and controversy over the U.S. Department of Education's wall chart indicates that there may be some movement in this direction.

Employers as Stakeholders. Employers seem to want many of the same absolute measures as society does, as well as wanting students to have some knowledge of or experience with the world of work, with punctuality, obedience to orders, and possibly some specific skills in such areas as word processing, computer usage, or auto mechanics. The existence of such work skills should be demonstrable at graduation. The other attributes, sometimes referred to as "good work habits," can probably be best shown after graduation, when the students' employers or next-level educational institutions make their assessments. High schools should collect such assessments of each of their graduating classes at least once in the first year or two after graduation.

The Local Community as Stakeholder. The local community may add some additional demands that concern students' behavior, such as respect for property, civil behavior in the streets and around town, and the like. In our mobile society it is difficult to obtain accurate measures of these kinds of activities as related to a specific school's student body. People from other neighborhoods can be contributing to crime rates or poor conduct in a given local community. But there can certainly be some accounting of crime statistics attributable to a given student body, complaints from local businesses and residents near the school buildings, behavior of students in groups, and perhaps other indicators of student behavior that could be identified, collected, and reported on periodically.

One of the troubles with these last indicators is that they are usually noticeable only in a negative sense and then often without adequate reference points for making judgments. For example, does a student group that gets unruly at a football game, creating a small amount of violence and a large amount of litter, once in a year exhibit a low, medium, or high respect for property and low, medium, or high behavior quality? Yet superintendents must be ready to discuss and help interpret such events if the community perceives them to be important and influenced in any way by the school system.

Staff and Administration as Stakeholders. The staff and administration of the school system are its education professionals, people who are supposed to understand the nature of the products and services of an educational system and the kinds of output that can result from employing certain processes and using certain input. Presumably, their training allows them to understand better than the lay public what the outcomes of various kinds of educational treatment might be. They may want the best for children just as parents do. But their motives are usually broader and their purposes aimed at group (the classroom) and societal benefits. For some, the attraction to the highly demanding but modestly financially rewarding job of teaching comes from the feeling of contribution and the satisfaction of watching children grow and develop or from being respected and looked up to by these children. Whatever the motives, the staff may want different results for students than the students or their parents want. And the teaching staff may want different results than the administrative staff wants.

Teachers, because of their knowledge of the limitations of standardized tests, may not put as much value as others do on higher achievement scores. They may put higher value on discipline, the intellectual interest of students, pleasant relationships among students and between students and staff. They may stress workbook completion, or they may alternatively stress creative pursuits. How does one measure the results that teachers value? Should a district measure these results if they are not especially valued by clients? If there is a difference between the results valued by the producer and the results valued by the customer, what is the responsibility of the professional administrator to educate either or both groups on the issues and implications of their varied demands and assessments? Again, the difficulty of getting complete and accurate measures of all the results a school achieves and the possible side effects of certain educational "treatments" make it important that some professional judgments and educational leadership be exercised to help the clients make the most intelligent demands possible for the longer-range benefit of the children, the community, and the society at large. This requires a great deal of skill on the part of the superintendent in consultative and consensus management, as discussed in Chapter Ten.

Parents and Students as Stakeholders. The final stakeholder groups, and from a marketing standpoint perhaps the most important, are parents and students. These groups are the more direct consumers of the services of schooling. Even when someone else is paying the bill (the state, the general taxpayer, and so on), the influence of the parent and student groups on the assessment of educational benefits is significant. What measures, other than those already discussed, do parents use to assess schools? Parents represent not one but several market segments. Each market segment or constituent group must be assessed in terms of its needs, the results that meet those needs, its ability to pay for certain services, and its ability to influence the school system's results.

Each school system should identify and classify its own market segments, perhaps by considering the end use of the service, the aspiration or income level of the consumer, the ability level of the student, and the motivation level or other special characteristics of the student and parent groups. Table 11 lists possible sets of parent and student market segments. School executives should think carefully about their own situations before using these same categories in their particular school systems.

Of course, some clients may fall into more than one category, and this necessitates subcategories such as single parents who work outside the home, single parents who are heavily involved with the schools, college-educated working parents, and so on.

Table 11. Client Market Segments.

STUDENT CATEGORIES
College-bound
Vocational school–bound
Work-bound
Those with special needs
Gifted and talented in math, science, and humanities
Gifted and talented in the performing arts and athletics
PARENT CATEGORIES
Parents actively involved with the schools
Single parents
Two-income, working parents
Parents of children with special needs
Parents of children with special talents

College-educated parents might be interested in SAT scores and acknowledgments that their children have participated in the kinds of individual or team activities that may help them gain admission to the "best" colleges. Such parents might also be interested in having their children associated with the "right" people and thus have some interest in the overall averages of the school's SAT scores and the percentage of students planning to go on to college, particularly to prestigious colleges and universities. Many less-educated parents might well have the same interests.

Single parents and working parents may be more concerned about the quality of the day-care services, the cocurricular programs, and the assistance that the school may be able to give to special needs in areas such as abuse dependency, health education, or moral development. That is not to say that these parents are not also interested in the same academic and social criteria that other groups are interested in and vice versa.

A sizable group of high school graduate parents may be most concerned with the school's reputation and performance in the area of discipline. Since this concern is so important to so many parents, as noted in the annual Gallup polls on education, it would seem imperative that a school system develop a reasonably objective and consistent measure of the system's performance in maintaining good discipline. This allows the district to report periodically to parents the discipline level in the schools and also to identify trends over time.

Other parents may be interested in the degree to which they are allowed to be involved in the decisions and activities of their children's school or how well they and other visitors are treated when they enter the school. Another very important market segment, whose voice is strong in many places, comprises the parents of children with ''special education'' requirements. This group is most interested in how the school handles children with special needs. Again, some consistent and regular method of reporting the school's status and trends in meeting these needs is called for in a complete accountability system.

With which of these measures should the school superintendent be concerned? If he or she has clients in each of the parent categories, then the answer is all of them. In reporting results and trends in the various outcome indicators discussed above, the superintendent is also telling the public something about the system's cost-effectiveness. In other words, how much is the school system providing for the money that taxpayers and others are investing in it? Are the various stakeholders receiving value for the investments they are making?

Other Views on Outputs. Many stakeholders, especially parents and students, are less concerned with general cost-effectiveness than they are with the size of the *total* benefit that they *personally* obtain from the school system. Thus, a superintendent might also be held accountable for the raising of additional funds by supporting referenda, selling services, and the like. In other words, the total output or the total perceived value of the results achieved by a school system may be more important to many key stakeholders than the efficiency of use of resources.

In the real world, of course, a school is judged by many perceptual factors. How good is the public presence of the administration? How well does it treat outsiders, students, parents? How happy are the students? Do they reflect that happiness when they come home from school and when they talk about their school experiences with members of the community? However, in the interest of continuing to focus on attempts to measure actual rather than perceived performance, at this point it seems useful to examine more closely some of the output measures that are or can be used by schools to assess performance.

An Annual Report to the Stakeholders

The preceding discussion leads to the subject of presenting an annual or periodic district report to the public. Such a
report should contain a brief summary of what the school system
has accomplished in the last year and what its goals are for the
future, along with some standardized statistics that are reported
systematically and consistently so that recipients of the report
can, if they wish, track progress from year to year. This kind
of report could be similar to the annual reports the Securities
and Exchange Commission requires of public corporations. The
resource section at the back of this book presents a framework
or outline for such an annual report in the form of a case, "Management Report to Stakeholders" (Mauriel, 1979b). This case
poses to a superintendent the question of what he should report
to the public, how, and how often. Although this case has more
detailed suggestions than any single school district would need
or want to follow, each item is worth the superintendent's study
before he decides whether and how to provide information about
it to stakeholders.

Of course, the questions of what to report and how to
report it become political as well as educational ones. Too much
data can confuse or mislead even the most educated reader, and
data are also subject to different interpretations. Some superintendents prefer to put their "annual reports" in the form of
an oral presentation at a public school board meeting, with very
little except a few basic statistics put in writing. Others use
newsletters, radio programs, the local press, or speeches to the
PTA, local service clubs, or other organizations as their means
of communicating. Most superintendents, however, use a combination of media to report to the public.

The problem with most of the informal means of reporting is that the public hears only what the administration wants
it to hear, and the public knows it. It is hard for people not to
view the communication as being self-serving rather than an
objective report of what is going well and what is not going well.
Are superintendents willing to report openly and fully about
the weaknesses as well as the strengths? An additional problem
with informal reporting in which the topics and format vary from

year to year is that there is little basis for comparison. It is hard for the public to judge statistics or testimonials and put them into a proper context in order to answer for themselves the question of how well this school is doing compared to other schools of its type or compared to how well it could be doing.

The problems of a lack of a standard for comparison and a lack of perceived objectivity are not necessarily solved by having an annual report. On the other hand, it is possible to have better accountability if (1) the state helps by requesting that school boards follow certain standard guidelines in collecting and reporting the data—I say "request" because mandates usually gain compliance without substance and trivialize a reporting process (Marcus, 1989), (2) several school systems provide similar data, and (3) an outside observer or analyst helps interpret those data for the reading public.

These are three big "ifs," but it is also fair to say that a great deal of pressure is building up among the taxpaying public for more accurate and standard forms of accountability. Furthermore, if consumers are to be given more choice in a deregulating economy, then the education monopoly will have to be weakened. When an industry is deregulated, the clients or consumers typically end up having more choices. More freedom of choice requires more information if it is to be used wisely. Remember the requisites of free competition from Economics 101: many suppliers and perfect information. People need information in order to be able to make intelligent choices about what sort of school best fits their children (or as a member of society, I could say *our* children). It is this need for information that will drive the pressures for more accurate and more complete accountability and reporting by public school systems. To deal with the possible information overload that could result from reporting everything suggested in the case at the end of the book, I recommend that administrators structure several different kinds of reports for the different key stakeholder groups. One way to divide the reporting system into manageable subparts is to consider the needs of each stakeholder group discussed in this chapter and to tailor a specific report for each one.

12

Leading Schools into the Future: Managing the Ongoing Process of Strategic Change

The strategic management framework provides a new approach for organizing and shaping the many processes and systems that are needed today to lead and manage the operation of a school system effectively. This approach provides a new perspective for superintendents, central office executives, and school board members as they attempt to establish order and structure in the complex world of the public schools.

Infusing purpose, harnessing human energy, and orchestrating the many tasks and groups involved in guiding and directing the affairs of a school system organization are challenging endeavors. They require a diverse set of talents, a great deal of patience, an exceptional amount of strength and stamina, a deep sense of caring, a sensitivity to the diverse needs and concerns of a wide variety of stakeholders, and many other skills and competencies. Superintendents, board members, and central office teams live in a world of demands and public expectations, a world that sometimes seems irrational, always presents competing pressures, is occasionally more exciting than the occupants of these positions wish, and is constantly changing.

My hope is that this book's discussion of frameworks and approaches to viewing issues and challenges school systems face will be of help to administrators in making sense out of a complex environment. The aim has been to provide some tools with which administrators can more effectively deal with the conflicting demands and challenging leadership and management imperatives they face. Before we examine next steps, it is useful to review what has been said so far.

Summarizing Strategy Formulation and Implementation

In the early part of this book, after the identification and description of major issues facing school superintendents today, a basic strategic management model was set forth and then applied to the school system context. The model provides a framework that leads through a process for formulating and executing a strategy for a school district. The formulation of strategy involves the articulation of a vision, a purpose, and a mission; an examination of environmental trends facing the education industry; an objective assessment of the strengths, capabilities, and limitations of the local school organization; and finally, the development of a set of goals and programs that describe the aspirations of the school system while providing a realistic set of plans for fulfilling those aspirations.

In assessing the external trends in the school system environment, you were asked to take a broader view of the education industry than that implied in the traditional definition of providing basic schooling for five- to eighteen-year-olds. Schools are already serving more markets and providing a wider array of services than this outdated definition embraces. Nonetheless, much program planning and technology and school district strategy is implicitly based on this narrow definition of schooling. The education industry, of which public schools are a part, is dynamic and growing, growing much faster than the population of school-age children. Furthermore, the kinds of economic, regulatory, political, social, and technological changes occurring today have resulted in many good alternatives for meeting needs that are now met by the traditional school organization. These competing alternatives are accessible to a growing portion of the population.

A framework for understanding the environment must be broad enough to allow school executives to see how society's education needs and the competing alternatives for meeting them are both changing. The framework must provide a way for such executives to examine how the changing environment will affect the school system of tomorrow so that they can begin to strategically plan for that tomorrow. This is what the approach to analyzing the external and internal environments presented in Chapters Three, Four, and Five attempted to do, while Chapter Six showed how to put together the environmental analyses and formulate a strategy for the enterprise called a local school system.

The process of implementing a strategy actually begins in the strategy formulation stage. Board members, the central office staff, other administrators, and selected members of the teaching staff and the community should be involved early in the development of the goals, the gathering of environmental data, and the examination of strategic alternatives. At this time, however, a consensus agreement should be reached by or attained from a wide range of constituencies on the school system's mission, purposes, and general operating philosophy. The mission might be articulated by the leadership or developed with broader participation. The mission or statement of purpose should not be controversial; therefore, a great deal of time need not be spent nit-picking over wording or trying to develop a final polished statement. The controversy arises in the selection of goals and the establishment of policies that allocate resources to programs for achieving those goals. It is important at selected times to employ consensus management and participative or consultative management as different stages of the process of developing the strategy unfold.

The second part of the book focused on implementation of strategy. Specific guidance on this implementation was provided in discussions about politics, marketing, and operations or instructional leadership and management, presented in Chapters Seven through Nine, respectively.

Chapter Seven used several anecdotal case situations to show how concerns about resource allocation, values, and power affect decisions and actions in schools and how conflicts are resolved. Discussion then proceeded to the subject of power and influence, with explanations of three types of power: social, economic, and legal. Power is only the potential to influence. The ability to turn power into influence is an important skill for a public school executive to have. Power can be enhanced by reframing an issue, changing the system through which decisions are made, augmenting the base of power, or influencing more stakeholders to participate.

Community power structures were described and labeled on the basis of the distribution and structure of power groups, the bases of power, the issues, the role and function of people in public office, and the customary political behavior in the community. The monolithic-elitist community has power concentrated in the hands of a few, is stable, tends to be relatively small, deals with all kinds of issues, and has a school board that is dominated by a few of its members and treats the superintendent as a functionary. The factional-competitive community has two or more coalitions or cliques in competition for influence, its leaders are involved in all issues, it tends to be larger and more heterogeneous, and has a factional school board and a superintendent who tends to be a political strategist. The plural-rational community has more cliques than the aforementioned communities, but its power structure is organized around clusters of issues, and the coalitions do not tend to be interested in the same issues and thus do not compete. The inert-latent community has no identifiable power structure or established leadership group, tends to be smaller, more stable, and more homogeneous than other communities, and tends to give its superintendent a great deal of authority.

There are at least four ways to collect information to help identify the type of power structure that exists in a given community: positional studies, event analysis studies, reputational studies, and demographic studies. Strategies for conflict resolution were discussed and classified by means of the case studies referred to above. Conflict is resolved by trying rational processes, then persuasion, then bargaining, and finally—as a last resort—a power play.

Political analysis includes the "who" (stakeholders), the "what" (stakes), and the "why" (values). Assumptions about politics and a discussion of the skills useful for political effectiveness were provided in the last section of Chapter Seven. Useful skills include strategic thinking and action taking, coalition building, adaptable action behavior, problem framing, and conceptual-theoretical knowledge building. The individual and group interactions and the interpersonal negotiations that are part of the day-to-day running of a school system are much better understood, dealt with, and managed when one has a deeper knowledge of the political processes and concepts conveyed in Chapter Seven.

The second leg of the three-legged strategy execution stool is marketing, which was discussed in Chapter Eight. A simple way to remember all the elements included in the marketing function is to think of the "four *P*'s" (product, pricing, place, and promotion) and the "four *C*'s" (consumer, cost, competition, and channels of distribution). These elements provide a framework for examining a marketing plan, something every school district should have. The development of a marketing plan starts with an extensive research effort aimed at identifying market "segments" and the needs and goals of each. Research can be conducted informally or more formally by means of depth and focus group interviews, surveys, and other techniques discussed in Chapters Five and Eight. The important fact to remember here is that marketing is not just selling and promoting. It is a process for understanding human wants and needs and designing and delivering affordable services to fill those needs. Promotion and selling usually come after the other functions of marketing are performed; if those other functions are performed well, promotion and selling may only be needed as a device for disseminating education and information.

A marketing plan must also have financial elements. Marketing strategies have financial implications, and the marketing plan should be developed concurrently with or within the parameters of a financial plan. Financial analysis involves an understanding of cost and revenue "drivers," the events or transactions that give rise to or create costs and revenues for a school system. By understanding the behavior of costs, the superintendent can project the implications of various alternative courses of action in financial terms at least, and more importantly, he or she can communicate these implications in effective and clear language to the district's various constituents.

Chapter Nine defined instructional leadership and delivery as the operations function of a school system. Operations management includes quality control and efficient delivery of services, responsibilities that have been getting more attention lately in all sectors of the U.S. economy because our competitive weaknesses in the global economy have become more obvious.

Operations management can be a factor in strategy formulation, not just a process for implementing a strategy, which is decided on separately. The point is that if schools develop innovative new services and delivery methods or processes by focusing on the potential for creative instructional concepts, the schools' strategy and market opportunities can be greatly expanded. In this case, leadership in operations management can drive the development of strategic plans rather than just follow from the strategy already determined.

Instructional leadership involves harnessing the great reservoir of energy and potential that normally exists in a school system's staff. It means carefully and appropriately introducing processes that allow appropriate groups to participate in key decisions. It does not have to mean losing control of the overall direction and driving purposes of the organization. Many myths are involved in the managerial use of participation. Certain jobs should ordinarily be done by administrators without consultation. Other actions require the cooperation and understanding of others, and their implementation is also dependent on others. These latter actions require at least consultation and at most consensual decision making.

Useful participation is based on assumptions about the inherent motivation of people to do a job well, to derive satisfaction from accomplishing goals they perceive as being worthwhile and inspiring, and to be members of successful teams. These are the Theory Y assumptions articulated by McGregor (1957) more than thirty years ago and still widely misunderstood.

Empirical evidence has not been gathered to support or refute the usefulness of these assumptions because academic research paradigms are not structured in this manner. The weight of the limited and indirect evidence we have, however, seems to support the validity of these assumptions, especially for knowledge workers and professionals who produce a result that is difficult to measure. Whether or not the assumptions are valid for a given situation, many practitioners and behavioral scientists believe that adopting them and truly putting them into action can be extremely useful in liberating the powerful forces for change and improvement that reside in most organizations. The trick is to internalize these beliefs and then to know how to act effectively on them. Doing this requires a great deal of skill and training of the kind that most educational administrators have not been exposed to, except perhaps at the intellectual or cognitive level.

The third and last part of this book discussed ways of introducing change, then ways of evaluating the performance to determine the degree of improvement, if any, that results from the change, and finally, approaches and methods for responding to the demands for accountability. Chapter Ten discussed first the roles of mission, vision, goals, strategy, and tactics in dealing with overall organizational change. These five terms are used in diverse ways by different people. Trying to define them may not solve the confusion this differential usage sometimes causes. I found it helpful, however, to distinguish three levels of usage of these concepts. At the first level a general vision is designed to enroll people and excite them about a future the organization can create. Examples for a school system might be "To help each child reach his or her full potential" or "To provide access to personal growth and development for all segments of society."

At the second level, somewhat more concrete purposes are enunciated, as well as some goals that state in general terms the mission or purpose that the organization will pursue. Examples here related to the visions suggested above might be "To maintain a closeness and sensitivity to the needs of clients," "To provide for 'cultural literacy' and basic skills," "To help each child become employable and self-sufficient," "To provide opportunities for development of esthetic capacities,'' ''To provide opportunities for athletic and physical development,'' ''To foster growth of positive self-image,'' and ''To provide special opportunities for culturally deprived children and children with special needs.''

At the third level, specific action programs are described. Examples here might be ''To develop a curriculum in basic skills that achieves enhanced test scores for our population of students,'' ''To support six major varsity girls' and boys' sports,'' and ''To have in each elementary school music, drama, and arts programs staffed by appropriate specialists.''

A fourth level of usage was discussed in Chapter Nine on operations management, where it was stated that the specifications for short-term goals should be specific, measurable, and attainable with some stretch and should involve instructional or curriculum matters (in other words, deal with the chief product or service being provided by the organization).

Given the background of a vision and a mission that enroll people and goals that they have participated in creating as vehicles for pursuing the mission and achieving the purposes of the school system, the organization can plan a change strategy to help it move from where it is to where it wants to be. An important part of this strategy involves a process termed transition management. This involves managing certain transition state dynamics, such as shifts in power and the resulting anxiety created by the prospects of change, the grieving process associated with loss, and issues regarding control. In the last dynamic, control, the need is for the executive to direct and guide the process while still providing for consultation and consensus decision making when appropriate. The management of transition requires a great deal of energy, a sensitivity to a wide variety of issues and groups, and close attention to many details that are often overlooked in the frenzy of activity created by the change effort.

There are forces that can facilitate change, and there are forces that can block change. Executives typically place most of their efforts on trying to increase the intensity of the positive forces. Participation in planning, articulating the new vision, rewarding behavior that supports the new processes and programs, and negotiating and bargaining with politically powerful groups are just some of the ways that executives can influence positive forces.

Another approach to change management is to lessen the intensity of negative or resistant forces. This includes paying special attention to the problems of loss and grieving and providing support that helps people cope with the stresses and anxiety they feel about the change. It can also involve an attempt to isolate powerful opponents with whom negotiating is not an option.

It is helpful to use the four frames mentioned in Chapter Ten—structural, political, human resource, and symbolic—for thinking about ways in which to deal with the forces that support and the forces that inhibit change.

Participation in decision making is an important tool in a variety of management and leadership situations but especially when it comes to issues of organizational change. In using participative methods, executives must take care to avoid the "sham" that is often involved in meetings called to obtain "input." They must communicate as clearly as possible in advance of a participative discussion just how much they are willing to delegate to the group, what the limits of the group's authority are, and how the final decision will be made. When there is wide support for certain actions, executives can show leadership by making the decisions themselves and not wasting the time of other staff members. If a superintendent's mind is made up in advance, then group members will resent the incursion on their busy schedules that active participation requires.

Research has shown that there are dangers in too much participation. Teachers want to be involved in curriculum and instructional decisions, where their professional knowledge can provide a meaningful contribution, but they seem to want neither to spend a great deal of time in long meetings nor to spend any time in minor administrative matters. On the other hand, two kinds of participative processes are useful to consider when major changes are planned: consultation and consensus building. Consultative methods are useful for planning and implementation issues. Consensus management is employed when the executive feels comfortable in vesting the group with total power for a given decision, when there is adequate time, when the decision is extremely important, and when collaboration and support of the entire group are needed. The last of these requires special skills and may entail the use of an outside consultant.

Building an effective work team is a vital role for the leader. The effectiveness of team effort can be important to the success of any organization. Chapter Ten briefly described the role of a "transition team" in guiding the change effort, but the concepts involved in building an effective work team have general application. Teams need both the technical knowledge required for whatever task they are charged to perform and the interpersonal competence to function synergistically as a group. This means paying attention to process dynamics at all stages of work. At the beginning, time must be taken to establish guidelines and rules for working together and norms of conduct and behavior. During the middle stages, members with the knowledge and skill needed in a given situation must be given an opportunity to be heard and to act. During the full-performing stages, appropriate support must be made available to the group, group members' efforts must be coordinated, and the group must be allowed to examine its behavior and results, make revisions in its processes, and learn from its experience.

Hackman (1987) provides a model for understanding the stages of work group development. It specifies four stages: (1) prework, when the task and group role are defined; (2) creating performance conditions, when the group is selected and organizes to do the task and obtains needed resources and support; (3) building the team, when the group must spend time (at the expense of frustrating its action-oriented members) establishing its norms, boundaries, and the specifics of its task definition; and (4) providing ongoing assistance, when the group requires continuing assistance from management to renegotiate its mission if necessary, to adjust its process to obtain synergy, and to help it exploit opportunities to learn from its experience.

Chapter Eleven described methods for assessing the success of a strategy, particularly with the success of any change

effort to improve the effectiveness of a school district. This led
to the topic of accountability, which was defined as both evaluation and reporting. A framework consisting of input, process,
and output was used in the discussion of assessment. I cautioned
school executives against giving in completely to the business
"results" model as the *only* means of assessing school districts'
performance. While outcomes or outputs are extremely important, the side effects of certain treatments are not well enough
understood and the results are not measurable in as complete
a manner as necessary to ignore completely an assessment of
process and input. On the other hand, the limitations of results
measures are not to be used as an excuse for paying less than
the fullest possible attention to the development, analysis, and
reporting of a variety of school system output measures.

After analysis of cost controls on input and of processes
and methods of teaching and their possible consequences, the
output of a school system can be viewed and reported on in terms
of three kinds of results: learner outcomes, client satisfaction
measures, and other indicators of outcomes achieved. When it
comes to output measures, we must ask, "Output for whom?"
That brings us back to the kind of stakeholder analysis prescribed
in Chapters Seven and Eight. Which of the following are the
clients and stakeholders of the school?

Society
The state
Employers
The local community
Parents and students
School staff and administration
All of the above

All of these groups share some common demands, but
each group also makes additional and sometimes conflicting
demands on the school. Society wants kind, considerate, law-
abiding, literate, knowledgeable, functional, and productive individuals who are equipped to intelligently participate in a democratic community. States want what society wants and also to

see measurable learning gains. Employers usually want people who are obedient to authority, prompt, and dependable, with good work habits and specific usable skills. The local community is concerned about its property and real estate values. Various segments of the parent and student groups focus on special program needs, on the opportunity to get into the "best" colleges, on vocational courses, on athletic successes, and on arts opportunities. Finally, the school's staff and administration are often interested in equal opportunity and access for all.

My last recommendation was that each school system develop an annual report to stakeholders. While the suggestions offered for items and data to collect, analyze, and report are too numerous for any single report, the recommendation to superintendents is that they use a variety of media and prepare a different kind of report for each major stakeholder group.

Getting Started

Strategic management and strategic leadership are processes that one does not just abruptly "start." They involve the skills and behaviors described in this book, attitudes of respect for the needs and ideas of other individuals and groups, a belief in Theory Y assumptions about people, a great deal of patience, and a willingness to speak out in public with inspirational words. These processes also demand firmness in staying with long-term goals, ideals, and values in the face of opposition to programs aimed at bringing ideals closer to reality; time and financial commitments; and extensive efforts aimed at educating and training school district personnel, including the board and superintendent. The following pages provide some guidelines and specific suggestions to school districts that wish to enhance their strategic direction and the leadership in their systems. I recommend that a school district start by initiating the development of a strategic plan that employs most or all of the specific steps outlined below. After the strategic planning process is well under way, the district can begin refining the mission and vision, formulating the strategy, and developing the action plan for implementation.

Steps to follow in strategic planning are as follows:

1. Form a strategic planning committee as suggested in Chapter Two.

2. Have this committee read Chapters Two and Three of this book.

3. Conduct several meetings of the planning committee (at least three to six meetings of about an hour and a half to three hours each) to discuss the assigned readings, to clarify issues and definitions, to add other local issues and trends, and then to agree on a process involving the later steps of strategic planning. (Adapt the sequence and structure of steps 4 through 10 to fit this agreement.)

4. Obtain full board approval of the process, with some general agreement on direction and deadlines for the committee's work.

5. Continue regular meetings of the committee (at least twice a month and preferably weekly), bringing in specialists in demography, education trends, technology, political, legislative, and school finance trends, and the like to provide input to and answer questions from the committee.

6. Examine the school system's strengths by using Chapter Four as a starting point for the committee's discussion and possibly bringing in key staff members and evaluation specialists. The planning committee may want additional staff assistance and consultants during this stage, depending on the budget available to them.

7. After completing steps 5 and 6 (these steps should not be rushed but probably should take no longer than six months to complete), make a progress report to the board and discuss the report at board and public meetings.

8. Conduct market research to ascertain the community's views and preferences for the pursuit of certain strategic options and for the methods of financing any new strategic initiatives. (This step will vary from school district to district, depending on size, homogeneity of the community, financial condition, seriousness of issues, and data already available on community needs and wants.) Use outside help to examine the final design of the surveys and to interpret the results. Be sure, however, that the superinten-

dent and board or the planning committee keeps control of the objectives and scope of the inquiry.

9. Have the planning committee prepare a report to the board. This report should contain some or all of the following: (a) an executive summary, (b) a discussion of some of the key options and their pros and cons, (c) a summary of the findings from any market research done, (d) some possible alternative scenarios, and (3) a recommendation and the reasons for it (optional). The report should be reasonably brief to allow for quick reading, with supporting data attached as exhibits or appendixes for those who want more detail.

10. Discuss the report at the board and community levels, possibly take a vote on specific issues, and then draft a statement to be voted on by the board. This statement should contain some or all of the following:

> A very brief mission or vision statement.
>
> A brief statement of the district's overall direction for the next five to ten years.
>
> Some specific goals and time schedules for the next three to five years, with some general goals for subsequent years.
>
> A preliminary statement as to the thrust of the implementation program in terms of political strategy, marketing plan, and operations and instructional plans. (My personal view is that this statement of strategy should be reasonably brief. Lots of detail can overwhelm or cloud the key strategic issues. Again use separate appendixes for details.)

To those districts engaging in strategic planning according to the above steps or other similar approaches, the following caveats are in order: Strategic planning is a continuous process. It is never "finished" just because the plan is agreed to and written down somewhere. The steps outlined above do not necessarily have to occur in the order noted. Simultaneous work can and should be proceeding on several steps at a time, and several adjustments in the output will have to be made along the way.

After a strategy is formulated and approved, next comes the working out of specific programs, systems, and structures for implementing that strategy. This involves following the kinds of recommendations given in Chapters Seven, Eight, and Nine. If a major change in strategy is involved, then the suggestions in Chapter Ten can be of great help. Even if major change is not involved, the ideas about work group development in Chapter Ten and the suggestions on when and how to use participative approaches in Chapters Nine and Ten should be helpful as the administration of the school works with various staff groups, citizens' committees, and other ad hoc groups formed to deal with the inevitable problems that arise in implementing a visionary plan.

The personal values of the board and the superintendent must be reflected in the strategy selected for implementation or it will have tough sledding. If they, in turn, do not reflect the values of the staff, the community, and other key stakeholders and cannot convince these stakeholders of the merits of the values reflected in the strategic plan, implementation will be even more difficult.

The task of articulating the mission and defining and shaping the organization's purpose is, as Andrews (1987) notes, perhaps the most important leadership function of the board and superintendent. If the leadership of a school system can excite its constituents and obtain their commitment to the purposes of the system, the job of implementing the strategy, while still challenging, will proceed much more smoothly.

After Strategy Formulation and Implementation, What Next?

After a process of strategy formulation has been engaged in and the implementation program is under way, it is tempting to step back and let the resulting programs run their course. More typically, school executives, who (despite some beliefs to the contrary) tend to be as energetic and work oriented as their business counterparts, wish to repeat the process all over again the following year. This can, much like the budget cycle, become an annual ritual. If this occurs, then the process is more like management control and monitoring, a very vital managerial activity for an organization but not "strategic" leadership. Strategic leadership is both a continuous activity and an irregular process. It is continuous because the job of formulating, pursuing, revising, and leading the strategic changes is never finished. It is irregular because it calls for momentous efforts and the focusing of a great deal of energy on specific needs and problems or opportunities that result from major changes in the environment. These changes come at irregular intervals and cannot be predicted in advance. Breakthroughs in technology, such as satellite and microwave transmission of courses, the sharp reduction in costs of the microcomputer, the social changes in the role of women—and the changes in colleges of education that these lead to—are all events that do not just arise when the annual planning cycle is beginning. They do not happen every year either. When they do occur, they signal a time for a major reexamination of the mission, purpose, and strategic plan of the school system.

After the first time a school system engages in a massive strategic management effort as prescribed in this book, constant monitoring of goal achievement, plans, and results should follow. My suggestion, however, is that a major reexamination of strategy and purpose should not become institutionalized into an annual event. Do this only when major changes in your economic, social, or technological climate occur or when your constituent groups change their goals and needs significantly. This means that the next steps after engaging in the initial formulation and implementation of strategy mainly involve monitoring and adjusting the strategy. I recommend that a school system's next steps be to set up a process for continually monitoring the trends discussed in Chapters Three and Four and to engage in marketing research and planning on a regular basis and that the district only consider reformulating strategy when environmental circumstances warrant it.

Professional Management

This book has been about the professional management and leadership of education organizations. Its focus has been on the general managers of local school systems. The concept of strategic management is the framework that one can use to help organize the process of managing local schools. When one understands more about the art and science of administration, one incurs a professional responsibility to practice that art as well as the latest knowledge and experience allow.

This book is just one milestone in what should be a lifelong search on the part of the professional manager, the reflective executive, for the best approaches for leading and managing effectively. This search extends to the best methods for directing and guiding education professionals engaged in the work of better serving public needs, to the best techniques and processes for activating and employing the resources needed to make a school system work most effectively and efficiently, and to finding the inner strength to inspire and excite others to higher levels of performance and achievement. The search is a lifelong journey for the dedicated school executive. My hope is that this book has contributed to progress on this journey and helped its readers to reignite their vision, regenerate their sense of purpose, and add additional power to their practical wisdom for achieving their significant and socially vital professional goals.

Resource:
Management Report
to Stakeholders

In early 1979, Harry Wallace, superintendent of schools in Lewis, a small midwestern town, was asked by his board to prepare an outline for an "annual report to 'stakeholders.'" Stakeholders were the "publics" or groups that had a stake in the quality and performance of the schools, that is, parents, students, teachers, administrators, the community, and so on. The idea was to have some consistent format for the superintendent to report to his publics on a regular basis.

In the preceding ten years, three superintendents had held Mr. Wallace's current job. Each had a different format for reporting to his citizens, stressing factors that he deemed important. For example, in 1971, when test scores were up, they were highlighted; in 1972, finance and budget were highlighted. The periodic reports to the board between 1974 and 1977 (not given on any regular schedule) focused on declining enrollment, teacher terminations, and discussion of alternatives for cost cutting and program reduction.

Prepared by John J. Mauriel. "Management Report to Stakeholders" is reproduced with permission of the Bush Public School Executive Fellows Program. Edited for inclusion here. All names are fictitious. This case was written from general experience and does not represent one specific school district.

331

In 1978, Mr. Wallace had tried to present a "report" to the public that emphasized the quality of education in Lewis and described some of its programs that were designed to optimize the use of limited resources in the classroom.

Mr. Wallace noted that there were no generally accepted criteria for comparing his schools' performance or quality this year with last year or comparing the performance of Lewis with that of nearby metropolitan, suburban, or smaller town schools. Often, some citizens in the community stated, "Our schools are good because _____" and then gave a variety of reasons. Other citizens would say, "Our schools aren't as we'd like because _____," and then they would give a variety of reasons, some of them similar to those stated by citizens who thought the Lewis schools were "good."

After reflecting on his past experiences and also on the fact that each citizen used different criteria for evaluating the schools, Mr. Wallace considered the report format shown in Exhibit 2. He was now contemplating presenting to his board for approval a policy requiring the administration to present to the public an annual report based on this format.

The content of his proposed annual report was broken down into eight general headings:

A. Customer-Client Satisfaction Levels
B. Student Performance Levels
C. Programs and Levels of Service Provided and Results
D. Staff Effectiveness
E. Budget Reports and Ratios
F. Openness to Change
G. General Observations
H. Summary and Interpretation by Superintendent

Under each heading he listed the items to be evaluated or measured and reported on in the annual message to "stakeholders."

The department of education of the state in which Lewis was located looked on with interest. If the plan worked well in Lewis, should the department *require* it elsewhere?

**Exhibit 2. Management Report to Publics (Parents,
Students, Teachers, Taxpayers, Board) of a School District.**

Note: It is understood that exact measures are not available on many of the items listed below. The point is that the superintendent must make some comment or judgment about each one, backing it up with quantitative data (where possible), carefully gathered professional opinions, objective judgments, and any other facts he or she can muster.

All items should be compared to the following:
>Last year
>State average or norm when available
>Other adjacent or similar school districts
>Other relevant reference points

A. Customer-Client Satisfaction Levels
>Items to be used for measurement and reporting:
>>Student evaluations
>>Parent surveys
>>Number and severity of complaints about school
>>Special commendations, gestures of appreciation

>(*Note:* Procedures must be developed for gathering data on complaints and commendations that are objective and consistent from year to year.)

>1. Attendance rate
>2. Dropout rate
>3. Percentage of students residing in district but attending nonpublic schools
>4. Number of community members involved in school activities and programs and kinds of involvement

B. Student Performance Levels
>1. Academic test scores
>(Several types, by grade, by building, compared to similar schools, and so on)
>2. Achievement related to ability
>3. Percentage of graduates going to
>>College (where?)
>>AVTI
>>Jobs (types?)
>>Other
>4. Alumni performance data
>(three, five, ten years later)
>5. Values test scores
>6. Evidence of concern for others, and so on
>7. "Citizenship" measures

C. Programs and Levels of Service Provided and Results
   1. Cocurricular
      (Activities and participation rates)
   2. Special education
      (Services provided, number served, assessment process, number and quality of parent conferences)
   3. Special teachers
      (Numbers, qualifications, and number of students served, quality measures, if possible)
   4. Aides and volunteers
      (Number used and how used)
   5. Electives
      (List twenty most popular offerings and percentage of students electing)
   6. Special Programs
      (Quality, type, number served, and so on)

D. Staff Effectiveness
   1. Evidence of motivation, dedication
   2. Extra service and so on
   3. New staff programs and efforts
   4. Training and development programs for staff completed last year
   5. Other

E. Budget Reports and Ratios

	Total Cost			Cost per Pupil		
	This Year	Last Year	% Inc. Decr.	This Year	Last Year	% Inc. Decr.
Classroom instruction						
Administration						
Special teachers						
Special education*						
Vocational education*						
Lunches: type and cost						
State-federal support						
Net cost to general fund						
Transportation—regular						
Transportation—special						
Net transportation cost after subsidy						
Cocurricular activities						
Revenue producing						
Number of participants						
Cost per participant						
Receipt per participant						
Nonrevenue producing						
Number of participants						
Cost per participant						
Receipt per participant						

	Total Cost			Cost per Pupil		
	This Year	Last Year	% Inc. Decr.	This Year	Last Year	% Inc. Decr.
Supplies						
Heat, light, power						
Other costs						
Total						
Total revenue						
Surplus or deficit						

*Net out against subsidy

Pupil/Teacher Ratios

	This Year	Your District Last Year	Adjacent District	Adjacent or Other Similar Sized or Type District	Adjacent or Other Similar Sized or Type District	State	Metr.	Out of State
HS, classroom only								
HS, including specials								
ES, classroom only								
ES, including specials								
Range of class size								
ES								
HS								

Notes: (1) Special ed. pupils should have separate classification, numbers per teacher, numbers mainstreamed, and so on. (2) List of instructional programs and cocurricular activities added or deleted should accompany this report.

F. Openness to Change
   1. Are relevant social changes in this district being examined and considered?
   2. By which of the following is new technology being examined?
   Teachers
   Community
   Administrators
   Pupils
   3. What basic changes in structure and delivery have occurred in the last five years or are planned? Are they related to the special environmental circumstances of the school?

G. General Observations
   1. Qualitative analysis of items not easily measurable
   2. Special items (legislation, state dept.) and responses by district
   3. Discussion of special factors not included above, with comparisons to last year and to other schools
   4. Analysis of strengths and weaknesses of school district as seen by administration, teachers, parents, students
   (May report on cooperative programs with other districts: successes, failures, numbers, and so on)

H. Summary and Interpretations by Superintendent
   (Limit 500-word narrative report)

References

Andrews, K. R. *The Concept of Corporate Strategy.* Homewood, Ill.: Dow-Jones, Irwin, 1987.

Beckhard, R., and Harris, R. *Organizational Transitions.* Reading, Mass.: Addison-Wesley, 1977.

Beer, M., *Oganization, Change, and Development.* Santa Monica: Goodyear, 1980.

Bennis, W. G., and Eisen, S. "Force-Field Analysis Inventory." In J. W. Pfeffer and J. E. Jones (eds.), *A Handbook of Structured Experiences for Human Relations Training.* Vol. 2. La Jolla, Calif.: University Associates, 1974.

Bennis, W. G., and Nanus, B. *Leaders: The Strategies for Taking Charge.* New York: Harper & Row, 1985.

Berkowitz, E., Kerin, R. A., and Rudelius, S. *Marketing.* (2nd ed.) Homewood, Ill.: Irwin, 1989.

Block, P. *The Empowered Manager: Positive Political Skills at Work.* San Francisco: Jossey-Bass, 1987.

Bolman, L. G., and Deal, T. E. *Modern Approaches to Understanding and Managing Organizations.* San Francisco: Jossey-Bass, 1984.

Brookover, W. B., and Lezotte, L. W. *Changes in School Characteristics Coincident with Changes in Student Achievement.* East Lansing: College of Urban Development, Michigan State University, 1977.

Brookover, W. B., and others. *School Social Systems and Student Achievement: Schools Can Make a Difference.* New York: Praeger, 1979.

Bryson, J. M. *Strategic Planning for Public and Nonprofit Organizations: A Guide to Strengthening and Sustaining Organizational Achievement.* San Francisco: Jossey-Bass, 1988.

Coch, L., and French, J. R. P., Jr. "Overcoming Resistance to Change." *Human Relations,* 1948, *1,* 512–533.

Conway, J. A. "The Myth, Mystery, and Mastery of Participative Decision Making in Education." *Educational Administration Quarterly,* 1984, *20,* 11–40.

Cuban, L. "Transforming the Frog into a Prince: Effective Schools Research, Policy, and Practice at the District Level." *Harvard Educational Review,* 1984, *54* (2), 129–151.

Cuban, L. *The Managerial Imperative and the Practice of Leadership in Schools.* Albany: State University of New York Press, 1988.

Dahl, R. E. *Who Governs?* New Haven, Conn.: Yale University Press, 1961.

Davidson, J. L. *The Superintendency: Leadership for Effective Schools.* Jackson, Miss.: Kelwyn, 1987.

Deal, T. E., and Kennedy, A. A. *Corporate Cultures: The Rites and Rituals of Corporate Life.* Reading, Mass.: Addison-Wesley, 1982.

Drucker, P. F. *The Practice of Management.* New York: Harper & Row, 1954.

Flesch, R. *Why Johnny Can't Read.* New York: Harper & Row, 1955.

Fritz, R. *The Path of Least Resistance.* Salem, Mass.: DMA, Inc., 1984.

Genck, F., and Klingenberg, A. *The School Board's Responsibility: Effective Schools Through Effective Management.* Springfield: Illinois Association of School Boards, 1978.

Gilbert, D., Hartman, E., Freeman, R. E., and Mauriel, J. J. *The Logic of Strategy.* Boston: Ballinger, 1988.

Ginsburg, A., Noell, J., and Plisko, V. "Lessons from the Wall Chart." *Educational Evaluation and Policy Analysis,* 1988, *10* (1), 1–12.

Hackman, J. R. "The Design of Work Teams." In J. W. Lorsch (ed.), *Handbook of Organizational Behavior.* Englewood Cliffs, N.J.: Prentice-Hall, 1987.

Hare, A. P. *Creativity in Small Groups.* Newbury Park, Calif.: Sage, 1982.

Herzberg, F. "One More Time: How Do You Motivate Employees?" *Harvard Business Review,* 1968, *1,* 53–62.

Homans, G. *The Human Group.* San Diego, Calif.: Harcourt Brace Jovanovich, 1950.

Hrebiniak, L., and Joyce, W. *Implementing Strategy.* New York: Macmillan, 1984.

Klebba, J., and Mauriel, J. J. *Golden Valley School District A–I.* St. Paul, Minn.: Bush Public School Executive Fellows Program, 1978. (Copies of these cases may be obtained by writing to the Bush Program, 1884 Como Avenue, St. Paul, Minnesota 55108.)

Kotler, P., and Fox, K. F. A. *Strategic Marketing for Educational Institutions.* Englewood Cliffs, N.J.: Prentice-Hall, 1985.

Kübler-Ross, E. *On Death and Dying.* New York: Macmillan, 1969.

Latane, B., Williams, K., and Harkins, S. "Many Hands Make Light the Work: The Causes and Consequences of Social Loafing." *Journal of Personality and Social Psychology,* 1979, *37,* 822–832.

Levin, H. "Cost-Effectiveness and Educational Policy." *Educational Evaluation and Policy Analysis,* 1988, *10* (1), 51–70.

Levy, P., and Goldstein, H. *Tests in Education: A Book of Critical Reviews.* Orlando, Fla.: Academic Press, 1986.

Lewin, K. *Field Theory in Social Science.* New York: Harper & Row, 1951.

Lightfoot, S. L. *The Good High School: Portraits of Character and Culture.* New York: Basic Books, 1983.

Lindblom, C. E. "The Science of 'Muddling Through.'" *Public Administration Review,* 1959, *19,* 79–88.

Lortie, D. C. *School Teacher: A Sociological Study.* Chicago: University of Chicago Press, 1975.

McCarty, D. G., and Ramsey, C. E. "Community Power, School Board Structure, and the Role of the Chief School Administrator." *Educational Administration Quarterly,* 1968, *4* (4), 19–33.

McGregor, D. *The Human Side of Enterprise.* New York: McGraw-Hill, 1957.

March, J., and Simon, H. *Organizations.* New York: Wiley, 1958.

Marcus, A. "Externally Induced Innovation." In A. Van de

Ven, H. Angle, and M. S. Poole (eds.), *Research on the Management of Innovation*. Boston: Ballinger, 1989.

Marris, P. *Loss and Change*. Boston: Routledge & Kegan Paul, 1974.

Mauriel, J. J. *Golden Valley G*. St. Paul, Minn.: Bush Public School Executive Fellows Program, 1979a.

Mauriel, J. J. *Management Report to Stakeholders*. St. Paul, Minn.: Bush Public School Executive Fellows Program, 1979b.

Miller, J. "Decision Making and Organizational Effectiveness—Participation and Perceptions." *Sociology of Work and Occupations*, 1980, *7* (1), 55–79.

Minnesota State Department of Education. *A Comprehensive Plan for School Effectiveness*. St. Paul: Minnesota State Department of Education, 1984.

Moynihan, D. P. *Family and Nation*. San Diego, Calif.: Harcourt Brace Jovanovich, 1986.

Nadler, D. A. *Feedback and Organization Development: Using Data-Based Methods*. Reading, Mass.: Addison-Wesley, 1977.

Nadler, D. A. "The Effective Management of Organizational Change." In J. W. Lorsch (ed.), *Handbook of Organizational Behavior*. Englewood Cliffs, N.J.: Prentice-Hall, 1987.

National Commission on Excellence in Education. *A Nation at Risk: The Imperative for Educational Reform*. Washington, D.C.: U.S. Government Printing Office, 1983.

Ouchi, W. *Theory Z*. New York: Avon Books, 1981.

Peters, T. J., and Waterman, R. H. *In Search of Excellence*. New York: Harper & Row, 1982.

Pittner, N. "The Study of Administrator Effects and Effectiveness." In N. J. Boyan (ed.), *Handbook of Research on Educational Administration*. New York: Longman, 1988.

Powers, R. C. *Identifying Community Power Structure*. North Central Regional Extension Publication, no. 19. Ames: Cooperative Extension Service, Iowa State University, 1965.

Quinn, J. B. *Strategies for Change: Logical Incrementalism*. Homewood, Ill.: Irwin, 1980.

Rudelius, C. W., Berkowitz, E., and Kerin, R. A. *Marketing*. St. Louis, Mo.: Times Mirror/Mosby, 1986.

Schein, E. H. *Process Consultation: Its Role in Organization Development.* Reading, Mass.: Addison-Wesley, 1969.

Schultz, T., and Mauriel, J. J. *The Northfield Case.* St. Paul, Minn.: Bush Public School Executive Fellows Program, 1981.

Silberman, C. E. *Crisis in the Classroom.* New York: Random House, 1970.

Simon, H. A. *Administrative Behavior.* (4th ed.) New York: Free Press, 1976.

Stufflebeam, D. L., and Shinkfield, A. J. *Systematic Evaluation: A Self-Instructional Guide to Theory and Practice.* Boston: Kluwer-Nijhoff, 1983.

Tannenbaum, R., Margulies, N., Massarik, F., and Associates. *Human Systems Development: New Perspectives on People and Organizations.* San Francisco: Jossey-Bass, 1985.

Tannenbaum, R., Weschler, I. R., and Massarik, F. *Leadership and Organization: A Behavioral Science Approach.* New York: McGraw-Hill, 1961.

"The Typical School Board Member: Still White, Male, Fortyish, and Well-Off." *American School Board Journal,* 1989, *176* (1), 21.

Vroom, V. H., and Yetton, P. W. "The Vroom and Yetton Model of Leadership: An Overview." In S. King and F. Fiedler (eds.), *Managerial Control and Organizational Democracy.* Washington, D.C.: Winston, 1978.

Waterman, R. H., Peters, T. J., and Phillips, J. R. "Structure Is Not Organization." *Business Horizons,* June 1980, pp. 14–26.

Weick, K. E. "Educational Organizations as Loosely Coupled Systems." *Administrative Science Quarterly,* 1976, *21,* 1–19.

Weinberg, R. A. "A Case of a Misplaced Conjunction: Nature or Nurture." *Journal of School Psychology,* 1983, *21,* 9–12.

Weisbord, M. R. *Productive Workplaces: Organizing and Managing for Dignity, Meaning, and Community.* San Francisco: Jossey-Bass, 1987.

Index

A

AASA (American Association of School Administrators), 304
Accountability: compliance with mandates vs. commitment to results, 287–288; demand for, 40–42, 304–311; described, 40, 287–290, 324; developing framework for, 291–292; for facilities and equipment resources, 297–298; for financial resources, 292–295; for processes, 298–299; for staff resources, 296–297; through annual reports to stakeholders, 312–313, 331–337; yardsticks for, 42, 299–304. *See also* Evaluation
Administrative staffs. *See* Staffs (administrative)
Adult education classes, 142
Advertising and promotion of marketable products, 222–226
After-school programs. *See* Preschool and after-school programs
AIDS education: and mission of schools, 23
American Association of School Administrators (AASA), 304
American School Board Journal, 84
Andrews, K. R., 45, 51, 145
Annual reports to stakeholders, 312–313, 325, 331–337

Anxiety: managing in transitional organization change, 268–271
Assessment. *See* Evaluation
Athletics: Golden Valley School System attitude toward, 91; and mission of schools, 22
Authority: for decision-making in schools, 17–20, 147; and participative management theory, 243–249; as shared/contested by school boards and superintendents, 84–86. *See also* Constituencies/Stakeholders; Politics; Power
Auto mechanics program example, 105, 111–112

B

Baby-sitting services. *See* Preschool and after-school programs
Band program example, 100, 105, 107, 109–111
Bargaining process of conflict resolution, 202–204
Beckhard, R., 264–265
Beer, M., 269
Bennis, W. G., 267
Berkowitz, E., 107–108
Block, P., 262
Bolman, L. G., 210, 275
"Bottom line" accountability: dangers of, 300, 302

Brookover, W. B., 31
Brown v. Topeka, 18
Bryson, J. M., 8
Budgets. See Accountability; Financial issues
Burn-out, 29
Bush Foundation, 15
Bush Public School Executive Fellows Program, 94, 120, 130

C

Central offices, See Staffs (central office)
CIPP (context: input, process, product) model, 251, 291
Citizens' committees: for strategic planning, 16, 113–116
Citizenship: and mission of schools, 21
Class size, 126, 140
Clients. See Constituencies/Stakeholders; Customers
Coch, L., 273
Cohort survival techniques, 54, 93
Collective bargaining, 19, 80, 140. See also Teachers' associations
Colleges of education: drops in enrollment and quality in, 30
Communities: identifying power holders in, 191–197; power structures in, 186–191. See also Constituencies/ Stakeholders
Competition: for educational services market, 59–64; for public resources, 48, 62
Computers. See Interactive cable programs; Technology
Conflict resolution, 176–177, 197–208
Consolidation of school districts, 123–124, 139–140
Constituencies/Stakeholders: annual reports to, 312–313, 325, 331–337; described, 12–13, 152, 306–311, 324–325; influence on schools of, 17–20, 168–169; involvment in decision making, 24–25, 151, 264–274; involvment in strategic planning, 16, 113–116; and public relations value of market surveys, 97, 114, 117, 128–129; stakes defined, 169–170. See also Accountability; Markets for education; Politics; Power, School boards; Teachers' associations
Consultants: cautions on use of, 116, 119, 121–122, 250
Control: loss of as anxiety-agent in organizational change, 271–274
Conway, J. A., 272
Cooperative school district arrangements. See Consolidation of school districts
Cost efficiency, cost-effectiveness, and cost-benefit analyses, 293–295, 311
Cost cutting measures, 140
Creationism, 165, 183
Crisis in the Classroom, 18–19
Cuban, L., 234
Culture within organizations, 232–233, 256
Customers: of schools' products, 214–216. See also Constituencies/Stakeholders; Parents; Students

D

Dahl, R. E., 194
Darwinian teachings, 165, 183
Davidson, J. L., 86, 276
Day-care programs, 21, 27, 144. See also Preschool and after-school programs
Deal, T. E., 210, 232, 275
Decision-making models, 145–151, 272
Delivery systems: alternate description of, 229; assessing, 127–129; designing, 221–226
Demographic studies of community power structures, 195–197
Demographics. See Social and economic trends
Department of Education wall chart, 295, 301, 304, 307
Depth interviews, 96, 98–101
Diversification of service areas, 138–139
Drop-out rates, 31
Drucker, P. F., 300
Drug education, 21–22, 27

E

Economic power, 179–180
Economic trends. *See* Social and economic trends
Edmonds, 78
Education: as an "industry", 45–51
The Empowered Manager, 262
Enrollments: predicting with cohort survival techniques, 54, 93; shrinking of, 25–26
Environment. *See* Home environment
Evaluation: annual reports to stakeholders as form of, 312–313, 325, 331–337; as device for change, 256–258; importance of anticipating results of, 250; and instructional improvement, 242–249; 252–254; and Northfield school system example, 249, 252–254; and program management, 249–252; school quality control with, 251, 254–255. *See also* Accountability; Instructional improvement
Event analysis studies of community power structures, 192–194
Evolution: teaching of, 165, 183

F

Factional-competitive power structures, 188–189
Federal government: and enrollment policies, 18; and handicapped rights policies, 18; and withdrawal of funds for state/local use, 26
Fee-for-service programs, 100, 105, 112, 124–125, 142
Field Theory in Social Science, 274
Financial issues: accountability for, 292–295; affording new technologies, 34–36; cost-cutting measures, 140; donations and fund raising, 142–143, 153; increasing revenues, 141–144; merit pay proposals, 28–29; pricing of new services offerings, 219–221, 318–319; squeeze on schools, 26, 225–226. *See also* Accountability; Social and economic trends

Flesch, R., 18
Focus group interviews, 96, 98–101
Force field analysis: and organizational change, 274–275
Formative evaluation, 249, 251
"Four C's (consolidate, cooperate, cut costs, cut program), 141
Fox, K.F.A., 213
Frameworks: for accountability, 291–304, 312–313, 331–337; for action plans, 11–13. *See also* Strategy formulation/implementation
Freeman, R. E., 145, 147
French, J.R.P., 273
Fritz, R., 270

G

Genck, F., 86
Gender issues: availability of women as teachers, 30, 329
Gilbert, D., 145, 147
Ginsburg, A., 295, 301, 304
Goals: establishing for instructional improvement, 237–242, 257. *See also* Mission; Vision
Golden Valley School System: described, 65–68, 152–155; market research conducted by, 113–122; planning committee size at, 282; resource audit of, 89–94; strategic decision-making in, 151, 155–160; trend analysis and interpretation for, 68–73
Goldstein, H., 301, 306–307
Groups: and participative management theory, 243–249, 271–274, 319–320, 322–323; working with, 24–25, 151, 265, 279–286

H

Hackman, J. R., 279–280, 283–285, 323
Handicapped rights policies: and federal government, 18; and mission of schools, 21, 23; as test of political strength, 164, 171

Hare, A. P., 286
Harkins, S., 281
Harris, R., 264-265
Hartman, E., 145, 147
Harvard Policy model, 145-147
Heredity: as factor in students' performance, 86
Herzberg, F., 242
Homans, G., 167
Home environment: as factor in student performance, 86-88. *See also* Parents; Poverty
Hrebiniak, L., 5
The Human Group, 167
Human resource perspective for organizational change, 276

I

Immigrants: provision of free education and acculturation to, 20
Inert-latent power structures, 190-191
Instructional improvement: establishing goals and expectations for, 237-242; evaluation and rewards for, 242-249; fostering within the organizational "culture", 232-233; importance of, 229-231, 319. *See also* Evaluation
Interactive cable programs: examples of, 105-106, 221, 242, 246, 329
Interviews: as means of market research, 96, 98-101, 107. *See also* Surveys
IQ: and student performance, 86-87

J

Joyce, W., 5
Jurisdictional shifting as form of conflict resolution, 207

K

Kennedy, A. A., 232
Kerin, R. A., 107-108
King: M. L., 133-134, 268
Klebba, J., 65
Klingenberg, A., 86

Kotler, P., 213
Kubler-Ross, E., 270

L

Languages program: examining need to expand, 98-100
Latane, B., 281
Leadership: compared to management, 5-7; as essential and lacking, 25, 44; for instructional improvement, 31-33. *See also* Strategic leadership
Learner outcomes: as school performance indicators, 31-32, 41-42, 81; as teacher performance indicators, 297; test scores as, 32, 79, 238, 255
Legal power, 180-181
Levin, H., 295, 302
Levy, P., 301, 306
Lewin, K., 274-275
Lezotte, 31
Lightfoot, S. L., 232
Lincoln: A., 133
Lindblom, C. E., 151, 208
Lortie, D. C., 242
Loss and Change, 270
Lunch programs, 23, 142

M

McCarty, D. G., 187
McGregor, D., 243, 319
Magnet schools: as curriculum specialists, 136, 138
Mail surveys, 96, 98. *See also* Surveys
Management: compared to leadership, 5-7, 42-43
Management planning, 137-138. *See also* Strategic planning
Management Report to Stakeholders, 312, 331-337
March, J., 185, 197
Marcus, A., 288, 313
Market research: advertising results of, 129-130; cautions on use of consultants for, 116, 119, 121-122, 250; data-gathering methods for, 96-103; described, 95, 318; design guidelines for, 102-103; design process for,

103–113; Golden Valley School System example of, 113–130; importance of anticipating results of, 97, 103–105, 110–111; public relations value/danger of, 97, 114, 117, 128–129, 218. *See also* Constituencies/Stakeholders; Marketing; Markets for education; Surveys

Marketing: advertising and promotion, 222–226; caution against ignoring "production" aspects of, 230–232; customers for services to be marketed, 214–217; delivery systems design, 221–226; described, 211–214, 318; developing a plan for, 227–228; product/service development, 216–219; school officials' apprehensions about, 211–213; selling and distribution of services, 226–227. *See also* Marketing; Markets for education

Markets for education: defining and pursuing, 36–40; described, 37–38; in Golden Valley School System example, 69; shrinking of, 25–26; trends in, 52, 69. *See also* Market research; Marketing

Marris, P., 270

Mauriel, J. J., 65, 94, 145, 147, 253, 312

Meal programs, 23, 27, 142

Megatrends, 143

Mergers of school districts. *See* Consolidation of school districts

Merit pay: disadvantages of, 28–29

Metaphors: in service of organizational change/vision, 267–268

Miller, J., 272

Minnesota State Department of Education, 78

Mission: defining, 262, 305, 316; reassessing, 20–24, 47–51, 88. *See also* Markets for education; Vision

Monolithic-elitist power structures, 187–188

Morale of school staffs, 29, 31, 242–243, 268–274

Motivation: intrinsic vs. extrinsic, 242–243

Moynihan, D. P., 27

Music programs: band program example, 100, 105, 107, 109–111

N

Nadler, D. A., 266, 269

NAEP (National Assessment of Education Progress), 295

Naisbett, 143

Nanus, B., 267

A Nation at Risk, 26, 36

National Assessment of Education Program (NAEP), 295

National Commission on Excellence in Education, 26

National School Boards Association, 83

Needs analysis. *See* Market research

Noell, J., 295, 301, 304

Northfield school system, 249, 252–254

O

Operations management, 229–230, 254–255, 319

Organizational change: creating momentum for, 275–277; managing transition stages of, 264–274, 277–279; and participative management theories, 245, 271–274, 319–320; transition structures for, 279–286; understanding forces that help and hinder, 274–279, 321–322

Organizations, 197

Organizations: and "culture" of, 232–233, 256

Ouchi, 252

"Ownership" (responsibility for control) of schools, 17–20, 147, 305–306. *See also* Constituencies/Stakeholders

P

Parents: and hereditary factors affecting student performance, 86–87; as influences on student performance, 87; as stakeholders, 309–311

Participative management theory, 243–249, 271–274, 319–320, 322–323

Persuasion process of conflict resolution, 200–202
Peters, T. J., 263
Physical facilities: accountability for, 297–298; assessing in Golden Valley School System example, 92; assessing usefulness of, 88, 126
Pittner, N., 234
Planning process model, 150–151
Plisko, V., 295, 301, 304
Plural-rational power structures, 189–190
Political perspective for organizational change, 276
Politics: affecting Golden Valley School System, 70; affecting schools, 53, 163–165; analyzing the who/what/why of, 165–173; and conflict resolution, 176–177, 197–208; described, 177–178, 208–209; skills needed for, 209–210, 318
Positional studies of community power structures, 192
Postponement as form of conflict resolution, 207
Poverty: and IQ, 87; and parent involvement in schools, 87; and underclass children, 26–28. See also Social and economic trends
Power: as element in politics, 175–176, 178; enhancing, 184–186; identifying in communities, 191–197, 317; managing in transitional organization change, 266–268; and means of conflict resolution, 176–177, 197–208, 317; as structured in communities, 186–191; types of, 178–181, 317; versus influence, 181–184, 317. See also Constituencies/Stakeholders; Politics
Power play process of conflict resolution, 204–206
Powers, R. C., 195
Prairie River case, 193–195
Prenatal care, 27
Preschool and after-school programs: baby-sitting, 21–22, 112; example of survey to add, 105; and mission of schools, 27; as revenue gainers, 142, 144

Pricing of new services, 219–221
Principals. See Staffs (principals)
Process gains/losses, 281–282
Problem-solving process of conflict resolution, 199–200
Programs: assessing in Golden Valley School System example, 90–91, 124–27; assessing quality/reputation/impact of, 81–82, 173–174; athletic, 22, 91; auto mechanics example, 105, 111–112; delivery systems for, 127–129, 221–226, 229; developing for marketing to customers, 216–219; eliminating to cut costs, 140; example of band expansion, 100, 105, 107, 109–111; example of languages, 98–100, 112; on a fee-for-service basis, 100, 105, 112, 124–125, 142; for increasing revenues, 141–144; options for, 136–145; preschool, 27, 105; pricing of new services, 219–221. See also Evaluation; Instructional improvement; Market research; Marketing; Markets for education; Resources
Promotion of marketable products, 222–226, 318
PTA: as activist group, 19
Pupils. See Students
Purposes. See Mission; Vision

Q

Quality. See Evaluation; Instructional improvement
Questionnaires. See Surveys
Quinn, J. B., 151

R

Racial issues: and mission of schools, 21
Ramsey, C. E., 187
Reading/writing/computing: as basic to mission of schools, 21–22
Reports to stakeholders, 312–313, 325, 331–337
Reputation of schools: assessing in Golden Valley School System example, 92–93; importance of, 55–56, 88–89

Reputational studies of community power structures, 194–195

Resources: accountability for, 291–298; audits of, 75–89; as element in politics, 175–176, 178

RFP (Request for Proposals), 121

RIF (reduction in force), 29

Rudelius, S., 107–108

S

Salaries: and collective bargaining, 19; and merit pay proposals, 28–29

SAT scores. *See* Test scores

SAT test. *See* Test scores

Schein, E. H., 286

School boards: assessing in Golden Valley School System example, 91–92; assessing quality of, 82–84; and board-superintendent relationship, 84–86; and budgeting for new technologies, 35; challenges to traditional authority of, 18–19; and community power structures, 187; and need to emphasize quality education, 33. *See also* Staffs

The School Board's Responsibility: Effective Schools Through Effective Management, 86

Schools: assessing capabilities and resources of, 40, 75–89; challenges facing, 15–44, 59–64; control or "Ownership" of, 17–20, 147, 305–306; defining as an "industry", 45–51; enhancing organizational capabilities of, 139–145; financial squeeze on, 26, 34–36; leadership/policy setting vs management/administration of, 5–7, 42–43; measuring performance of, 81–82; mission of, 20–24, 47–51, 88, 136–145, 262, 305, 316; quality and effectiveness of, 31–33, 78–79; reputation of, 55–56, 88–89. *See also* Constituencies/Stakeholders; Golden Valley School System; Organizational change; School boards; Staffs; Students

Schultz, T., 253

Selling and distributing education products, 226–227, 318

Selling the products of schools. *See* Marketing

Seniority: as sole basis for layoffs, 29

SES (socioeconomic status), 294

Shifting jurisdictions as form of conflict resolution, 207

Shinkfield, A. J., 251, 291

Silberman, C. E., 19

Simon, H. A., 151, 185, 197

Simulations, 96, 101–102

Six E's (equity/excellence/efficiency/election/"eccountability"/effectiveness), 170–172

Social and economic trends: analysis of, 38–39, 51–59, 315–316; availability of women as teachers, 30; in Golden Valley School System example, 68–73; shrinking of market and budgets for education, 25–26. *See also* Financial issues; Poverty

Social "loafing", 281

Social power, 179

Socialization: and mission of schools, 21–22

Staffs (administrative): assessing as school resource, 75–81; role in market research, 97, 110–111; as stakeholders, 308–309; and teacher evaluations, 255

Staffs (central office): and instructional improvement, 6–7, 11–12, 32–33, 235–237; motivating to work with constituencies, 24–25; and political trend analysis, 53

Staffs (principals): as leaders in instructional improvement, 31–32, 235–236

Staffs (superintendents): assessing in Golden Valley School System example, 91–92; and budgeting for new technologies, 35; challenges to traditional authority of, 18–20; and community groups/power structures, 24–25, 118–120, 187; and relationship with school boards, 84–86, 288–289; role in instructional improvement, 6–8, 11–12, 32–33, 233–237, 249; role in market research, 97, 110–111, 119, 122; role in organizational change, 256–

258, 271; role in preparation of vision statement, 134–135; role in raising critical questions, 144–145, 148; skills needed for political leadership, 209–210, 257–258. *See also* Accountability; Evaluation; Instructional improvement; Strategic leadership

Staffs (teachers): accountability for performance of, 296–297; ageing of, 29–30; assessing in Golden Valley School System example, 89–90; assessing as school resource, 75–81; and gender issues, 30, 329; increasing/measuring performance of, 31–33, 41–42, 242; involving in instructional improvement goal-setting, 238–240, 252–254; as learning motivators, 59; and merit pay proposals, 28–29; salaries of, 19, 28–29, 296; as stakeholders, 308–209. *See also* Evaluation; Instructional improvement; Students

Stakeholder model, 147–150

Stakeholders. *See* Constituencies/Stakeholders

Strategic leadership: analyzing political factors for, 165–173, 175–178, 208–210; cases of political impact on, 163–165; described, 3–4, 9, 45, 325, 329; need for vision in, 3, 42–43; program/political/market perspectives of, 173–175. *See also* Conflict resolution; Instructional improvement; Politics; Power; Strategic planning

Strategic planning: additional questions affecting, 144–145; analysis of external trends affecting, 45–46; analysis of internal capabilities affecting, 75; available options for, 136–144; decision-making models for, 145–151; Golden Valley School System example of, 151–160; sequence of steps for, 8, 15–17, 325–328; timing of, 329; working with committee for, 16, 113–116. *See also* Market research; Organizational change

Strategy formulation/implementation: decision-making models for, 145–

151; described, 5, 139, 161, 315–325, 328; options for enhancing organizational capability, 139–145. *See also* Marketing; Organizational change; Politics

Structural perspective for organizational change, 275–276

Student outcomes: as school performance indicators, 31–32, 41–42, 81; as teacher performance indicators, 297; test scores as, 32, 79, 238, 255

Students: assessing backgrounds in Golden Valley School System example, 92; assessing heredity and environmental factors affecting, 86–88; attracting from other areas, 143; children from underclasses as, 26–28; children of immigrants as, 20; declining numbers of, 25–26; and drop-outs, 31; handicapped, 18, 21, 23, 164, 171; predicting enrollment of, 54, 93; as stakeholders, 309–311

Stufflebeam, D. L., 251, 291

Summative evaluation, 251

The Superintendency: Leadership for Effective Schools, 86

Superintendents. *See* Staffs (superintendents)

Support networks: for handling organizational change, 278–286

Surveys: by Golden Valley School System, 113–118; by simulations, 96, 101–102; cautions on design of, 113–118, 145; of consumer satisfaction, 103, 106, 116–117, 303; interview, 96, 98–101, 107; mail, 96, 98; sample questionnaire for, 55–56; survey feedback as change agent, 269; telephone, 96–97. *See also* Market research

SWOT (strengths, weaknesses, opportunities, and threats) analysis, 131, 145

Symbolic perspective for organizational change, 277

T

Tannenbaum, R., 277

Teachers. *See* Staffs (teachers)

Teachers' associations: and binding arbitration statute, 164, 176; emer-
gence of, 19, 80; pros and cons to
schools of, 80–81; and seniority as
sole basis for lay-offs, 29. *See also*
Staffs (teachers)
Team efforts, 24–25, 151, 265, 279–
286. *See also* Organizational change
Technology: at Golden Valley School
System example, 72; bringing to
schools, 34–36, 49–50, 57–59; and
interactive cable program, 105–106
Telephone surveys, 96–97
Television. *See* Interactive cable programs; Technology
Test scores: in accountability reports,
294, 297; inadequacy as measure-
ments of effectiveness, 32, 79, 238,
255
Textbooks: pressure to revise, 164, 176
Theory X vs. Theory Y on motivators,
243–249, 252, 256, 319–320
Transitional management, 321. *See also*
Organizational change
Trends. *See* Social and economic trends

U

U.S. Department of Education wall
chart, 295, 301, 304, 307
Underclass children: and mission of
schools, 26–28
Unions. *See* Teachers' associations
United nations, 165, 183, 202

V

Values: acountability for instilling,
298–299; as agents for change, 270;
described, 170; as element in politics, 175–176, 178; need to consider,
13–14, 145, 147–148, 173, 328. *See
also* Mission
Vision: defined, 4–5, 262; developing
statement of, 132–136, 320–321;
responsibility and authority for,
17–20, 134–135; and role in strategic
leadership, 3, 42–43. *See also* Mission
Voucher system, 220
Vroom, V. H., 272

W

Wall chart of U.S. Department of Edu-
cation, 295, 301, 304, 307
Waterman, R. H., 263
Weick, K. E., 284
Weinberg, R. A., 86
Weisbord, M., 275
Who Governs?, 194
Why Johnny Can't Read, 18
Williams, K., 281
Women in education, 30, 329

Y

Yetton, P. W., 272